THE INDUSTRIALIZATION OF AGRICULTURE

The Industrialization of Agriculture

Vertical coordination in the U.S. food system

Edited by
JEFFREY S. ROYER
University of Nebraska—Lincoln

RICHARD T. ROGERS
University of Massachusetts—Amherst

Ashgate

Aldershot • Brookfield USA • Singapore • Sydney

Published by
Ashgate Publishing Ltd
Gower House
Croft Road
Aldershot
Hants GU11 3HR
England

Ashgate Publishing Company
Old Post Road
Brookfield
Vermont 05036
USA

British Library Cataloguing in Publication Data
The industrialization of agriculture : vertical
    coordination in the U.S. food system
    1. Agriculture - Economic aspects - United States
    2. Agricultural innovations - United States
    I.Royer, Jeffrey S. II.Rogers, Richard T.
    338.1'0973

Library of Congress Catalog Card Number: 98-73510

ISBN 1 84014 382 7

Printed in Great Britain by The Ipswich Book Company, Suffolk

Contents

Contributors

Jeanine Koenig Balbach, Robert A. Levy Fellow in Law and Liberty, George Mason University School of Law.

Kingsley Bash, strategic planning specialist, Chemonics International.

Michael Boehlje, professor, Department of Agricultural Economics, Purdue University.

Stephen P. Davies, associate professor, Department of Agricultural and Resource Economics, Colorado State University.

Satish Y. Deodhar, post-doctoral research associate, Department of Agricultural and Applied Economics, University of Georgia.

Stanley M. Fletcher, professor, Department of Agricultural and Applied Economics, University of Georgia.

William E. Foster, professor, Department of Agricultural Economics, Pontificia Universidad Catolica de Chile.

Stuart D. Frank, agricultural economist, Grain Inspection, Packers and Stockyards Administration, U.S. Department of Agriculture.

Roger G. Ginder, professor, Department of Economics, Iowa State University.

Dennis R. Henderson, professor emeritus, Department of Agricultural Economics, Ohio State University.

David A. Hennessy, assistant professor, Department of Economics, Iowa State University.

Garth John Holloway, assistant professor, Department of Agricultural Economics, University of California–Davis.

John E. Ikerd, extension professor, Department of Agricultural Economics, University of Missouri–Columbia.

Carolyn Betts Liebrand, agricultural economist, Rural Business–Cooperative Service, U.S. Department of Agriculture.

K. Charles Ling, agricultural economist, Rural Business–Cooperative Service, U.S. Department of Agriculture.

V. James Rhodes, professor emeritus, Department of Agricultural Economics, University of Missouri–Columbia.

Jeffrey S. Royer, professor, Department of Agricultural Economics, University of Nebraska–Lincoln.

Loïc Sauvée, associate professor, Department of Management Sciences, Institut Supérieur Agricole de Beauvais.

Lee F. Schrader, professor, Department of Agricultural Economics, Purdue University.

Tomislav Vukina, associate professor, Department of Agricultural and Resource Economics, North Carolina State University.

Kelly Zering, associate professor, Department of Agricultural and Resource Economics, North Carolina State University.

Preface

Earlier versions of the papers included in this volume were presented at the NE-165 Research Conference, "Vertical Coordination in the Food System," held in Washington, D.C., June 5–6, 1995. Since the conference, several of the papers have been significantly revised or updated.

The conference was organized by the NE-165 Regional Research Project, "Private Strategies, Public Policies, and Food System Performance." Financial support for the conference was provided by the Food Marketing Policy Center of the University of Connecticut, the Cooperative State Research, Education, and Extension Service of the U.S. Department of Agriculture, and the Farm Foundation. The conference organizing committee consisted of Jeffrey S. Royer, Richard T. Rogers, Ronald W. Cotterill, and Dennis R. Henderson.

We would like to thank Teddee Grace of Pro-Ed, Phoenix, Arizona, for technical editing assistance, Pamela Holmes of the Department of Agricultural Economics of the University of Nebraska–Lincoln for word processing services, and Darleen Slysz of the Department of Resource Economics of the University of Massachusetts–Amherst for proofreading help. Financial support for the publication of this book was provided by the Department of Agricultural Economics of the University of Nebraska–Lincoln, the Department of Resource Economics of the University of Massachusetts–Amherst, and the Food Marketing Policy Center of the University of Connecticut through the Special Grant Program of the Cooperative State Research, Education, and Extension Service of the U.S. Department of Agriculture.

PART I
OVERVIEW OF VERTICAL
COORDINATION

1 The Industrialization of Agriculture: Questions of Coordination

MICHAEL BOEHLJE and LEE F. SCHRADER

Major structural changes are occurring in food production and distribution. Changing linkages between producers, those firms or entities that provide inputs to producers, and those who buy their products are key elements of this structural change. Increased interdependence among the entities that deliver the final consumer product—food with specific attributes desired by consumers—has major implications for the efficiency of the food sector, the independence and power of various entities, and the sharing of risks and rewards from food production and distribution.

The focus of this discussion is the changing nature of linkages in the food chain. First, with particular reference to the production of agricultural commodities, the number of linkages has generally increased—producers are sourcing more inputs from off the farm and performing fewer activities or processes along the chain that result in the final food product. They are buying not only chemicals and fertilizer, but also purchasing breeding stock, application services, transportation services, and numerous other products and services previously produced on the farm. At other points in the food chain, linkages have been internalized—functions such as wholesaling, retailing, and distribution of inputs or food products, previously performed by independent firms, have now been integrated.

Not only are the number of linkages changing (both increasing and decreasing), but the nature of those linkages is also changing. Open, impersonal spot markets are being replaced by negotiated, personal, and sometimes closed, contractual linkages. Some linkages between stages in the food chain that once were external have now become internal through acquisitions and integration, resulting in unique problems of cost allocation and transfer pricing within firms.

3

The changing nature of linkages between the stages and the consolidation of firms in the food production and distribution system have been popularly referred to as the industrialization of agriculture (Urban; Barry, Sonka, and Lajili; Council on Food, Agricultural, and Resource Economics). Most analysts expect coordination between stages within the food chain to be characterized less by open spot markets and more by negotiated contracts or integration. These changes in the coordination system generate a number of questions: (1) When and under what conditions will contractual or ownership coordination occur? (2) What stages of the food chain will be linked through such coordination mechanisms? (3) Who will have the most control or power in the contract- or ownership-coordinated system? (4) How will the risk and rewards be shared among various participants in the contract- or ownership-coordinated system? (5) What concepts are available to evaluate and understand these changes and provide answers to the above questions?

These questions are particularly relevant for the swine subsector, given the rapid growth of large-scale, contract-coordinated production in recent years. As long ago as the early 1960s, many economists expected some form of contract- or ownership-coordinated system soon to predominate in the swine industry. It was considered likely that the swine subsector would eventually resemble that of poultry, but that has not yet happened. Today there are similar predictions not only for swine, but also for other subsectors. Are these predictions more accurate today?

This discussion will speculate about the system coordination issues rather than provide empirical answers to these questions since little empirical work is available on this topic. However, the hypotheses and concepts presented here may provide the basis for more definitive empirical work.

Life Cycles: The Window of Opportunity

Structural change occurs more rapidly when both a window of opportunity and economic pressures or incentives exist. The window of opportunity for rapid structural change in the swine industry is the result of a convergence of four cycles: (1) the product life cycle, (2) the investment/replacement life cycle, (3) the manager/producer life cycle, and (4) the technological life cycle. Individually these cycles provide windows of opportunity for structural change in an industry; when they converge, as they have in the swine industry, the structural change is both dramatic and rapid.

The Product Life Cycle

Live hogs have been a commodity product fundamentally with most of the preferred consumer attributes added in the sorting and processing activity. Increasingly, certain attributes such as leanness and specific size portions such as loin eyes are difficult to obtain efficiently through processing. A more efficient way of obtaining these attributes is by changing the raw material—the live animal. This transformation of the hog from a commodity to a specific-attribute raw material (SARM) is major and provides the opportunity for (or requires) new coordination options and structural change to obtain and merchandise the new product.

Investment/Replacement Cycle

A significant portion of the current plant capacity—particularly in the production stage of the pork industry and specifically in the Midwest—is in need of replacement or modernization if it is to remain productive. Many small and mid-size Midwest production facilities are of a size and technology that can continue to produce if capital and investment costs have already been recovered, but will likely not be profitable if major remodeling or upgrading of investments is necessary to remain in operation. Because of technological, size, environmental, or managerial conditions and limitations, many of these production facilities (which embody the technology of the early 1980s) are likely to be phased out of production rather than upgraded and modernized in place.

Manager/Producer Life Cycle

Until recently, most pork production has occurred in owner/operator firms in which the entrepreneur provides most of the labor and management for the production enterprise—the classic family farm. For many of these family farms, the human as well as physical resources are aging. For example, the 1992 Census of Agriculture reveals that 40.5 percent of Iowa family farmers are 55 years of age and older (U.S. Department of Commerce). Unless the firm has plans for managerial succession, producers of this age logically have a shorter planning horizon than those who are younger when considering major expansion or replacement decisions. Particularly with small and modest-size livestock operations, fewer family members or others are available and/or interested in taking over the business. For a number of family farmers, the logical strategy is to sequence human and physical resources so they wear out at the same time—that is, when the farmer is ready to retire, the building and facilities can be shut down with the investment costs fully recovered.

Technological Life Cycle

Dramatic changes have occurred in the technology of pork production, processing, and distribution. Genetic and nutrition technologies allow pork producers to produce those specific attributes consumers want. Until recently, the knowledge and technology to do so were not available on a practical, commercial scale. And technical change in production facilities and structures in the past five to seven years has been profound. The traditional approach for many producers has been to integrate the farrowing, nursery, growing, and finishing phases of pork production in one interconnected plant at a single location. For disease control and biosecurity, modern technology suggests farrowing facilities be physically separated from nursery facilities with growing/finishing facilities at a third site. Production of breeding stock may occur at a fourth location. And feed may be produced in a separate location by a separate firm as well. This separation of physical production facilities stands in stark contrast to the traditional approach of facilities integration. Note that physical separation of facilities and economic stages of production facilitates (but does not require) separate firms being responsible for each stage of production. Additional technological advances, such as split-sex feeding, all-in/all-out production, feeding different rations during different phases of the growing/finishing process, etc., render obsolete much of the technology embodied in production facilities constructed even in the late 1980s. Similar, if less dramatic, changes in technology are evident in other commodity systems.

Benefits/Constraints to Contract/Ownership Coordination

Arguments favoring contract or ownership coordination include both potential economic rewards and biological capacity to exploit this potential. One of the prime benefits perceived is the reward gained from responding to increased specificity in consumer demand. Richer consumers are more demanding consumers. They expect quality-controlled products with specific characteristics to be available when desired. Demand for product diversity is increasing. Products are differentiated based on what they do not contain as well as what they do. Low fat, low salt, and low cholesterol claims are common. Some attributes are achieved through processing, others in production. Consumers are also specifying how products are produced—examples include free-range chicken and organic vegetables and grains. Given the expected continued increase in the standard of living and the increased ethnic diversity of markets, the trend toward product diversity will continue.

Continued substitution of capital (fixed cost) for labor (variable) at all stages of processing provides a stronger incentive to stabilize volume processed. Flow scheduling and capacity utilization are essential to cost control. Plants and animals bred or engineered for specific end uses will also require production practices tuned to the specific end use.

Conformance to specific quality standards may be more easily accomplished with a contract- or ownership-coordinated system. Compliance with regulations on the use of drugs and chemicals also requires a greater degree of coordination of activities at more than one level of the food system. Some technologies, such as the use of specialized feed mixing and blending equipment to manufacture specific rations, may not be economical at the scale of a single farm.

Risk has been a hallmark of the agricultural sector, and business strategies to reduce risk have significant structure and coordination implications. One risk is that of prices of inputs or products. A common business strategy is to reduce the risk of high prices for inputs by contracting for supplies. A related strategy is to reduce the price risk exposure on products by contracting product sales. Some firms reduce price risks by vertically integrating into the input supply or product distribution channels. These coordination methods attempt to reduce the impact of market fluctuations that are part of the open-market spot pricing system.

Firm-level risk may be reduced by contract coordination or integration. However, the assurance of a supply of SARM may require planning production somewhat greater than expected needs to allow for yield variation or larger-than-expected demand. The excess would be placed on the commodity market, perhaps increasing the variability of the commodity product price.

A second source of risk is related to quantity and/or quality features. Food packaging and processing unit costs have become very sensitive to operating at full plant capacity; thus flow scheduling is critical to being cost competitive. Matching the physical capacity of various stages (for example, hog finishing capacity with packing plant kill capacity, or turkey grower space with processing capacity) is critical to the overall efficiency of the system. This coordination may be more difficult to attain in open markets. Furthermore, some food distribution channels may require particular quality characteristics that may not be available in predictable quantities in open spot markets. The coordination needed to ensure both quality and quantity for efficient operations can be achieved through contracts, ownership of more than one stage, joint ventures, or similar arrangements in the food production and distribution chain.

A third source or type of risk in the food chain that has become more serious in recent years is food product safety. This risk has two dimensions—the health risk of food-borne disease and the risk of polluting water, air, and land resources in the food production processes. These risks can result in significant direct costs and liability exposure for not only the responsible firm in the food chain, but also firms that supply related inputs and purchase products from the "responsible" firm in the case of strict (joint and severable) environmental liability related to chemical use. Thus system coordination to reduce or control these risks may be in part a response to the broad sweep of product and environmental liability law.

Each of these factors accentuates the degree of interdependence among different levels of the food system. They suggest the need for closer coordination than the produce-first-and-then-sell strategy that has characterized much of agricultural commodity production. Standard yellow dent corn and soybeans are examples of the latter. Other products, such as chicken, turkey, popcorn, waxy maize, specialty soybeans, and, increasingly, hogs, are produced under contracts of varying specificity. The ability to produce to specification will increase, as will the ability to measure product characteristics. Thus the cost of producing the diversity demanded by consumers and responding to the risks likely will be lower in a more closely coordinated system.

The need for greater diversity, more exacting quality control, and flow control will tax the ability of spot markets to coordinate production and processing effectively. Open spot markets increasingly encounter difficulty in conveying the full message concerning attributes (quantity, quality, timing, etc.) of a product and characteristics (including services) of a transaction. Where open markets fail to achieve the needed coordination, other options, such as contracts, integration, or joint ventures, will be used. Thus relationships between input suppliers, producers, and processors are expected to become less impersonal and more personal.

In general, negotiated or administered coordination results in more rapid transmission of information between the various economic stages and consequently enhanced ability of the system to adjust to changing consumer demands, economic conditions, or technological improvements. The ability of the production and distribution system to be more responsive and adjust rapidly to changing conditions is increasingly important with the increased rate of change in economic and social systems worldwide.

This ability to respond quickly to changes in the economic climate is critical to maintaining profit margins as well as extracting innovator's profits. Likewise, quickly recognizing erroneous decisions and making appropriate adjustments and corrections are essential to survival and success. Market coordination of systems characterized by biological lags cannot respond to changing conditions as quickly as an integrated or contract-coordinated system. That is, the response at one stage can be initiated only after price signals the need for change, and the change in quantity or quality may be realized only after a full production cycle. Negotiated coordination systems require more frequent and direct communication between decision makers at each stage on a wider variety of product/service characteristics than is typically possible with more traditional spot markets. Thus the improved information flows and more rapid adoption or adjustment allow negotiated coordination systems to function more effectively in rapidly changing markets.

The relationship between raw product value to a processor and quality attributes of the raw product affects the relative efficiency of alternative coordination systems. Figure 1.1 illustrates the relationship of raw value (i.e., price paid to the producer) to a product-attribute score for two cases; one with value less sensitive to the attribute (A) and the other more sensitive (B). For example, A might represent the value of a live hog to a pork processor related to lean yield percentage if the desired final product attribute can be achieved by trimming cuts from carcasses of variable quality. If final product quality is directly related to carcass composition and requires carcasses within a narrow quality range to be achieved, the relation would resemble curve B. When the value/attribute relationship is less sensitive, as in A, open-market coordination would be more efficient than for the more sensitive value/attribute relationship B.

These arguments suggest that in situations in which specific attributes are not demanded, supplies are fully adequate and can be obtained from various sources, and information flows between the various stages are minimal, traditional spot commodity markets can function effectively and efficiently. As one deviates from these conditions—which is increasingly the case with more specificity in raw materials, information flows, and fewer potential sources of acceptable supplies—various forms of negotiated coordination

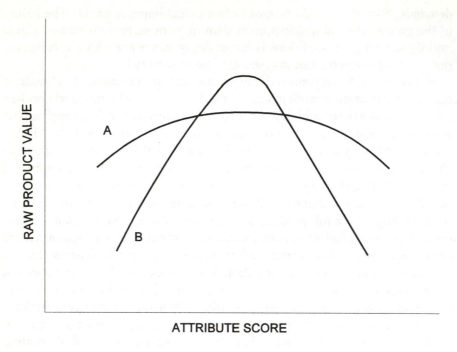

Figure 1.1 Relationships of raw product value to quality

systems become more effective and necessary for efficient functioning of the production and distribution system.

Finally, a key determinant of contract or ownership coordination (perhaps the prime explanation for why it has not occurred as rapidly as predicted for the hog/pork complex) is the biological capacity to respond to consumer demand for specific attributes. Recent advances in genetics, nutrition, reproduction, etc., have resulted in more control and predictability, thus increased capacity to biologically engineer the products consumers want. In essence, biological capacity to respond to consumer demands may be the linchpin to capturing the benefits of contract/ownership coordination.

What are the constraints to increased contract or ownership coordination? The first of these might be changes in the economic environment that would eliminate the economic incentives and rewards noted earlier or increase the costs of such forms of coordination so as to offset those rewards. Thus, in cases in which less specificity and more variation in both product and process throughout the food chain are acceptable (i.e., specificity is not rewarded), contract or ownership coordination is less likely to occur. Or, if the specific attribute desired can be more efficiently sourced by sorting through the various raw materials produced by the commodity markets, more explicit linkages are less likely. Likewise, if the transaction costs of contract or ownership coordination are high, such coordination is less likely to occur. High transaction costs may occur because of the difficulty of agreement between various parties to acceptable contract terms, or because of inaccurate transfer pricing between divisions within a company. Disagreement on the acceptable sharing of the risk and rewards between the various parties in a contract- or ownership-coordinated system may also result in high transaction costs and reduce the net benefits of, or ability to use, these coordination methods. Improvements in the performance of open, impersonal spot markets that provide more complete signals concerning the value of specific food attributes (quality, freshness, taste, perishability, availability, etc.) and provide such information in a timely fashion would make other forms of coordination less attractive.

One would expect transaction costs to be lower with vertical integration than with contract coordination. However, it is important to recognize that coordination of integrated stages is not without costs.

Contract coordination or integration of markets also will not occur unless there is a perception that an economic advantage exists. Not being committed (i.e., flexibility) has value. Once a commitment has been made, the option to do something else is foregone. Both parties to a contract give up this option; thus both parties must see an advantage to make the commitment.

Public policy might also constrain increased use of contract or ownership coordination. Concerns about market power and concentration might result in increased scrutiny under antitrust laws and regulations. More likely, state legislators concerned about the future of family farmers and the threat of corporate farming may constrain forms of coordination arrangements such as contract farming or integrated ownership of various stages of production. Note, however, that such limitations are more likely to influence the location of various activities in the food production and distribution chain rather than the method of coordination unless such legislation is national in scope.

What Stages?

Not all stages in a subsector are likely to be integrated or coordinated by the same means. Figure 1.2 illustrates the stages, coordination means, and

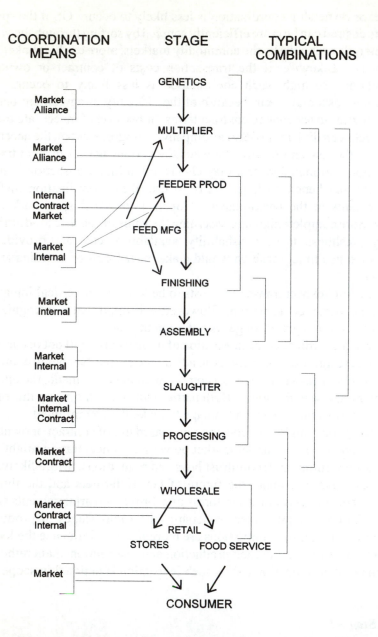

Figure 1.2 Stages, coordination, and integration in the hog/pork subsector

integration patterns currently found in the hog/pork subsector. Coordination means at each stage interface are listed to the left in order of use as perceived by the authors. The share of each alternative is not known, little data exist on the extent of nonmarket linkages in the subsector. Typical stage combinations found in the subsector are noted to the right of Figure 1.2. For example, the genetics and multiplier stages are likely to be linked by an open market or through some alliance of firms at the two stages.

Recently, attention has focused on the integration of the multiplier and feeder pig production stages with contract coordination of finishing by the same firms. To date there has been relatively little nonmarket coordination of the finishing-slaughter linkage, which the foregoing analysis would lead one to expect. As pork becomes less of a commodity, earlier arguments would suggest more negotiated linkages between finishing and slaughter and throughout the chain.

Who Will Control?

A fundamental issue in any negotiation-based coordinated system is the point (or points) and source of power or control. Who dictates, or has the most control, over the performance of the system, of the sharing of risk and rewards? And what is the source of that power or control?

Traditionally, discussions of power or control in an economic system have focused on issues of size and the ability to exercise monopoly or monopsony power as a function of volume or size—in essence, market dominance. With the increasing importance of the role of information in economic decision making combined with more negotiated coordination systems, the potential of economic power associated with a particular stage in the production/distribution process has surfaced. The question is whether there is economic power or control associated with a particular stage in the production/distribution system—is there *position* power as well as *size* power!

The basic argument is that there are two fundamental points of control and one fundamental source of power in a negotiation-based coordinated food production and distribution system. The first point of control is the end user or consumer and those firms that have intimate contact with the consumer. Consumers are more discriminating in their food purchases, want a broader spectrum of attributes in their food products, and increasingly have the purchasing power to convert wants into effective demand. It is not news that the consumer is the ultimate determinant of the attributes that food products must contain. Those firms that know consumers and understand the increased specificity of their demands have a unique capacity to communicate or dictate those demands to the rest of the food chain. This knowledge of consumer wants, needs, and purchasing capacity is a source of power (and rent) and provides one point of influence in the food production and distribution system.

The second point of power in the food production and distribution system is the raw material supplier. But not all raw material suppliers have the same degree of power. The relative power of raw material suppliers depends upon the degree of substitutability for their input or contribution to the production/distribution process. Labor is substitutable for capital (although imperfectly); fertilizer is substitutable for land and vice versa. Machines can substitute (again imperfectly) for chemicals, and labor for money. The one input with the fewest substitutes—that is, the most essential in the food production/distribution chain—is the genetic material in plant and animal production, the seed and breeding stock. Biotechnology and increased predictability and control of genetic manipulation provide additional power to those who control genetic material. Thus the second point of control in the food production and distribution system is the owner of the genetics.

Note that the points of power concentration in the food production and distribution chain are at the beginning and the end—the genetics and the consumer. In both cases, the source of this power is knowledge. At the consumption end, it is knowledge of ultimate consumers' wants and needs that can be communicated through the chain; at the opposite end, it is knowledge and information about, and the ability to manipulate, the genetic material that will produce the specific attributes for which consumers are willing to pay. The genetics company with a differentiated gene pool and the firms with closest contact with consumers have the access to information at these points of control. Given that the source of control is knowledge and information (not physical resources, not capital, not land), then the only way a firm between the end points of the consumer and the genetics company can obtain control is through superior information. Who knows the consumer best is an open question. Slotting allowances are often cited as an indicator of retailer power. However, manufacturers and processors do more marketing research and make the product decisions. Private labels and retailer-specified products have not taken over the supermarket shelves.

At this early stage in the process of shifting from impersonal markets to contract/ownership coordination, there may be a first-mover advantage for organizations such as the very large producers or producers' cooperatives to play the control role. Thus initiative now at the intermediate firm level may offset the perceived advantage of firms at the end points. Coordination by producers' cooperatives has the potential for the more traditional producers to retain a more prominent role. But unless such firms make preemptive moves early in the transformation from open markets to closed systems, the opportunity for control likely will be lost.

Discussions of vertical linkages by such analysts as Williamson; Mahoney; and Milgrom and Roberts emphasize the importance of various characteristics of the firm and industry such as asset specificity, task programmability, and performance-measurement separability to the type and form of coordination between various stages in the production-processing-distribution chain. The arguments presented here concerning the critical role of knowledge and information as a source of power and control in the food chain are an extension of those concepts. Unique knowledge and information are a specific asset (an idiosyncratic asset in Williamson's terms) that facilitates task programmability and encourages contractual or ownership vertical linkages. And the firm with the most unique knowledge and information (with the greatest asset specificity) relative to other firms in the chain has the most relative power and control of the system.

At present, food systems coordination is accomplished primarily by processors when not by open markets. Recent indications of weakening brand loyalty have been attributed to a lessening of real product differences and a consequent emphasis on price (*The Economist*). This shift positions the retailer for a larger role in nonmarket coordination. Fast food restaurant firms already exercise extensive system coordination and control of their major suppliers, reflecting consumer preferences. Diminished brand loyalties may diminish the power of processors to extract extraordinary profits; however, the processor is likely to continue to play an important role even as power shifts toward genetics firms and consumers.

Information/Knowledge—The Key Driver

Although numerous forces are contributing to the industrialization expected to occur in the swine sector, the key driver of this change is information and knowledge. As in other industries, those with unique and accurate information and knowledge have increasing power and control. And with power and control comes the capacity to capture profits from, and transfer risk to, others with less power.

The increasing role that knowledge and information play in obtaining control, increasing profits, and reducing risk in the hog/pork subsector is occurring for two fundamental reasons. First, *manufacturing pork* has become an increasingly sophisticated and complex business in contrast to *raising hogs*. This increased complexity means that those with more knowledge and information about the detailed processes as well as how to combine those processes in a total system will have a comparative advantage. The second development is the dramatic growth in knowledge of the chemical, biological, and physical processes involved in pork production. This vast expansion in knowledge means that those who can exploit that knowledge in a practical context have a further comparative advantage. Thus the role of knowledge and information in success in the hog/pork subsector is more important today than ever before.

The logical question for individuals in the pork manufacturing chain is how to obtain access to this knowledge and information. Historically, particularly for the production sector, this knowledge and information have been obtained from public agencies and institutions such as universities and the land-grant system as well as from external sources such as genetics companies, feed companies, building and equipment manufacturers, packers, and processors. In general, independent producers have obtained information from external sources in much the same fashion as they have sourced physical and financial resources and inputs. In contrast, ownership- or contract-coordinated production-processing-distribution systems get their knowledge and information from a combination of internal and external sources. Many of these firms or alliances of firms have internal research and development staffs. And the knowledge they obtain is obviously proprietary and not shared outside the firm or alliance; it is a source of strategic competitive advantage. Furthermore, the research and development activities in coordinated systems are more focused on total system efficiency and effectiveness rather than on only individual components of that system.

In addition to more effective research and development, such alliances or integrated firms have the capacity to implement knowledge or information and technological breakthroughs more rapidly over a larger volume of output to obtain a larger volume of innovator's profits. And in the case of a defective new technology, ownership- or contract-coordinated systems generally have more monitoring and control procedures in place and can detect deteriorating performance earlier and make adjustments more quickly compared to a system with impersonal market coordination.

As knowledge and information become a more important source of strategic competitive advantage, those who have access to it will be more successful than those who do not have that access. Given declining public sector funding for research and knowledge dissemination, which has been the major source of these resources for independent producers, the expanded capacity of integrated systems to generate proprietary knowledge and technology and to adopt it rapidly enables the participants in that system to more regularly *create* and *capture* innovator's profits while simultaneously increasing control and reducing risk. This provides a formidable advantage to the ownership- or contract-coordinated production system compared to the system of independent stages and decision making.

How Do We Study Coordination?

How can we obtain empirical answers and make concrete predictions concerning the numerous hypotheses and questions that are now only the focal point of speculation in this and most discussions concerning the new forms of coordination in the hog/pork production and distribution system and in the food chain in general? Traditional microeconomic theory provides limited help because it assumes open markets and independent firms that react to market determined prices. Concepts of industrial organization are only partially helpful in that they assist in understanding the relationships between stage structure and performance, but do little to explain the dynamics of firm behavior and the interactions between and among firms at different stages within the production and distribution system.

Concepts from three fields of behavioral science may provide useful components of a conceptual framework to study coordination systems. These three fields are broadly defined as: (1) transaction cost and principal-agent theory, (2) strategic management, and (3) negotiation/power and performance incentives. Each of these fields will be briefly introduced; the challenge is to integrate the appropriate concepts along with those from economics into a comprehensive analytical framework.

The concepts of transaction cost and principal-agent theory as conceived by Coase and expanded by Williamson and others indicate that the form of vertical linkages or coordination in an economic system (impersonal markets versus ownership or contracts) depends not only on economies of size and scope as suggested by conventional theory, but also on costs incurred in completing transactions using various coordination mechanisms. Furthermore, these costs and the performance of various coordination mechanisms depend in part on the incentives and relationships between the transacting parties in the system—the principal and the agent. Under various conditions, the agent may exhibit shirking behavior (i.e., not performing expected tasks) or moral hazard behavior (i.e., the incentives are so perverse as to encourage behavior by the agent and results that are not consistent with, or valued by, the other party to the transaction—the principal).

Given these fundamental behavioral principles, Mahoney suggests that the form of coordination or business linkages will be a function of three characteristics of the transactions and the industry: (1) asset specificity, (2) task programmability, and (3) task separability. Asset specificity refers to the specialized nature of the human or physical assets that are required to complete the transaction; the more idiosyncratic the asset, the stronger the linkage or bond required for the transacting parties to invest in that asset. Task programmability indicates that a transaction is well understood by all parties and often repeated, thus not requiring intense discussions or negotiations and easily accomplished by impersonal coordination mechanisms. Separability refers to the ability to determine and measure the value of the contribution and thus the reward that should be given to each participant in the transaction. If that can be accomplished easily (and thus the transaction is separable), coordination systems that are less personal are relatively more efficient and effective than when separability does not exist. Based on these arguments as extended by Milgrom and Roberts and Martin et al., a taxonomy of expected coordination mechanisms can be developed as summarized in Table 1.1.

The second set of arguments that might assist in understanding and predicting coordination mechanisms comes from the strategic management literature. In essence, these concepts are derived from Porter's value chain (the value-added activities that result in the transformation of raw materials into finished goods), strategies to develop a strategic competitive advantage, and the criteria or considerations in the integration (buy-versus-build) decision. In general, this literature indicates that the buy-versus-build decision is driven by: (1) internal considerations of costs, technology, and financial and managerial resources, and (2) external competitive considerations of synergies, differentiation, and market power and positioning. Harrigan has captured the essence of the strategic management vertical integration arguments for the build-rather-than-buy decision and, thus, the determinants of the most effective coordination mechanism as summarized in Table 1.2.

Table 1.1 Predicting organizational forms of alternative business linkages

	Low programmability		High programmability	
	Low asset specificity	High asset specificity	Low asset specificity	High asset specificity
Low nonseparability	Spot market	Long-term contract	Spot market	Joint venture
High nonseparability	Cooperation (strategic alliance)	Cooperation or vertical ownership	Inside contract (hybrid)	Vertical ownership

Source: Martin et al.

Table 1.2 Some advantages and disadvantages of vertical integration

Advantages	Disadvantages
Internal benefits	*Internal costs*
Integration economies reduce costs by eliminating steps, reducing duplicate overhead, and cutting costs (technology dependent).	Need for overhead to coordinate vertical integration increased costs.
Improved coordination of activities reduces inventorying and other costs.	Burden of excess capacity from unevenly balanced minimum-efficient-scale plants (technology-dependent).
Avoid time-consuming tasks, such as price shopping, communicating design details, or negotiating contracts.	Poorly organized vertically integrated firms do not enjoy synergies that compensate for higher costs.
Competitive benefits	*Competitive dangers*
Avoid foreclosure to inputs, services, or markets.	Obsolete processes may be perpetuated.
Improved marketing or technological intelligence.	Creates mobility (or exit) barriers.
Opportunity creates product differentiation (increased value-added).	Links firm to sick adjacent businesses.

Superior control of firm's economic environment (market power).	Lose access to information from suppliers or distributors.
Create credibility for new products.	Synergies created through vertical integration may be overrated.
Synergies could be created by coordinating vertical activities skillfully.	Managers integrated before thinking through the most appropriate way to do so.

Source: Harrigan.

The third set of arguments that may help explain the choice and implications of various coordination mechanisms relates to the concepts of negotiation and performance incentives. With personal, negotiated coordination among stages in the food chain, the invisible hand of the market is replaced by the very visible hands of buyers and sellers negotiating the terms of trade, in many cases prior to the production or manufacturing process. In such a system, phenomena such as negotiation strategy and skill, power, conflict resolution, trust, and performance monitoring and assessment become central to effective and efficient functioning of the economic system and the sharing of risks and rewards in the system. Concepts of negotiation strategy and tactics as developed by Donohue; Fisher; Putnam and Jones; and others may assist in understanding not only what form a negotiated coordination will take, but also how the risks and rewards will be shared.

Recent work on various approaches to provide performance incentives, as proposed by Casson but rarely referenced in the literature on vertical integration and coordination of economic systems, may also be useful. The basic presumption of Casson's work is that overall economic performance of any system depends on transaction costs and these costs mainly reflect the level of trust that exists in the economy. The level of trust in turn depends upon culture. An effective culture has a strong moral content. Morality can overcome problems that formal procedures based on monitoring and compliance with rules and regulations cannot. A strong culture that respects the spirit as well as letter of the law reduces transaction costs and enhances performance; consequently, the basic success of an economic system depends on the quality of its culture.

A key concept in this argument is that of trust. A crucial question in any economic transaction, and particularly in those that are personal and negotiated, is whether the other party to the transaction can be trusted. There are two fundamental approaches to engineering or creating trust. The one most commonly used in much of the Western world is to monitor performance through the institutional and legal system and penalize those parties that do not fulfill their negotiated commitments. An alternative approach to engineering trust is to manipulate the incentive structure so that individuals fulfill their commitments based on rewards they receive rather than penalties they incur. These incentives can be economic or emotional; the economic incentives are standard fare for economists. The emotional incentives of guilt or satisfaction have not been the focal point of economic analysis, but are part of the psychology of individuals and influence their participation in business transactions. This is particularly important in personally negotiated transactions in contract markets and less so in impersonal transactions common in open spot markets. Casson argues that emotional rewards and penalties are part of the preference structure, can be manipulated, and thus can be optimized. The effectiveness of emotional incentives as they influence business transactions depends on the moral sensitivity of the participants and the effectiveness of the "leader," i.e., the manager. Honesty and moral sensitivity are crucial to the emotional incentive system. In essence, people who commit themselves to honesty punish themselves with guilt when they cheat and reward themselves with satisfaction when they perform according to expectations. The manager can impact participants' self-perception of honesty by emphasizing the moral dimensions of honest behavior. In reality, the leader/manager plays two critical roles in developing an efficient system: (1) to make each individual as trustworthy as possible by emphasizing the moral dimensions of honesty and (2) to make each individual optimistic about other people's honesty to instill trust in the system.

The manager has two fundamentally different strategies available to encourage efficiency/productivity/performance—a manipulation strategy and a monitoring strategy. The choice of which strategy to use clearly depends upon cost and effectiveness. Casson argues that, generally, a monitoring strategy is preferred when manipulation is costly. This is more frequently the case if information and communication services are expensive, the manager lacks charisma or persuasive skills, or the manipulation intensity required is very high such as in hazardous situations or those in which personal/emotional safety and health are a consideration. Monitoring may also be more effective in cases of routine/definable tasks common in the manufacturing or distribution process. A manipulation strategy works best when monitoring costs are high, communication costs are low, the manager has persuasive skills and charisma, and performance is more difficult to measure and monitor as is frequently the case in service industries and when intellectual skills are involved in contrast to mechanical/manual skills.

The impossibility of writing a complete contract and asset specificity associated with modern agricultural production accentuates the role of trust in contract coordination. In a continuing game even the large contractor who is recognized as being in control must maintain a reputation for fairness. The contractor needs the set of contractees as much as the contractees need the contractor. And a contractee's reputation may well determine whether she/he gets the benefit of doubt in an unusual situation.

How might these concepts be applied in understanding and analyzing issues of contract or ownership coordination? One approach is to use them in a game-theoretic framework to analyze coordination behavior. Data for the analysis might come from simulation exercises, decision-making games and personal questionnaires; sources of observable real-world data are less clear. The transaction cost of negotiating contracts, strategic alliances, or transfer pricing systems would be included in the analysis and compared to the information search and discovery process to complete a similar transaction using open spot markets. Emotional as well as material rewards would be included in the payoff matrices for the various negotiating parties. Performance on negotiated transactions could be analyzed by comparing monitoring costs using the legal and institutional system compared to manipulation strategies that rely on leadership and trust. The use of various manipulation strategies in cases of repeated or sequential transactions, including public pronouncements to reinforce emotional rewards or penalties, or reciprocity and revenge, would also be included. The role of the leader/manager in using announcements or emotional awards to manipulate participants and encourage honesty and dedication rather than slacking or cheating could also be analyzed.

In essence, a model to analyze and predict changes in the coordination systems for the hog/pork subsector and agriculture in general must combine concepts of economic incentives and costs, emotional rewards, and penalties as influenced by culture and social mores, transaction costs, negotiation skills, and power to understand: (1) when contract/ownership coordination rather than open spot-market coordination might occur, (2) the dynamics of personal negotiation in a contract- or ownership-coordinated system, (3) the cost and benefits of various strategies for enforcing performance relative to negotiated transactions, (4) the sharing of risk and rewards in a negotiated contract- or ownership-coordinated system, and (5) the overall economic and financial performance of a contract- or ownership-coordinated system.

A Final Comment

Our discussion of the issues of alternative coordination systems for industrialized food systems has been as promised—speculative! The fundamental themes of this speculation as illustrated in the hog/pork sector are:

1. The transformation of the coordination system in the hog/pork sector from impersonal markets to personal, negotiated contract/ownership will be rapid because of both the incentive and economic benefits of closer coordination and the windows of opportunity provided by the

product, investment, human resource/manager, and technological life cycles.

2. Information is a major driver and determinant of the form of coordination as well as of who has power in the food production/distribution system. The improved flow of information from consumer to raw material supplier with a contract/ownership coordination approach results in significant advantages for this form of coordination since consumers increasingly demand attributes in their food products that can be most effectively and efficiently sourced as characteristics of the raw material. For commodities without these specific attributes, impersonal, open markets are quite effective in transferring the limited information needed for efficient system coordination. As consumers become increasingly demanding of the attributes in pork and food products in general, contract/ownership-coordinated production and distribution systems will have a comparative advantage and dominate market coordination of independent firms.

3. In a negotiation-based (contract- or ownership-) coordinated system, the relative uniqueness of the information/knowledge resource (not the physical resources) will be the basis for system power and control, and allow those firms or stages with unique and appropriate knowledge to extract larger relative rewards and transfer more risk to other participants in the system. We argue that in the food production-distribution chain, the most unique information/knowledge, and consequently the most power and control, can be exercised by those who know the consumer best.

4. The issues of coordination can best be understood and analyzed by combining the concepts of transaction cost and principal-agent theory, strategic management, and negotiation/power and performance incentives with those from traditional market-focused concepts of economic theory and industrial organization.

References

Barkema A., and M. L. Cook. 1993. "The Changing Pork Industry: A Dilemma For Public Policy." *Economic Review*, Second Quarter, pp. 49–65. Kansas City, Mo.: Federal Reserve Bank of Kansas City.

Barry, P. J., S. T. Sonka, and K. Lajili. 1992. "Vertical Coordination, Financial Structure, and the Changing Theory of the Firm." *American Journal of Agricultural Economics* 74:1219–25.

Casson, M. 1991. *The Economics of Business Culture: Game Theory, Transaction Costs and Economic Performance*. Oxford, England: Clarendon Press.

Coase, R. H. 1937. "The Nature of the Firm." *Economica* 4:386–405.

Council on Food, Agricultural, and Resource Economics. 1994. *The Industrialization of Agriculture: Policy, Research, and Education Needs*. Synopsis of symposium held in Washington, D.C., July.

Donohue, W. A. 1978. "An Empirical Framework for Examining Negotiation Processes and Outcomes." *Communication Monographs* 45:247–57.

The Economist. 1994. "Don't Get Left on the Shelf," July 2, pp. 11–12.

Fisher, R. 1983. "Negotiating Power: Getting and Using Influence." *American Behavioral Scientist* 27:149–66.

Greenhalgh, L. 1987. "Relationships in Negotiations." *Negotiation Journal* 3:235–43.

Harrigan, K. R. 1985. *Strategic Flexibility: A Management Guide for Changing Times*. New York, N.Y.: Lexington Books.

King, R. P. 1992. "Management and Financing of Vertical Coordination in Agriculture: An Overview." *American Journal of Agricultural Economics* 74:1217–18.

Mahoney, J. T. 1992. "The Choice of Organizational Form: Vertical Financial Ownership versus Other Methods of Vertical Integration." *Strategic Management Journal* 13:559–84.

Martin, L., R. Westgren, L. Schrader, L. Cousineau, N. Le Roc'h, R. Paguaga, and V. Amanor-Boadu. 1993. "Alternative Business Linkages: The Case of the Poultry Industry." Working Paper 10-93, Food Industry Research Group, George Morris Centre, University of Guelph, June.

Milgrom, P., and J. Roberts. 1992. *Economics, Organization and Management*. Englewood Cliffs, N.J.: Prentice Hall.

Porter, M. E. 1985. *Competitive Advantage: Creating and Sustaining Superior Performance*. New York, N.Y.: Free Press.

Putnam, L. L., and T. S. Jones. 1982. "The Role of Communication in Bargaining." *Human Communication Research* 8:262–80.

Urban, T. 1991. "Agricultural Industrialization: It's Inevitable." *Choices*, Fourth Quarter, pp. 4–6.

U.S. Department of Commerce. *1992 Census of Agriculture—Iowa State and County Data*, vol. 1, part 15, p. 22. Washington, D.C.: Bureau of the Census.

Williamson, O. 1973. "Markets and Hierarchies: Some Elementary Considerations." *American Economic Review* 63:316–25.

2 Toward an Institutional Analysis of Vertical Coordination in Agribusiness

LOÏC SAUVÉE[1]

Vertical coordination[2] has always been a major field of economic research, both theoretical and empirical. Industrial organization theory has focused on vertical integration and make-or-buy decisions and is mainly built on a technological and imperfect competition basis. The transaction cost theory has developed a contractual vision of firms and markets and has opened new perspectives for the study of vertical coordination. Complementary and sometimes critical researchers from the fields of agency theory, strategic management, and organization theory have pushed further and extended the Williamsonian paradigm and some industrial organization insights.

We will see that the field of New Institutional Economics could provide renewed theoretical foundations on which to base understanding and analysis of the complex and polymorphic phenomenon of relationships between firms. In the same vein, integrative approaches implementing strategic dimensions and organizational economics appear to be a promising way of research. Our objective is to show that these recent contributions can lead to new perspectives on vertical coordination, seen as a *result of strategic planning choices*. Consequently, the purpose of the analysis is to understand *how* the decisions are made and to propose a framework for firms' decision making.

The paper is divided in three parts. The first part is mainly a review of the literature on institutional approaches to vertical coordination. It explains the concepts, from the most significant works, used in the study of vertical coordination between firms. Indeed, each theory focuses on certain aspects of the phenomenon in order to represent it in an intelligible way and in a specific perspective. The emphasis is put on recent syncretic institutional and strategy-oriented theories,[3] notably on their conceptual contributions to the understanding of vertical coordination. The second part addresses the main implications of these theories for the study of vertical coordination and identifies their methodological contributions. The vertical chain structure of agricultural subsectors, the heterogeneity of their vertical coordination mechanisms, and the importance of quality and chain management issues have interested many agricultural economists[4] in applying or testing theoretical hypotheses. Consequently, we attempt to determine a possible methodological framework for the study of vertical coordination in agribusiness, with an illustration applied to the alternative business linkages of the broiler industry.

Institutional Analysis: Main Theoretical Backgrounds

Transaction Cost Economics and Related Approaches

The governance structures of vertical transactions Instead of studying the firm as an entity, Williamson (1979, 1985, 1989) considers the transaction as the basic unit of analysis. Under behavioral assumptions of opportunity and bounded rationality of economic agents, this theory affirms that "institutions of economic organization have a transaction-cost origin" (Williamson 1979), where the transaction costs are the costs of carrying out transactions.

The central hypothesis of Williamson's work is that "transactions, which differ in their attributes, are assigned to *governance structures*, which differ in their costs and competencies, in a discriminating—mainly transaction cost economizing—way" (Williamson 1979). Therefore, knowing the significant dimensions of transactions will allow one to predict governance structures. According to Williamson, the critical dimensions of transactions are the frequency with which they recur, the degree and type of uncertainty to which they are subject, and the condition of asset specificity.[5]

Four generic governance structures and three contracting forms are considered: market (classical contracting), trilateral (neoclassical contracting), bilateral and unified (relational contracting) (Table 2.1).

The market governance structure is the main structure for "non specific transactions of both occasional and recurrent contracting" (Williamson 1989). In these particular types of transactions, markets are seen to be efficient and the specific identity of the parties is unimportant.

Trilateral governance involves two types of transactions: occasional frequency of both mixed and idiosyncratic assets. In these cases, "the interests of the principals in sustaining the relation are especially great" (Williamson 1979). Then, "given the limits of classical contract law (the market governance) for sustaining these transactions and the prohibitive costs of

Table 2.1 Characteristics of transactions and governance structure

	Investment characteristics		
Frequency	Nonspecific	Mixed	Idiosyncratic
Occasional	Market governance (Classical contracting)	Trilateral governance (Neoclassical contracting)	
Recurrent		Bilateral governance (Relational contracting)	Unified governance (Relational contracting)

Source: Williamson (1979).

transaction-specific governance, an intermediate institutional form is needed" (Williamson 1979). A third-party assistance will resolve disputes and evaluate performance.

The bilateral and unified governance structures are both considered to be relational contracting forms. They occur when transactions are recurrent and involve mixed or idiosyncratic assets. Williamson distinguishes between the case in which the autonomy of the parties is maintained (bilateral governance) and that in which the transaction is organized within the firm (unified governance or vertical integration). Bilateral governance occurs in the case of mixed assets and recurrent transactions; both parties have a strong incentive to sustain the relationship. What is needed here are "some ways for declaring admissible dimensions for adjustment such that flexibility is provided under terms in which both parties have confidence" (Williamson 1979). Unified governance is required when transaction-specific assets become more idiosyncratic and therefore when incentives for trading weaken. A complete vertical integration allows adaptations without the need to "consult, complete or revise interfirm agreements" (Williamson 1979).

In the transaction cost theory, each type of vertical governance structure will stem from the characteristics of transactions. Under the assumption of economic efficiency and competition, the chosen governance structure will minimize the total transaction costs.[6]

According to Milgrom and Roberts, it is useful to separate the transaction costs into two categories: coordination costs and motivation costs. The coordination costs are the costs of "monitoring the environment, planning and bargaining to decide what needs to be done" (precontractual costs). The motivation costs are the costs of "measuring performance, providing incentives, and enforcing agreements to ensure that people follow instructions, honor commitments, and keep agreements" (postcontractual costs).

In a complementary work, Williamson (1991) notes the dimension of governance structures related to adaptation to economic changes, which, according to him, is the source of organizational dynamics. He considers two types of adaptation:

1. Adaptation type A (autonomy) in which "consumers and producers respond independently to parametric price changes so as to maximize their utility and profits, respectively."
2. Adaptation type C (cooperation) wherein "the needs for coordinated investments and for uncontested (or less contested) coordinated

realignments increase in frequency and consequentiality" (Williamson 1991).

Governance structures will vary in their efficiency to adapt to economic changes (type A or type C) because they rely on instruments of control with variable *incentive intensity*. Market governance structure is particularly efficient in adaptation A, while hierarchy is better to orchestrate coordinated actions in adaptation C. Table 2.2 gives the main distinguishing attributes of three generic forms of governance structure: market, hybrid, and hierarchy. The choice of a governance structure is not only linked to characteristics of transactions, but also to external conditions.

Transaction cost theory gives a contractual representation of vertical coordination. The central notion of governance structure is the ability to join economic and legal aspects. But, taking into account many criticisms and being aware of the limitations of his own framework, Williamson (1993b, 1994b) progressively broadened the scope of transaction cost theory to a more general theory of economic organizations. Indeed, his concept of market or organization *failures* as the only determinant of vertical integration decisions is probably too restrictive. As shown by Medema,[7] the treatment of opportun-

Table 2.2 Distinguishing attributes of market, hybrid, and hierarchy governance structures

Attributes	Governance structure		
	Market	Hybrid	Hierarchy
Instruments			
Incentive intensity	++	+	0
Administrative control	0	+	++
Performance attributes			
Adaptation (A)	++	+	0
Adaptation (C)	0	+	++
Contract law	++	+	0

++=strong   +=semi-strong   0=weak

Source: Williamson (1991).

ism is incomplete and the minimization of transaction costs is only one of the motives for vertical integration. He argues that "the governance structure is the product of an evolutionary process which is worked out over time, a many period game characterized by power play." He suggests, for example, that opportunism is the exercise of power or authority from one firm vis-à-vis the other. We will see that, in spite of these limitations, theorists from other fields heavily use transaction cost concepts and perspectives.

The design of vertical control Agency theory deals with the relationship between two parties in which one party (the principal) delegates work to another (the agent). The theory is focused on the contract between these two parties and seeks to determine the optimal contract, i.e., the contract with the most efficient organization of information and the lowest costs. This agency structure is found in a wide range of settings such as relations between employers and employees, owners and managers, insurance companies and their customers, buyers and suppliers, etc.

Eisenhardt (1985, 1989), borrowing from Ouchi and from Barney and Ouchi, shows that agency theory and organization theory have important links and complementarities, mainly because both of them deal with ambivalent cooperative/conflictual behaviors. We will see that this complementarity is particularly relevant for the study of control strategies between firms.

Two branches in agency theory are generally recognized (Eisenhardt 1989): the positivist theory and the principal-agent theory.[8] The two streams of thought share a common unit of analysis (the contract between a principal and an agent) and similar assumptions, but differ in the formal treatment. The first branch is more descriptive and mainly concerned by the relevant variables, the "governance mechanisms," of contracts. The second branch develops models—under a wide range of quantitative variables—and defines the contracting optimum solutions.

According to Eisenhardt (1989), these differences are not crucial for organization theory. The contracting problem remains with its two dimensions: the agency problem and the risk-sharing problem. The agency problem arises because of information asymmetry between the parties. *Adverse selection* occurs when one party (principal or agent) is better informed than the other about the characteristics of the transaction. For Milgrom and Roberts, adverse selection is "a kind of precontractual opportunism that arises when one party to a bargain has private information about something that affects the other's net benefit from the contract and when those whose private information implies that the contract will be especially disadvantageous for the other party agree to a contract." *Moral hazard* refers to the lack of effort on the part of the agent because the task is too complex to be completely controlled. Milgrom and Roberts define it as a "form of postcontractual opportunism that arises when actions required or desired under contract are not freely observable." Besides, the agents may differ in their behavior vis-à-vis risk; agency theory tries to resolve both the question of risk sharing and of the cost of transferring that risk.

For Eisenhardt (1989), "the heart of principal-agent theory is the trade-off between (a) the cost of measuring behavior and (b) the cost of measuring outcomes and transferring risk to the agent." Instead of the traditional approaches focusing on structural alternatives such as matrix, decentralization, and divisionalization, Eisenhardt (1985) puts the stress on control characteristics and mechanisms.

The organizational approach to control suggests that two strategies are available:

1. Assessing the performance of the agent, measured either by the behavior or its outcome. The cost of this performance evaluation depends upon the information characteristics of the performed tasks. According to Eisenhardt, these characteristics are the ability to know the transformation process (*task programmability*) and the ability to measure outcomes (*separability*).[9]
2. Minimizing the divergence of interests and/or preferences among the members. In that case, the need to control members is lessened because they "understand and have internalized the goals" (Eisenhardt 1985). Numerous means could achieve this objective, among them the selection of members, training, etc.

The choice between these two strategies is essentially determined by the ease of performance evaluation, i.e., readability of tasks in both their programmability and separability dimensions.

In a simple low/high framework applied to the dimensions of task characteristics, the control strategies can be classified in three categories (Table 2.3). This representation of control design may be usefully completed by several elements borrowed from agency theory perspectives. First of all, in agency theory, information as well as information systems have a dynamic role: they are considered commodities that can be purchased or sold. Thus they play an active role in the choice and design of control strategies. Second, agency theory shows that uncertainty plays a central role in the definition of

Table 2.3 Organizational theory and control strategy

Outcome measurability	Task programmability	
	Perfect	Imperfect
High	Behavior/outcome control	Outcome control
Low	Behavior control	Socialization (clan control)

Source: Eisenhardt (1985).

a contract. Indeed, the optimal contract must minimize the control costs plus the residual loss due to an imperfect control. Uncertainty, for instance in performance evaluation, affects directly the choice of a control mechanism.

Finally, Eisenhardt's syncretic approach leads one to consider the task characteristics and the measurement system characteristics as the key dimensions for explaining the choice of a control strategy. This choice of a control strategy is an important aspect of the linkages between vertically interrelated organizations. Her approach enhances understanding of the choice between alternative control mechanisms, as well as consideration of the continuum of contract forms between the two extremes of outcome-based and behavior-based control strategies. For instance, a control strategy can combine behavior control with compensation of efforts through multiple rewards.

A syncretic approach: Mahoney's framework Mahoney's work provides a general framework for predicting and prescribing the alternative governance structures of vertical integration. Mahoney recognizes a continuum of governance structures, including spot markets, short-term contracts, franchising, joint ventures, and vertical financial ownership (hierarchy). His approach constitutes an attempt to aggregate agency-related perspectives (such as Eisenhardt's) and transaction cost theory.

His review of the strategic management literature shows that the motives for vertical integration may be classified into three categories: strategic considerations, output and/or input advantages, and uncertainties in costs and/or prices. According to Mahoney, these factors constitute explanations for vertical integration strategies, but "they do not provide insight on the choice of organizational form" (i.e., the governance structure).

The missing link to predict this choice is the existence of transaction costs. In fact, as Mahoney suggests, "in absence of transaction costs, vertical contracting can replicate the advantages of vertical financial ownership." In other words, the effective form of vertical corporate control cannot be predicted when transaction costs are ignored.

In order to understand the choice of governance structure, Mahoney affirms that "measurement costs and transaction costs should be considered simultaneously." Then the governance structure chosen to implement the vertical coordination strategy will minimize the costs of "negotiating, adapting, monitoring, and enforcing buyer-supplier relationships." From this point of view, a comparative institutional analysis between different forms of governance structure will allow consideration of the advantages and the disadvantages of vertical integration strategies.

We have seen that frequency, uncertainty, and asset specificity are the critical criteria of Williamson's framework. For Mahoney, frequency can influence the choice of governance structure especially in case of intermediate asset specificity. But, following Williamson, Mahoney considers that when asset specificity is either low or high, frequency influence is indeterminate. Then two key dimensions remain: asset specificity and demand and/or technological uncertainty.

On the other hand, research on control in organization (especially Eisenhardt and Ouchi) adds two critical variables: programmability and separability of tasks. According to Mahoney, external uncertainties (for example, demand and technological uncertainties) have an indeterminate influence[10] on governance structures and are not included in his framework. Hence, three dimensions are combined in an eight-case chart to predict the governance structure (Table 2.4).

For Mahoney, a combination of three determinant variables is sufficient to explain the choice of a vertical coordination mechanism. His framework allows the prediction of six different forms of vertical contracts (in eight generic situations). His approach is very similar to Williamson's; he considers that "the transaction-cost approach provides insight into the key role of asset specificity." But, he adds, "[this approach] neglects the interactive effects of measurement problems that have been highlighted by agency theory. On the other hand, positive agency theory emphasizes measurement costs but neglects asset specificity. Combining these two efficiency perspectives enables us to make predictions and offer prescriptions on the make-or-buy decision."

Table 2.4 The organizational form of vertical control/ownership

	Low programmability		High programmability	
	Low asset specificity	High asset specificity	Low asset specificity	High asset specificity
Low nonseparability	Spot market	Long-term contract	Spot market	Joint venture
High nonseparability	Relational contract	Clan (hierarchy)	Inside contract	Hierarchy

Source: Mahoney.

Strategic Management Theory and Institutional Analysis

Porter's interest in vertical integration strategies initiated abundant research in the strategic management field. His 1991 article summarizes his main concepts. For Porter, the basic unit of competitive advantage is the discrete activity. The firm is a "collection of discrete, but interrelated economic activities such as products being assembled, salespeople making sales visits, and orders being processed. A firm's strategy defines its configuration of activities and how they interrelate." Consequently, competitive advantage will result "from a firm's ability to perform the required activities at a collectively lower cost than rivals, or perform some activities in unique ways that create buyer value and hence allow the firm to command a premium price" (Porter 1991).

Porter defines the value chain as "activities that directly produce, market, and deliver the product and those that create or source inputs or factors (including planning and management) required to do so. The firm's strategy is manifested in the way in which it configures and links the many activities in its value chain relative to the competitors" (Porter 1991).

The central interest of Porter's approach is his concept of vertical coordination (along a value chain) as a result of a firm's behavior. Stimulated by this approach, strategic management scholars will adopt this perspective and will focus their research on the links between environmental circumstances and a firm's strategy. Hence, the study of strategy appears to be an in-house means of investigation into the vertical coordination process.

Harrigan (1984, 1986) represents a classical strategic management perspective on vertical integration. She develops a complete framework for the formulation of vertical integration strategies. She proposes an extended model of choice, including the breadth of integrated activities undertaken; the number of stages of integrated activities; the degree of internal transfer for every vertical linkage; and the form of ownership used to control the vertical relationship. Substantial additions have been made to the simple make-or-buy decision model, but the main factors that determine the choice of vertical integration strategy are coherent with industrial organization assumptions and Porter's theory of strategy. These factors are demand uncertainties, nature of competition (on the buyer/supplier interfaces), and corporate strategy requirements.

Recent contributions are more directly connected with new microeconomics research (essentially in transaction cost and agency fields), or at least concerned with the possible bridges between the two areas of strategic management and organizational economics. Four of the most recent and significant works are particularly stressed here.[11]

The tendency toward vertical disintegration frequently observed in manufacturing industries is the starting point of Boone and Verbeke's 1991 analysis. According to them, a simple transaction cost analysis does not provide a full explanation of this phenomenon because the Williamsonian paradigm underestimates the bureaucratic costs and the incentive problems of hierarchy. Moreover, the strategic implications of vertical integration are ignored. Thus they extend transaction cost theory through the introduction of "conceptual elements" from organization theory and strategic management theory.

While economizing on transaction costs, vertical integration may, on the other hand, significantly increase the bureaucratic costs. According to Boone and Verbeke, "the competitive strategy chosen by the firm largely determines the level of bureaucratic costs and may thus influence the optimal level of vertical integration." Their main statement is that bureaucratic costs are not automatically determined by the structural conditions of internalization, but are, on the contrary, related to the strategic choices of the firm. Consequently, the incomplete character of transaction cost analysis leads to an overestimation of the advantages of vertical integration.

For Boone and Verbeke, the optimal degree of vertical integration stems from two core variables: asset specificity and the importance of innovation and flexibility in competitive strategy. The level of asset specificity is coherent with the original transaction cost model. The degree of flexibility of the competitive strategy is a particularly relevant variable because it is highly interrelated with costs due to the internalization of the transaction.

In the cases of intermediate or high asset specificity and innovation strategies, hybrid forms of vertical coordination are likely to occur. Indeed, the two extremes (hierarchy and market) are both inefficient because of too high bureaucratic costs in the former case or uncertainty of the transaction in the latter case. Thus the main challenge for the firm is to "develop strategic networks of contractual arrangements, so as to build reciprocal commitments with suppliers." This is what Boone and Verbeke call the "strategic management of contractual relations" wherein "benefits normally associated with a hierarchical organization (coordination and control) can be obtained, but without incurring the bureaucratic costs of such a hierarchy." Various forms of long-term contracts will benefit from the high power incentives of the market, but in case of dissatisfaction, contractual arrangements may be canceled.

Finally, for Boone and Verbeke, vertical coordination cannot be explained solely in terms of transaction costs. The necessity for a firm to have "flexibility and innovation (of its) corporate strategies (partly as a reaction to environmental dynamism—such as rapid changes in demand or new information technologies)" lessens considerably the theoretical advantages of vertical integration.

Hennart (1993, 1994), on his side, addresses two main criticisms of transaction cost analysis. First, this theory is only a theory of market failure and does not explain why a particular firm will succeed. Second, the two classical categories of market and hierarchy are irrelevant because most of the governance structures cannot be classified under these two categories. Utilizing concepts from agency and organization theories, Hennart's view is an attempt to extend transaction cost theory to a general model of competitive advantage through organization.

First, Hennart (1993) distinguishes two notions that are usually confused: (1) the methods of organizing, i.e., the mechanisms utilized to conduct the transactions (price constraints or behavior constraints), and (2) the institution, i.e., the organization that implements a particular set of organizing methods. While markets rely principally on prices and firms on hierarchy, Hennart (1993) insists that "there is not a one-to-one correspondence between prices and markets, and hierarchy and firms."

Then, Hennart broadens the definition of transaction costs in defining the shirking costs (the costs of constraining behavior plus the residual amount of shirking due to imperfect behavior constraints) and cheating costs (the costs of using price-constraint systems—i.e., of measuring output—plus the losses due to imperfect measurement). While the choice of a price-constraint system minimizes shirking but encourages (or at least allows) cheating, the choice of a behavior-constraint system, on the contrary, minimizes cheating but encourages shirking. Under particular transaction conditions (see Williamson 1979, 1985), and considering the existence of diminishing returns to measuring output and constraining behavior, institutions will try to combine price and behavior constraints in order to reach the lowest global costs. This extended concept of "organizing costs" is the foundation of Hennart's theory of the firm.

The distinction between intra- and interfirm transactions is "that intra-firm transactions are mediated by employment contracts, while inter-firm transactions are contracts for outputs. Choosing the appropriate mix of contracts and improving the efficiency of each type is a source of competitive advantage" (Hennart 1994). The source of rents is the ability of a firm to better coordinate its activities. In fact, three strategies are available: reduce organizing costs within firms, increase efficiency of external contracts, and assess more efficiently the costs of alternative strategies.

In other words, competitive advantage arises from "inter-firm differences in their organizing capabilities" (Hennart 1994). In that sense, the role of strategy is essentially one of implementation and coordination, in "reducing both internal and external transaction costs and achieving the lowest total level of organizing costs by developing better internal and external contracts" (Hennart 1994).

Dosi et al. provide a general theory of corporate coherence, i.e., an explanation of the boundaries of the modern corporation. Although not exclusively concerned with vertical integration issues, this theory is very useful to understand vertical corporate coherence, such as the multiproduct scope, the distribution of product portfolios inside firms, and the relative stability of these portfolios. Vertically integrated firms appear, in this view, as one out of several models of corporate coherence.

In traditional theories of the firm, market power and economies of scope are the common explanations of corporate coherence. But, according to Dosi et al., such theories are unable to explain "why a set of contractual relationships among specialist firms could not accomplish the same objectives." With economies of scope, for instance, the organizational dimensions are not considered; a wide variety of organizational arrangements could provide the same effects. Technological economies explain the make-or-buy decisions, but not the choice of specific contractual forms. Transaction cost economics may have some capacity to explain vertical relationship, but does not provide, for the same reasons, an explanation of a firm's diversification.

Fundamentally, the inability of these theories to fully explain the multidimensions of corporate coherence lies in the fact that the firm is seen either as a production function or as a nexus of contracts involving vertically interrelated factors of production. For these authors, an organization is more than a minimization of production and/or transaction costs.

In their attempts to understand coherence, Dosi et al. add new criteria. Borrowing from organizational economics, these authors affirm that four factors are relevant to study: complementary assets, enterprise learning, technological opportunities, and selection. These four factors determine the "evolutionary path" of the firm and the fluctuation of its activities' boundary over time.

Existence of *complementary assets* is probably the strongest factor that explains the contour of the evolutionary path. Typically, complementary assets lay upstream or downstream "from product-process development in the value added chain." *Enterprise learning* is the ability of a firm to learn through its economic activity (learning by doing). This knowledge is cumulative and concerns organizational skills rather than individual skills.[12] But enterprise learning is not omniscience. This necessarily local feature limits what a firm is able to do. Moreover, the choice of new activities will be dependent on what has already been done; there are path dependencies. In fact, Williamson's concept of idiosyncratic assets and their impact on organizational design is broadened by the introduction of irreversibility and dependencies.

As a result, "firms can be thought of as an integrated cluster of core competencies and supporting complementary assets. The degree of coherence one would expect to observe at a particular point in time depends on the relationships between learning, path dependencies, opportunities, inherited complementary assets, and selection." Dosi et al. distinguish six forms of corporate coherence: specialist firms, vertically integrated firms, coherent diversifiers, conglomerates, network firms, and hollow corporations (see Table 2.5). The vertically integrated firms, for instance, are characterized by "slow learning but high path dependencies and specialized assets etc; older firms are likely to be more vertically integrated than young firms because start-ups are less common in industries where learning is slow" (Dosi et al.).

Zajac and Olsen, while stressing the interorganizational strategies of firms, propose another variant of integration between strategic management and transaction cost perspectives. For them, the standard transaction cost theory is only a "single-party analysis of cost minimization and neglects the interdependence between partners." They suggest that an exchange, instead of being passive and costly, can also be a means to construct and create value even if the exchange comes with new transaction costs. They consider that "the transaction-cost theory overemphasizes the structural analysis of interorganizational exchange relationship without taking into account the processual/behavioral aspects."

Instead, their transactional value analysis shows that an exchange can create value that "could otherwise not be created by either firm independently." The classical Williamsonian analysis appears to be relevant in the particular case of a single firm's make-or-buy decision wherein the main (or exclusive) objective is the minimization of costs. But in many other cases, two firms involved in a transaction could also try to develop a common strategy of, for instance, product differentiation. Therefore, the central question will be how to create/maximize this value and how to claim it.

Table 2.5 Corporate coherence matrix

Evolutionary path	Slow learning/ Restricted opportunities	Rapid learning/ Rich opportunities
Wide	Coherent diversifiers (low growth)	Coherent diversifiers (high growth)
Narrow	Vertically integrated firms	Specialist firms
Converging	Network firms (low growth)	Network firms (high growth)

Source: Dosi et al.

This new perspective has another implication: Zajac and Olsen focus on the process of decision making. Indeed, because of its highly strategic and behavioral content, the choice of a governance structure is seen as largely unpredictable. Instead, Zajac and Olsen propose a model of interorganizational process, configuring the stages of decision making, useful in understanding the likely choice of vertical structure (see Table 2.6).

From the essentially structural and deterministic transaction cost framework, the authors moved to a strategic and processual framework, not denying but extending and, in a sense, reinterpreting the transaction cost foundations.

French Institutional Analysis: Convention Theory and Contract Economics

To be complete on the recent theoretical developments particularly relevant for the study of vertical coordination, one must consider the two following approaches: (1) convention theory and (2) Brousseau's contract economics.

Convention theory is not yet structured in a single theoretical paradigm. We will refer to Eymard-Duvernay's article focused on the central role of quality uncertainty in structuring interfirm relationships. For Eymard-Duvernay, "prices do not constitute a determinant variable anymore to ensure coordination, but one of the links of industrial organization subject to conventional rules. When markets work properly, quality will be assessed

Table 2.6 A stages model of interorganizational processes

Initializing stage	Processing stage	Reconfiguring stage
Summary of key issues:		
Weighing exchange alternatives	Accelerating learning	Reaching end of expected duration
Projecting exchange into future	Managing conflict	Assessing performance gap
Clarifying exchange parameters	Creating relational norms	Redefining type of strategy
Engaging in preliminary exchange, communications and negotiations	Developing trust	Redefining nature of exchange process
Conducting initial exchange rounds		

Source: Zajac and Olsen.

without ambiguity by a given price. But quality conventions are necessary when the price alone cannot evaluate quality."

Eymard-Duvernay distinguishes four generic forms of coordination: domestic, industrial, civic, and market. *Domestic coordination* occurs when uncertainty about quality is solved through trust: for example, long-term relations between agents or use of private brands that increase the quality reputation of products. In *industrial coordination*, quality is not defined by the agents themselves, but by a third party outside the market who determines common norms or standards. Economic agents, in their exchanges, will refer to these objective definitions. If prices are sufficient indicators to evaluate quality, i.e., if there is no uncertainty about quality, then the market works by itself: this is *market coordination*. *Civic coordination* occurs when there is a collective commitment to avoid conflicts (Table 2.7).

In this theory, conventions are a set of mechanisms and rules that involve private agents as well as public institutions. Therefore, the analysis focuses on the way quality uncertainty is solved. The content of product specification, the nature and genesis of third parties involved, the strategy of product differentiation or labeling, or other empirical observations about quality, clarify the conventions. Convention theory shows that quality conventions are a strong factor structuring industrial organization. Far from being static or noncompetitive, these conventions belong to the competitive process. Influenced by strategic management approaches, convention theorists insist that coordination mechanisms determine the degree of cooperation or competition between agents. Eymard-Duvernay, for instance, emphasizes the similarity between Porter's strategic groups and models of coordination. As soon as they are set up, quality conventions constitute, in a sense, a particular

Table 2.7 Quality, quality conventions, and coordination

Way of defining quality	Way of recognizing quality	
	With uncertainty	Without uncertainty
Externalized (standards, norms)	Industrial coordination	Market coordination
Internalized (trust, authority)	Domestic coordination	Civic coordination

category of mobility barriers. Moreover, the convention theory approach shows that the definition of contracts cannot be understood exclusively at a microeconomic level, i.e., between two single parts. A convention is also a mode of regulation found at a collective level, for instance, a region or an industry. In return, the choice of specific conventions is not neutral; it affects greatly the basic conditions of competition.

Unlike neoclassical economists, convention theorists do not consider nonprice exchanges between firms as market failure or imperfections. Instead, adopting a positive approach, they integrate the diversity and the complexity of the quality issue and build their analysis on it. They insist on the institutional and strategic dimensions of quality and are able to explain the existence and juxtaposition of several coordination modes in the same industry. In spite of methodological incompleteness, this approach usefully links quality questions with industrial structure.

Convention theory has been used in the study of quality conventions found in agricultural subsectors. Two authors, Valceschini (1993) and Sylvander (1995), have applied this theory to the study of economic coordination.[13] Valceschini (1993) demonstrates that, in the French vegetable processing industry, the traditional articulation between civic and industrial coordinations —where price discovery and definition of quality are centralized—is no longer relevant. In this sector, production contracts between vegetable producers and processors have been established at a collective level in a national interprofessional organization. For Valceschini, this contract economy is "not reducible to a (simple) contract minimizing technological and strategic uncertainties between agents, but is a conventional arrangement whose goal is to create value through cooperative behavior and to share (ex ante) this value."

Valceschini (1993) shows that the definition of these "institutional arrangements" is contingent upon the economic and political context. In the 1960s, these conditions (and notably a high economic growth) led to a centralized and civic interprofessional organization. This organization defined a standard contract that specified price discovery, risk sharing, production planning, and technical monitoring. This quasi-complete contract aims to limit conflicts and competition between producers. But Valceschini insists this industrial/civic form of coordination, far from eliminating competition between processing companies, exacerbates it among the only remaining variables: investment policy and production-cost minimization. In the 1980s, a new competitive environment (high concentration ratio, high substitution effects between canned and frozen vegetables, etc.) invalidated the traditional rules of value creation and risk sharing. Increased competition between companies and between producers led to new quality standards (defined by the market, i.e., consumer needs) and to more flexible price discovery mechanisms. In fact, the industrial/civic coordination was progressively replaced by an industrial/market coordination.

Sylvander (1995) demonstrates that in the French poultry processing industry, "quality specifications influence the choice of coordination mechanisms" and, consequently, the way firms compete and cooperate. Notably, this is the emergence and the strengthening of an industrial convention that determines the economic behavior of the firms. In this industrial convention, quality is defined and controlled by a third party. Each grower is held to a strict set of standards and requirements about feed, genetic stocks, housing conditions, etc.

This convention played an important role in the development of the subsector and particularly in restoring trust among consumers about the product quality. This convention progressively shaped competition between processing companies. Indeed, the competitive advantage in such a system is mainly found in the ability to improve its quality management and its productivity (at the production level, in order to decrease costs). For Sylvander (1995) only the biggest companies were able to improve significantly these constraints because of financial availability and marketing skills. They benefited from the rapid growth of consumption.

Coherent with convention theory assumptions, Valceschini's and Sylvander's approaches have three methodological consequences for the study of vertical coordination. First, the comprehensibility of a contract's genesis cannot be understood exclusively at the microeconomic level; indeed, the content of contractual arrangements (micro level) may stem from institutional arrangements and institutional organizations (macro level). Secondly, these institutional arrangements greatly contribute to shape the competition in the sector. Contracts are not outside the competitive process but are a part of it. Third, the genesis of these arrangements is itself dependent upon external and internal factors. Therefore, a complete vertical coordination analysis should include the study of interplay between basic conditions and strategic behaviors and the effect of their consequences on the institutional environment.

Brousseau's (1993) contract economics extends the Williamsonian paradigm but reconsiders some of his fundamental assumptions in a positivist way. He proposes a general theory of bilateral economic relations and combines, in an original fashion, transaction cost theory and elements of industrial organization. His contribution completes the Williamsonian paradigm in two main directions: (1) the description of contracts and (2) the way these contracts are chosen.

First, Brousseau proposes a discrete and descriptive grammar of contracts. Contracts are complex, and a unified framework to describe this complexity is needed. For Brousseau, every contract can be interpreted as a set of clauses, with several possibilities for each clause. These clauses are based on the main functional characteristics of contracts.[14] Then each particular contract is fully described by a specific combination of the alternatives of the seven clauses. This common grammar allows the description of a wide range of contracts. According to Brousseau, this discrete and strictly descriptive approach avoids ambiguities and analogical limits of categories such as market, hybrid, or hierarchy. The process of choice involved in a particular contract will be more understandable. Indeed, the final choice is, in fact, the sum of all the clauses' choices.

The second contribution by Brousseau to the transaction cost framework concerns the definition of a decision-making model. Although strongly influenced, Brousseau differs from Williamson on several important matters. His definition of costs is more extensive. To the traditional transaction costs, he adds two categories of costs: production and incentive. These three categories of costs are the basic elements for the evaluation of contract efficiency.

Unlike Williamson, Brousseau does not consider that the choice of a governance structure is strictly determined by the structural conditions of the transactions. One must consider the *objectives* of the contracting process, which will depend greatly upon the asset specificity and distribution. Different objectives lead to different optimization rules: the simple transaction cost minimization objective is completed by rent maximization of either the coalition or of the agent having bargaining power.

Brousseau combines and completes Williamsonian concepts with strategic and organizational considerations. A redefined notion of contracts replaces the governance structure. He focuses on the comprehension of the decision process instead of defining a determinist model of governance structure.

Implications for the Study of Vertical Coordination

Institutional and Strategic Perspectives on Vertical Coordination

As Spulber (1992) suggests, "Vertical integration provides in varying degrees the beginning of a theory of the firm because [it] addresses the rationale for including specific activities within the firm." Mahoney, in the same vein, considers that vertical coordination and theory of the firm are "largely isomorphic." Indeed, if vertical coordination can be seen as a process of selecting and organizing activities, the questions of the boundaries and of the conceptual essence of the firm inevitably arise.[15]

Starting from a neoclassical point of view, theorists became more and more preoccupied with questions such as imperfect competition, uncertainty, and control. The status of the firm itself evolves; the production function makes room for the institutional form in which economic and legal aspects are inseparable. But how could these theories be articulated for the study of vertical coordination? And to what extent are they irreducible? In spite of this diversity and complexity, it is possible to highlight the main contributions of these theories through discussion of two issues: (1) the complementarity between economic and institutional approaches, and (2) the strategic dimension of economic coordination. A critical discussion about these points will lead to our own assumptions and hypotheses.

The industrial organization approach shows that technological and market structure considerations are relevant, but insufficient to understand the choice of a coordination system. Indeed, control strategies, for instance, involve legal aspects and are not reducible to the choice of a technological sequence through an optimization of costs.

In fact, what institutional theories, in their diversity, show is that economic and legal aspects cannot be easily separated. Organizational issues need specific concepts. The contract, as an economic concept, is a particularly pertinent subject for the study of economic organizations. Pertinence of new concepts lies in the fact that they provide a different vision of reality and that specific facts, until now neglected, are taken into account. Strictly microeconomic perspectives consider the organization as a black box. More important, no common conceptual bridge links organizations and markets. No microeconomic concepts allow their study simultaneously as alternative forms of institutions. Indeed, if the market is the only reference, nothing, or very little, can be said about organizations.

The contract provides this unified vision and it becomes the central unit of analysis. Some discrepancies exist between economic and contractualist approaches, but some convergences are already significant. We have seen that some integrative approaches emerged. Works such as Milgrom and Roberts; Ménard (1989, 1995); and Barney and Ouchi show that organizational economics is already valid.

The main interest of contractual approaches is their ability to introduce in the analysis more realistic assumptions about agents' behaviors, such as *bounded rationality* and *opportunism*. Coordination issues permanently cope with the existence of an uncertain environment and with the fact that individuals or firms seek to satisfy their own interests and try to use advantageous positions. Another pertinent contribution of contractual approaches is the concept of *institution*. An institution combines a particular distribution of power over assets with specific exchange mechanisms. All socioeconomic "structures" can be seen through the prism of this *institutional analysis*[16] and one can emphasize the institutional nature of vertical coordination. These approaches are at their beginning but, as Williamson (1990) affirms, "The main axis (of future research) will be economics and organization theory, where the former provides an economizing orientation and the latter supplies added behavioral and organizational content."

Vertical coordination is the result of a highly complex process. With a dynamic and uncertain environment, and incomplete information about opportunistic partners and competitors, the choice of a coordination mechanism surely cannot be understood in a purely determinist way.

In fact, strategic management scholars[17] and economists like Brousseau share a common interest in the study of the decision process. Opposed to determinist models of choice, they open the way for a specific concept of coordination, deliberately focusing on the planning process. For them, the choice of alternative linkages is a result of goal-directed collaboration or conflict among the economic agents who make the exchange, but not (or not only) the result of external/structural forces. Consequently, the building of a *determinist* framework appears to be unrealistic. In an uncertain environment, there is no optimal equilibrium. Instead, economic agents are radically opportunistic and will adopt strategies that will maximize their own utility.[18]

This approach has important consequences and modifies underlying assumptions of economic analysis. Its role is therefore to understand and explain the behavior of agents. The choice of an organizational structure reflects not only the basis of cost, but also the existence of hierarchy and power relationships. One cannot predict the result of economic agents' behavior, but it is possible to better understand how they will make their decisions and what is their process of choice.

This procedural concept of rationality leads one to reconsider the question of efficiency. Notably, the traditional criterion of transaction cost minimization must be reexamined for several reasons. First, bargaining power within the coalition will benefit the dominant agent, who may have other objectives than a transaction cost minimization. Secondly, the goal of the coordination process may differ greatly as a function of the competitive situation. And the two more common generic strategies, cost domination and product differentiation, suggest that the objectives assigned to a particular vertical coordination process could be either cost minimization or value maximization. Third, as shown by the convention theory, institutional arrangements can affect greatly this notion of efficiency; collective rules will define specific coordination mechanisms involving factors not necessarily economic.

The fundamental methodological implication is that competitive analysis is a necessary step in the study of coordination. Indeed, firms' behaviors are specific to circumstances. For Oster, "Strategies that are able to help an organization move forward in response to changing times and integrate and disseminate the corporate vision are necessarily conditioned by the circumstances of the organization, its history and its environment."

Spulber (1992) insists on the role of strategic management research in the building of an extended model of choice. He says, "A unified theory of the firm can address in detail how managers answer the questions of what to produce, how to produce it, and for whom . . . [that] may eventually lead to a richer description of competitive markets by introducing some of the organizational issues missing from the neoclassical and industrial theories of the firm. At the same time, a clearer understanding of incentives and delegation of authority will emerge from the introduction of competitive forces into a multiple organization framework. Finally, and most significantly, greater integration of competitive and organizational issues will allow increased application of economic analysis to practical problems in management strategy."

Participating in this debate, Williamson (1994a) argues that "many errors of myopic strategic reasoning can be avoided by approaching the problem of economic organization as one of incomplete contracting in its entirety. . . . Parties to an incomplete contract are assumed to behave perceptively with respect to present and prospective benefits and hazards, whence they decide simultaneously on the technology to be employed, the price under which a good or service will be transferred, and the governance structure within which a transaction is located." Thus the central question in the study of vertical coordination will lie in the decision-making process where economic, strategic, and organizational issues are at stake.

A Descriptive and Modular View of Vertical Coordination

One of the main interests of institutional analysis is to provide new categories to describe economic reality. Ménard (1995), for example, suggests that "The deep significance of the New Institutional Economics is to have delineated fundamental differences among the complex components of a market economy, and to have initiated studies leading to a subtle articulation of these dimensions." In fact, a description of vertical coordination mechanisms gives us a tool to understand the diversity of these mechanisms.

The first step of this description is the identification of two institutional levels: *institutional environment* and *institutional arrangements*. Williamson, in a recent paper, insists deeply on this distinction. "The institutional environment is the set of fundamental political, social and legal ground rules that establishes the basis for production, exchange and distribution. Rules governing elections, property rights and the right of contract are examples. . . . An institutional arrangement is an arrangement between economic units that governs the ways in which these units can cooperate and/or compete. It . . . (can) provide a structure within which its members can cooperate, or (it can) provide a mechanism that can affect a change in laws and property rights" (Williamson 1993a).

Ménard (1995) also uses this distinction and clarifies the contents of these concepts. For him, "institutions—i.e., the institutional environment—on one hand, markets and organizations—i.e., the two types of institutional arrangements—on the other hand, operate at different levels, with institutions being an overarching class that subsumes both organizations and markets." He gives the following definitions:

An *institution* is manifested in a long-standing historically determined set of stable, abstract, and impersonal rules, crystallized in traditions, customs, or laws, so as to implement and enforce patterns of behavior governing the relationships between separate social constituencies.

A *market* is a specific institutional arrangement consisting of rules and conventions that make possible a large number of voluntary transfers of property rights on a regular basis, these reversible transfers being implemented and enforced through a specific mechanism of regulation, the competitive price system.

An *organization* is an institutional arrangement designed to make possible the conscious and deliberate coordination of activities within identifiable boundaries, in which members associate on a regular basis through a set of implicit and explicit agreements, and commit themselves to collective actions for the purpose of creating and allocating resources and capabilities by a combination of command and cooperation.

The category of institutional environment could be seen as external from the firms, but this does not mean that the definitions of rules or quality conventions, as shown earlier, are outside the competitive process and not a part of firms' behavior. But an important conceptual ambiguity remains: this institutional environment is itself very complex and heterogeneous. Some rules (or conventions) operate at macroscopic level while others are found at industry or even interfirm level.

The second step of the description is to delineate precisely the different types of vertical institutional arrangements of the firm and to classify these vertical linkages.[19] In the following section, we will consider an hypothetical model of bilateral coalition, i.e., of two economic agents entering a process of exchange.

Two dimensions are sufficient to describe the entire possibility of institutional arrangements: (1) the distribution of ownership/control over assets and (2) the mechanisms involved in the exchange.

First, one considers the "ownership" dimension. In our bilateral model, two extreme cases are possible: unified (common) or bilateral (separated) ownership. But agency literature points out the complementary notion of control as another relevant concept in the study of bilateral contracts. When ownership over assets is unified, the control will be, obviously, internal. A third party may complete this procedure without modifying the approach. In the case of bilateral ownership, control between assets can be either external (the case of principal-agent relationship) or absent. In the former case, two independent agents enter in an exchange relationship and one of them has a direct ex ante control over the other. In the latter case, there is no ex ante control (but an ex post control—over the products, for instance—is likely to exist).

The second relevant dimension of coordination is the exchange mechanism. Organization theory literature distinguishes two extreme forms of mechanisms: price and behavior constraints, separated by a continuum of combination between these two generic forms.

As shown by Table 2.8, a diagram matching the ownership/control and the exchange mechanism dimensions allows the description of a wide range of vertical coordination *institutions*. An institution can be defined *by the way authority(ies) is(are) distributed over a specific sequence of assets and by a particular choice of exchange methods between these assets.*

Table 2.8 A modular and descriptive concept of institutional arrangements

Mechanism of exchange and/or control	Ownership and control		
	Unified	Bilateral	
	Internal control	External control	No control
Price constraints	Vertical integration: profit-center firm	Vertical contracting: piecework	Pure market
Mix price/behavior constraints	Vertical integration: price + behavior control	Vertical contracting: piecework + monitoring	Alliance or agreement
Behavior constraints	Pure vertical integration	Vertical contracting: monitoring	Alliance or agreement

The table gives nine hypothetical variants of vertical coordination. With unified ownership, we find three generic forms. If this unified structure uses the price-constraint system, this is the case of the "profit-center" firm. Pure vertical integration occurs when all the exchanges within the firm are under behavior constraints. A third intermediate form is possible when the firm uses a combination of price and behavior constraints. With bilateral ownership but external control, this is the case of the vertical contracting mode of coordination. The two parties are legally independent, but one has an authority over the other. The exchange can be done under exclusive price constraints (piecework), exclusive behavior constraints (monitored work), or under an intermediate mechanism. In the case of bilateral ownership and without ex ante control, two independent and autonomous economic agents exchange. The "pure market" is found when the price is the only reference. But this exchange can also involve behavioral elements (on a reciprocal basis); the coordination is a type of agreement or alliance between the parties. Theoretically, a third party could also control the transactions.

Vertical Coordination as a Positive Framework of a Firm's Decision Making

Porter (1991) gives an excellent definition of a framework and its construction: "A framework encompasses many variables and seeks to capture much of the complexity of actual competition. Frameworks identify the relevant variables and the questions which the user must answer in order to develop conclusions tailored to a particular industry and company. In a sense, they can be seen almost as expert systems. . . . The theory embodied in frameworks is contained in the choices of included variables, the way variables are organized, the interactions among variables, and the way in which alternative patterns of variables and company choices affect outcomes."

The framework developed here contains two main objectives: (1) to provide a full description of vertical coordination in its main institutional characteristics and (2) to propose a model of decision making within the firm concerning the choice of these characteristics. In a process of decision making, a wide range of variables acts simultaneously. But, for the analysis, we propose a two-step model, in correspondence with the two main dimensions of our coordination description. A successful analysis of coordination problems lies in a complete description of what may influence the decision process. It must include, as Brousseau (1993) emphasizes, both production *and* exchange.

Transaction cost economics theory is concerned with exchanges between technologically independent entities. The process of asset segmentation and distribution between entities is not taken into account. On the other hand, industrial organization economics, with the notion of vertical market structure, includes the comparative market structure on the buyer/supplier interface, and the situation of competition between the coalition and the other competitors (level of entry and exit barriers). The two approaches may be articulated, and Brousseau's framework is an attempt to do so.[20] The objective of such an attempt is, therefore, to better understand the authority relationship and the objectives assigned to the vertical coordination process.

In the first step, the goal is to analyze the situation of asset distribution and specificity. The particular layout of stages of an industry chain are likely to be the reflection of scale and scope economies. Agents are already specialized, but this situation is not static; new technologies may affect this layout. Asset specificity is also an important feature of production characteristics within the coalition. Like asset distribution, asset specificity does not remain static. Many factors may modify this specificity; in fact, the choice of vertical coordination mechanisms itself often reflects an attempt to modify this specificity. In this perspective, transaction cost and industrial organization theories are complementary. They help explain how authority will emerge between the parties and what the objectives of vertical coordination strategies could be.

The second step focuses on the exchange (and control) mechanisms of the transactions between the parties. The characteristic of uncertainty in the transaction is probably one of the determining variables that affect the design of control mechanisms. The definition of uncertainty is highly contingent upon the conditions of competition, the strategies of the agents, and the characteristics of technologies. The contract must set up and define, at the lowest costs, what is expected from the agents, reduce their opportunism, and equitably share the risks. Given a particular context, the analysis, as the organization theory approach suggests, must focus on the criteria that most affect the control costs. The objective is to understand the choice between the various forms of control strategies—outcome-based, behavior-based, or a combination of these two generic forms.

Programmability and *separability* are such criteria. Indeed, programmability is the evaluation of task readability, that is the (more or less costly) feasibility to see what is done by the agent and how. For example, particular product specifications will be more or less programmable—easy to control. But programmability itself can be modified. A redefinition of an agent's tasks can improve the task readability. On the other hand, separability is the evaluation of individual performance readability, that is the (more or less costly) feasibility to see who has done the work. With low separability, the principal will face either high control costs or intense cheating. Like programmability, separability can be modified. For instance, the selection of agents or the set-up of an information system can increase separability.

The choice of a control mechanism is the result of a complex evaluation process. Hennart (1994) notes that the ability to assess precisely (or more precisely than competitors) the cost of a wide range of alternative control mechanisms is probably a key dimension of competitive advantage. And this knowledge is likely to be highly related to organizational learning. As Hilmer and Quinn suggest, this choice is also dependent upon competitive conditions. Indeed, they consider that companies deal with "a constant trade-off between flexibility and control." Companies have to compare their needs between rapid adaptations to environmental conditions and their needs to be directly involved in the partner's activities.

Still, the question of risk sharing remains. An optimal contract must be able to distinguish idiosyncratic risks (agent-specific) and nonspecific risks. Then the nonspecific risk can be equitably shared between the parties. But when it is not possible to separate these two types of risks, it could be preferable to adopt either a pure market or a full integration solution. Thus the analysis must stress the feasibility of the separation between specific and nonspecific risks.[21] One finds a similar problem already seen above: that is the feasibility of identifying idiosyncratic features (like risk, task, individual behavior, etc.) and the cost of modifying these features. Problems of programmability and separability are also found here.

Table 2.9 summarizes the main characteristics of the analysis. The first step is industrial organization/competitive analysis oriented. Results from this first step play as "basic conditions" of vertical coordination: existence of authority relations, firm's strategic objectives, number of technological stages, etc. The second step focuses on the contract's design. Indeed, there is a full spectrum of possible outsourcing arrangements, and one must consider the nature of transactions (uncertainty, opportunism, etc.) to understand this choice. In fact, this two-step model is largely a matter of perspective. At a first level, the focus is on the firm's situation in its environment; at a second level, the focus is on a particular transaction. But the interplay between these two levels does not permit a partial analysis.

An Illustration in Agribusiness: The U.S. Broiler Industry

The framework developed above can be applied to a particular subsector in order to understand how a firm will choose its vertical coordination strategy.

Table 2.9 Vertical coordination as a decision-making process: An analytical framework

Focus	First step Production (assets)	Second step Exchange (transactions)
Objectives	Understand the layout stages of the industry chain Understand the emergency of authority relations Determine the strategic objectives of the coordination process	Analyze the control and exchange mechanisms Describe the agency problems (if any): • Adverse selection • Moral hazard Analyze the incentives problems
Variables	Technological variables Asset specificity of agents and of the coalition versus the competitive environment	Transaction characteristics Uncertainty Tasks' programmability and separability
Approaches	IO analysis Competitive/institutional analysis Convention theory analysis	Transaction/coordination costs analysis

From the empirical studies available,[22] we will use this framework to understand the specific vertical linkages of the U.S. broiler industry.[23]

The U.S. broiler industry is highly competitive and has benefited from a constant shift in substitution effects from other types of meats. Indeed, during the period 1960–1994, the consumption per person increased from 19.2 to 49.7 pounds for broilers, while increasing only from 59.8 to 63.6 pounds for beef (all figures are boneless weights). Many socioeconomic factors have favored this trend (Rogers), but the ability of firms to increase productivity and reach new consumer needs is likely to be a determinant. The industry concentration remains relatively low. According to Rogers, the four-firm concentration ratio is about 40 percent. In the beef industry (slaughter level), the same ratio is 70 percent (see Kim and Marion). The constant rise in the concentration ratio during the past ten years is mainly the result of mergers among leading firms (Kim and Marion). These leading firms are Tyson Foods with a 20 percent market share and ConAgra with an 8.5 percent market share. These companies develop strategies of cost domination and product differentiation. In a context of high competition, rapid technical change, and a relatively low degree of product differentiation, the search for the lowest costs—both in production/processing and coordination—is absolutely necessary. But the leading firms, notably Perdue Farms, ConAgra, and Tyson Foods, try to differentiate their products through advertising or product innovation (Rogers).

One of the most distinguishing characteristics of the broiler industry is probably its vertical organization. Indeed, the spot markets are virtually absent and the totality of vertical exchanges between production and processing stages occurs through vertical contracting and integration. According to several inquiries (Rogers; Christensen et al.), the resource-providing type of vertical contracting is largely predominant (from 80 percent to 90 percent) while pure vertical integration is around 10 percent of the total value of farm-originated inputs. In a resource-providing contract, the processing company provides feed, chicks, medicine, a management program, and technical and management advice services. The grower provides housing, labor, and management and technical skills.

According to our thought processes, one must understand the genesis of such a configuration or, in other words, analyze the successive economic and strategic choices (and constraints) that led to what is observed. The main features of this configuration are: (1) three main technological stages in the industry: feed mill, grow-out farm, processing plant; (2) the existence of vertical integration between the feed mill and the processing plant; (3) the existence of a principal-agent relationship between processors and growers; (4) the definition, by the principal, of cost-domination/differentiation strategies; (5) a high degree of competition between the coalitions (and a low degree of concentration); and (6) a vertical contract between growers and processors with resource-providing contracts.

Economies of scale and scope explain the particular market structure of the broiler industry (Rogers). The size of processing and milling plants are large compared to a single grow-out farm because of the internalization of specific technological economies in the respective stages. Very high in the case of processing and milling activities, these economies rapidly reach a maximum in the growing activities.

Asset specificity is high in this industry. This is essentially a site specificity: feed milling, growing, and processing activities are tied together through their proximity. Indeed, high costs of transportation of both feed, chicks, and live chickens prevent a dispersion of the operations. And the transportation of a processed product is relatively less costly. As shown by Rogers, the situation in the Broiler Belt, located in the southeastern United States, allows efficient shipping to the population centers without being too far from the supply sources (corn and soybean meal from the Midwest states). This particular asset specificity suggests there is no real asset-specificity asymmetry between the economic agents; rather they depend upon each other. But the vertical market structure is asymmetric. One processing company deals with a large number of grow-out farms. This indicates a likely source of authority in the relationship and explains the principal-agent situation. The asset distribution, along the industry chain, can be featured as a *bilateral dependency*: about twenty coalitions (that account for about 80 percent of the domestic market) that are highly vertically dependent and facing a competitive environment.[24]

The principal-agent relationship found here has to resolve the generic problems of agency theory: uncertainty about the agents, opportunism of the agents, uncertainty about product quality, incentives for a good performance, risk sharing between the parties. An optimum contract is expected to solve these problems at the lowest cost.

The first uncertainty, for the processor, is the choice of skillful growers. A response would be to internalize totally the growing operations and to monitor directly the labor force—through a labor contract. But the cost of monitoring such work would be costly, and the choice of good workers remains problematic. An efficient ex ante selection of growers is necessarily related to the possibility of assessing the skills of these growers, which is difficult to measure. With the choice of resource-providing contracts, the grower has to invest in housing facilities. Highly specific, this investment will have a low value outside the coalition, and, consequently, the incentive for the grower to succeed will be enforced.

The second uncertainty for the processor is the product quality. The ability to sell products with a constant quality and very precise characteristics is absolutely necessary in a competitive environment. Among the factors affecting this quality, the composition of feed and the genetics of broilers have a great influence. As usual, many alternatives are available. The first one would be an ex ante control of the inputs (feed, chicks, medicine, etc.), which would be costly and probably difficult to set up. It is also possible to control the products ex post (for instance at the farm gate). Likewise, it will be very costly to control all the products if one wants to limit as much uncertainty as possible and avoid bad products. But, perhaps more important, the risk for the growers not to sell their products would be too high and would prevent them from investing in such a business.

Finally, a resource-providing contract is a better alternative. If the principal directly tailors and, consequently, perfectly knows the feed and chicks, the growers' tasks become more programmable. Management and technical advice are also a means to limit heterogeneous behavior. Reproduced on a large scale, these operations are not costly. And the need for control exists only at a significantly more centralized level (the feed mill or the hatchery). Therefore, the control costs are lessened.

As we can see in this case, contracting is a means to modify task programmability, and thus control costs. An important dimension in the choice of vertical contracting is probably the way a particular contract will affect task programmability.[25]

The question of price discovery remains. Knoeber describes the contract commonly found in the broiler industry: the performance-order tournament. The grower is paid per pound of live broiler produced. This is a piece-rate contract with outcome-based control. The size of this per-pound rate is not fixed but is instead determined by the relative performance of the grower compared with other contestants.

A tournament may be rank-ordered in which case it is only the grower's performance rank that matters. But more frequently, the tournament is based on a cardinal measure of performance. In that case, a grower's settlement cost (inputs consumption—i.e., chicks and feed—divided by the production of live broilers) is "compared with the average of several flocks' settlement cost (at least ten), and the payment per pound is determined as the sum of a base payment minus a portion (sometimes all) of the deviation between the grower's performance and the average" (Knoeber).

This type of relative performance-order tournament has several advantages. First, it requires a relatively simple and cheap measure of performance. A comparison of, for instance, fifteen growers' inputs consumption and output production, will be sufficient. The processor company, being the supplier/buyer, has a perfect knowledge of this consumption/production. Moreover the separability problem is minimized: the company determines easily each individual performance. But, more importantly, this contract has high incentives. Knoeber shows in his example that some of the payment per pound depends upon relative performance.

As an outcome-based contract, problems of cheating may occur. Several features of the contract will discourage them. First, the grower(s) whose settlement costs are substantially above the average is (are) not included in its calculation. Thus the tendency to sabotage a grower to increase the average cost will be limited or avoided. Wide collusion between growers to reduce efforts collectively is also prevented. Indeed, the processor company will select and decide secretly what growers, at a particular moment, will enter in the same tournament and, consequently, will compete with each other. Not knowing who their competitors are, the growers would need to collude with all of them, which is either too costly or practically impossible.

The question of risk sharing between the parties must be considered. The grower may agree to bear idiosyncratic risks (specific to his own behavior), but not those—or at least only one part—inherent to external shocks (climate, disease, etc.). Nor will he agree to bear the risk of low productivity inputs. For instance, a grower's low performance may result from deficient chicks or unbalanced feed, which are provided by the principal. In the case of external shocks, they are likely to affect all the growers of the tournament, increasing the average settlement cost and, consequently, not greatly modifying each grower's relative performance. In the case of input problems, the company tries to limit as much as possible the heterogeneity of inputs. In fact, the problem is not to have variation in input productivity—variation is impossible to avoid—but to provide all the tournament contestants with inputs of the same characteristics. The company does so in delivering the contestants at the same time with the same products (chicks from the same hatchery and the same breeding, feed from the same milling operation).

These contracts are short term, usually one year. But in order to minimize opportunism and risk for both principal and agents, they are tacitly renewed each year, unless repetitive poor performance occurs.

The existence of a small proportion of pure vertical integration is problematic. But it could be interpreted in many ways. It gives an objective indicator of the settlement costs without the bias of growers' behavior. It can be a means to innovate with new inputs and new management programs more easily than with an independent grower. Finally, a direct control over a small part of the production will allow the company to respond more quickly to the demand fluctuations. In these two latter cases, growers are too risk averse and cannot bear such risks as innovation or frequent surplus.[26]

This example shows that an integrative framework using insights from different theoretical backgrounds[27] helps to better understand the genesis and shape of vertical coordination in a particular subsector. Obviously, this partial theoretical interpretation of case studies does not demonstrate the validity of the results proposed, nor does it provide explanations for the entirety of coordination features. But the purpose here is to illustrate the relevance of a framework focused on the strategic planning process. It also gives an example of how these theories could be implemented (Table 2.10).

Conclusion

Our understanding of vertical coordination benefits greatly from new approaches in institutional economics, organizational economics, and strategic management. New concepts and new assumptions allow a more realistic and more complete vision of coordination and broaden considerably the scope of the analysis. But schools of thought are diverse and far from being unified. The main methodological oppositions are found between organizational economics and strategic literature perspectives; the intense debate existing between these two fields is symptomatic.[28]

In spite of important progress, many questions remain unsolved. Among these problems, the question of organizational efficiency and of its assessment is particularly problematic. Indeed, as soon as the source of organizational dynamics and change can no longer be found in the optimization of a production function, theorists must provide new explanations. For instance, economic treatment of incentive problems in organizational economics is incomplete. Indeed, as Simon suggests, "economic rewards are not the only means of motivation available." Notions such as loyalty, commitment, and trust explain greatly the behavior of economic agents (and therefore organizational efficiency) but do not fit easily in economic concepts. For Simon, "Organization size and degree of integration, and the boundaries between

Table 2.10 Vertical coordination in the U.S. broiler industry: An interpretation of the process of choice

First step			Second step		
Facts	Implications	Results	Facts	Implications	Results
• Three main technological stages • Unbalanced vertical market structure • Low concentration	• Interdependent coalitions • Authority relationship • High competition	• Vertical integration (feed mills/ processing plants) • Vertical contracting (processing companies/ growers)	• Highly recurrent transactions • Uncertainty about quality • Uncertainty about behavior	• Programmability and separability problems • Incentives problems • Opportunism • Risk-sharing problems	• Resource-providing contracts between growers and processing companies

organizations and markets, are determined by rather subtle forces. The wide range of organizational arrangements observable in the world suggests that the equilibrium between these two alternatives often be almost neutral, with the level highly contingent on a system's history. A traditional arrangement may be preserved until its inefficiencies become overwhelming—or even beyond."

Interestingly, Casson considers that the notion of trust is central to organizational problems.[29] Indeed, for Casson, trust reduces transaction costs and improves the allocation of resources. This notion of trust is itself embedded in the cultural environment (both local, at a corporate level, and in society). Simon's "subtle forces" probably find a part of their explanation on this level of trust; organizational arrangements are contingent not only upon a system's history, but also on its social and corporate values.

Another fundamental question lies in the methodological assumptions. In agency and transaction cost theories, vertical coordination is fully understandable at a microeconomic level. For convention and organization theories, and strategic management perspectives, the building of an intermediate level is an indispensable step in the analysis.[30] Indeed, the "structure" is more than its components and has emergent properties.[31] We think it is necessary to take into account structural criteria for a full understanding of vertical coordination mechanisms. But, as Brousseau (1993) suggests, this structural analysis should not prevent one from using transaction cost economics concepts.

The ability to explain why heterogeneous vertical business linkages emerge, remain, and compete is far from being achieved. Vertical coordination decisions are the result of complex procedures. Despite promising concepts and significant results, a full understanding of this phenomenon challenges future research. The progressive building of an institutional analysis, implementing organizational economics and strategic management, should contribute to this future research.

Notes

1   The author thanks Michael D. Boehlje, Catherine A. Durham, and Lee F. Schrader, Department of Agricultural Economics, Purdue University, for their helpful comments on earlier drafts of this paper. The author would also like to thank Andrea K. Pigey who proofread several drafts of this paper. None of them are responsible for any misleading ideas. This research was made possible by the Institut Supérieur Agricole de Beauvais (ISAB), France, and by an invitation from the Department of Agricultural Economics, Purdue University.

2   We will define vertical coordination as the process of specifying—for a reference firm and activity—a particular configuration of ownership, control, and exchange over up-

stream/downstream activities. Upstream/downstream activities are "activities that precede/follow the reference activity in the sequence of steps from producing raw materials to delivering a finished product to a customer" (Milgrom and Roberts).

3   For a review of vertical coordination issues through industrial organization, see Henderson.

4   Since the seminal works by Mighell and Jones and by Goldberg, the study of vertical coordination in agricultural subsectors has been particularly rich. For complete surveys, see Sheldon, and Valceschini (1995). The relevance of contractual and institutional approaches of vertical coordination in agribusiness is stressed by numerous works. See, for instance, Torgerson; Schrader; Cotterill; Hudson, Sonka, and Streeter; and Barry, Sonka, and Lajili.

5   Five kinds of asset specificity are found: site specificity, physical asset specificity, human asset specificity, dedicated assets, and brand name capital (Williamson 1989).

6   This concept of efficiency is closed to neoclassical assumptions; perfect competition conditions lead to economic efficiency.

7   This author provides a good synthesis on transaction cost limitations about vertical integration issues. He considers that "transaction-cost theory has not departed very far from static, neoclassical optimization analysis. . . . A more complete theory will contain a substantial evolutionary component, with a greater emphasis on the roles of factors such as forbearance, goodwill, interdependence, and power in the transaction process." Brousseau (1993) and many strategic management scholars share a relatively close view (see Table 2.2 and Table 2.3).

8   The main authors of these two streams are Jensen and Meckling, for the former, and Grossman and Hart, for the latter.

9   Programmability is the ability to observe what and how the work is done. Separability is the ability to observe/identify who has done the work.

10   External uncertainties can either favor or prevent a vertical integration strategy.

11   Among other works close to this perspective, see Reve, and Ring and Van De Ven (1992, 1994).

12   Langlois also stresses the importance of learning, but with a different approach. For him, firms and markets are "alternative—and sometimes overlapping—institutions of learning." These institutions will differ in their ability to learn—at a particular cost—new capabilities over time. In that perspective, learning costs are another type of transaction cost.

13   Two edited volumes provide several applications of convention theories: Allaire and Boyer; Nicolas and Valceschini. Gomez gives a methodological framework for the study of economic conventions.

14   These clauses are strategic coordination, organizational coordination, operational coordination, guarantee system, control mechanism, risk sharing, and duration.

15   This theoretical contingency between theories of the firm and representation of vertical coordination is shown in Sauvée (1994).

16   This concept of institution allows a "comparative institutional analysis" (Hennart 1994), and this thought process, as shown by Hennart (1994), can be applied to a wide range of organizational issues.

17   And notably Hennart (1993, 1994); Zajac and Olsen; and Reve.

18   A similar concept is found among organizational economics scholars. Milgrom and Roberts "do not presume that organizations per se have goals that they seek to realize." These authors are careful "to treat organizational decisions and actions as the outcomes either of strategic interplay among self-interested people responding to incentives designed to influence their behavior, or of collective or managerial attempts to compromise the

interests of parties affected by the decisions." They add: "using *efficiency as a positive principle* requires taking care about whose interests are being served."

19 A similar approach is found in Barkema, Drabenstott, and Cook, in which the authors propose a "taxonomy of vertical coordination."

20 A similar construction, but with a different set of variables, is found in Stuckey and White and in Venkatesan.

21 Boehlje suggests another dichotomy between strategic and nonstrategic risks.

22 These empirical studies are: Marion, Schrader, and Ward; Christensen et al.; Koonce and Thomas; Knoeber; Kim and Marion; Rogers; and Martin et al. Elements of comparison are drawn from Sauvée (1989) and Sylvander (1992).

23 The stress here is put on the analysis of institutional arrangements. To be complete, one should include the analysis of how the institutional environment affects—and is affected by—the behavior of economic agents.

24 A comparison with the Dole Fresh Vegetables Company, a shipper, and its vegetable producers provides interesting insights (for a complete analysis, see Martin et al.). In that case, and despite an unbalanced vertical market structure (one shipper for many producers), there is no significant authority relationship but, instead, a vertical alliance. Indeed, the producers are much less asset-specific than the shipper, both because they can easily find another shipper and because other marketing channels are available.

25 Again, the comparison with the Dole Fresh Vegetables Company is enlightening. This company invested heavily in information systems in order to "identify the source of quality problems and recognize the contributions of both farmers and Dole to delivering high valued products to the markets" (Martin et al.). This case study shows that the problem of "separability—who is responsible for quality—can be alleviated with information" (Martin et al.).

26 In fact, this is a case of "plural form," defined by Bradach and Eccles as "an arrangement where distinct organizational control mechanisms are operated simultaneously for *the same function* by *the same firm*." For a complete analysis, see these authors.

27 Principally, Mahoney; Crank, Lajili, and Mahoney; Hennart (1993, 1994); Brousseau (1993); and Zajac and Olsen. For a general perspective on organizational economics through strategy issues, see Oster.

28 See, for instance, important contributions to this debate in Rumelt, Schendel, and Teece and, especially, Williamson (1994b) and Nelson.

29 Baudry (1992, 1993) also insists on the importance of this notion of trust. Boehlje and Schrader recommend a similar approach. Barney and Hansen show that socioeconomic analysis of trust "can be seen as an extension of transaction-cost theory."

30 One finds here the traditional opposition between the methodological individualism and the methodological holism.

31 In the same vein, Bradach and Eccles consider that "the analytic focus must be moved away from exclusive attention to individual transactions. Instead, the dynamics of whole structures must be examined since the transactional context affects the control that can be brought to bear on individual transactions."

References

Allaire, G., and R. Boyer, eds. 1995. *La Grande Transformation de l'Agriculture: Lectures Conventionnalistes et Régulationnistes.* Paris, France: National Institute for Agronomic Research–Economica.

Amanor-Boadu, V., and L. J. Martin. 1992. *Enhancing the Competitiveness of Canadian Agri-Food Industries Through Vertical Strategic Alliances.* George Morris Centre, University of Guelph, November.

Barkema, A., M. Drabenstott, and M. Cook. 1993. "The Industrialization of the U.S. Food System." *Food and Agricultural Marketing Issues for the 21st Century*, ed. D. I. Padberg, pp. 3–20. Food and Agricultural Marketing Consortium 93-1, Texas A&M University.

Barkema, A., M. Drabenstott, and K. Welch. 1991. "The Quiet Revolution in the U.S. Food Market." *Economic Review*, May-June, pp. 25–41. Kansas City, Mo.: Federal Reserve Bank of Kansas City.

Barney, J. B., and M. H. Hansen. 1994. "Trustworthiness as a Source of Competitive Advantage." *Strategic Management Journal* 15:175–90.

Barney, J. B., and W. G. Ouchi, eds. 1986. *Organizational Economics.* San Francisco, Calif.: Jossey-Bass.

Barry, P. J., S. T. Sonka, and K. Lajili. 1992. "Vertical Coordination, Financial Structure, and the Changing Theory of the Firm." *American Journal of Agricultural Economics* 74:1219–25.

Baudry, B. 1992. "Contrat, Autorité, Confiance: La Relation de Sous-Traitance est-elle Assimilable à la Relation d'Emploi?" *Revue Economique* 5:871–94.

———. 1993. "Partenariat et Sous Traitance: Une Approche par la Théorie des Incitations." *Revue d'Economie Industrielle* 66(4):51–68.

Boehlje, M. 1994. "Managing Multiple Business Risks for Agribusiness Firms." Paper presented at Summit on Risk Management in American Agriculture, Washington D.C., November 29.

Boehlje, M., and L. F. Schrader. 1998. "The Industrialization of Agriculture: Questions of Coordination." In this volume, pp. 3–26.

Boone, C., and A. Verbeke. 1991. "Strategic Management and Vertical Disintegration: A Transaction Cost Approach." *Microeconomic Contribution to Strategic Management*, ed. J. Thepot and R. A. Thietard, pp. 185–205. Amsterdam, The Netherlands: Elsevier Science.

Bradach, J. L., and R. G. Eccles. 1989. "Price, Authority and Trust: From Ideal Types to Plural Forms." *Annual Review of Sociology* 15:97–118.

Brousseau, E. 1993. *L'Economie des Contrats: Technologies de l'Information et Coordination Interentreprises.* Paris, France: Presses Universitaires de France.

———. 1994. "Contracts as Modular Mechanisms: Some Propositions for the Study of Hybrid Forms." Working Paper 94-01, Centre d'Analyse Théorique des Organisations et des Marchés, Université de Paris I Panthéon–Sorbonne.

Casson, M. 1991. *The Economics of Business Culture: Game Theory, Transaction Costs and Economic Performance.* Oxford, England: Clarendon Press.

Christensen, L. A., E. H. Easterling, H. B. Harold, and A . F. Lasley. 1988. *The U.S. Broiler Industry.* Washington, D.C.: U.S. Department of Agriculture, Economic Research Service, Agricultural Economic Report 591, November.

Coase, R. H. 1993. "The Institutional Structure of Production." *The Nature of the Firm: Origins, Evolution, and Development*, ed. O. E. Williamson and S. G. Winter, pp. 227–35. New York, N.Y.: Oxford University Press.

Cotterill, R. W. 1987. "The Economic Efficiency of Alternative Forms of Business Enterprise." *Economic Efficiency in Agricultural and Food Marketing*, ed. W. J. Armbruster and R. L. Kilmer, pp. 107–33. Ames, Iowa: Iowa State University Press.

Crank, D. A., K. Lajili, and J. Mahoney. 1994. "Spot Markets, Vertical Contracting, and Financial Ownership: Competition among Organizational Forms." Paper presented at NE-

165/WRCC-192 research conference, Interactions between Public Policies and Private Strategies in the Food Industries, Montréal, Québec, Canada, June 27–28.

Dosi, G., R. Rumelt, D. Teece, and S. Winter. 1994. "Understanding Corporate Coherence: Theory and Evidence." *Journal of Economic Behavior and Organization* 23:1–30.

Eisenhardt, K. 1985. "Control: Organizational and Economic Approaches." *Management Science* 31:134–49.

———. 1989. "Agency Theory: An Assessment and Review." *Academy of Management Review* 14:57–74.

Eymard-Duvernay, F. 1989. "Conventions de Qualité et Formes de Coordination." *Revue Economique* 2:329–59

Foss, N. J. 1994. "Why Transaction Cost Economics Needs Evolutionary Economics." *Revue d'Economie Industrielle* 68(2):7–26.

Frank, S. D., and D. R. Henderson. 1993. "Vertical Coordination and the Competitive Performance of the U.S. Food Industries." *Competitive Strategy Analysis in the Food System*, ed. R. W. Cotterill, pp. 45–68. Boulder, Colo.: Westview Press.

Goldberg, R. A. 1968. *Agribusiness Coordination: A Systems Approach to the Wheat, Soybean and Florida Orange Economies.* Boston, Mass.: Harvard University Graduate School of Business Administration.

Gomez, P. Y. 1994. *Qualité et Théorie des Conventions.* Paris, France: Economica.

Grossman, S. J., and O. D. Hart. 1986. "The Costs and Benefits of Ownership: A Theory of Vertical and Lateral Integration." *Journal of Political Economy* 94:691–719.

Harrigan, K. R. 1984. "Formulating Vertical Integration Strategies." *Academy of Management Review* 4:638–52.

———. 1986. "Matching Vertical Integration Strategies to Competitive Conditions." *Strategic Management Journal* 9:535–56.

Henderson, D. R. 1991. "Industrial Organization Theory and Vertical Coordination." Paper presented at NC-194 symposium, Examining the Economic Theory Base for Vertical Coordination, Chicago, Ill., October 17–18.

Henderson, D. R., S. McCorriston, and I. M. Sheldon. 1993. "Vertical Coordination: Concept, Practice, Theory and Policy Implications for the Agro-Food Sector." North Central Regional Research Project 194 Occasional Paper OP-50, Ohio State University, September.

Hennart, J. F. 1993. "Explaining the Swollen Middle: Why Most Transactions Are a Mix of Markets and Hierarchies." *Organization Science* 4:529–47.

———. 1994. "The 'Comparative Institutional' Theory of the Firm: Some Implications for Corporate Strategy." *Journal of Management Studies* 31:193–207.

Hilmer, F. G., and J. B. Quinn. 1994. "Strategic Outsourcing." *Sloan Management Review*, Summer, pp. 43–55.

Hudson, M. A., S. T. Sonka, and D. H. Streeter. 1991. "Information Technology, Coordination, and Competitiveness in the Food and Agribusiness Sector." *American Journal of Agricultural Economics* 73:1465–71.

Jensen, M. C., and W. H. Meckling. 1986. "Theory of the Firm: Managerial Behavior, Agency Costs and Ownership Structure." *Organizational Economics*, ed. J. Barney and W. G. Ouchi, pp. 214–75. San Francisco, Calif.: Jossey-Bass.

Kilmer, R. L. 1986. "Vertical Integration in Agricultural and Food Marketing." *American Journal of Agricultural Economics* 68:1155–60.

Kim, D., and B. W. Marion. 1991. "Concentration Change in Selected Food Manufacturing Industries: The Influence of Mergers Versus Internal Growth." *Agribusiness* 7:415–31.

Knoeber, C. R. 1989. "A Real Game of Chicken: Contracts, Tournaments, and the Production of Broilers." *Journal of Law, Economics and Organization* 5:271–92.

Koonce, J. M., and J. G. Thomas. 1989. "Differentating a Commodity: Lessons from Tyson Foods." *Planning Review*, September-October, pp. 24–29.

Langlois, R. N. 1992. "Transaction-Cost Economics in Real Time." *Industrial and Corporate Change* 1:99–127.

Mahoney, J. T. 1992. "The Choice of Organizational Form: Vertical Financial Ownership versus Other Methods of Vertical Integration." *Strategic Management Journal* 13:559–84.

Marion, B. W. 1976. "Vertical Coordination and Exchange Arrangements: Concepts and Hypotheses." *Coordination and Exchange in Agricultural Subsectors*, pp. 179–95. North Central Regional Research Project NC- 117 Publication 228, University of Wisconsin–Madison, January.

Marion, B., L. Schrader, and R. Ward. 1986. "Food System Coordination." *The Organization and Performance of the U.S. Food System*, ed. B. W. Marion, pp. 51–196. Lexington, Mass: D. C. Heath and Co.

Martin, L. J., R. Westgren, L. F. Schrader, L. Cousineau, N. Le Roc'h, R. Paguaga, and V. Amanor-Boadu. 1993. "Alternative Business Linkages: The Case of the Poultry Industry." Working Paper 10-93, Food Industry Research Group, George Morris Centre, University of Guelph, June.

Medema, S. G. 1992. "Transactions, Transaction Costs and Vertical Integration: A Re-Examination." *Review of Political Economy* 4:291–316.

Ménard, C. 1989. *L'Economie des Organisations*. Paris, France: La Découverte.

———. 1995. "Markets as Institutions Versus Organizations as Markets? Disentangling Some Fundamental Concepts." *Journal of Economic Behavior and Organization* 28:161–82.

Mighell, R. L., and L. A. Jones. *Vertical Coordination in Agriculture*. Washington, D.C.: U.S. Department of Agriculture, Economic Research Service, Agricultural Economic Report 19, February.

Milgrom, P., and J. Roberts. 1992. *Economics, Organization and Management*. Englewood Cliffs, N.J.: Prentice Hall.

Nelson, R. R. 1994. "Why Do Firms Differ, and How Does It Matter?" *Fundamental Issues in Strategy: A Research Agenda*, ed. R. P. Rumelt, D. E. Schendel, and D. J. Teece, pp. 247–69. Boston, Mass: Harvard Business School Press.

Nicolas, F., and E. Valceschini, eds. 1995. *Agro-Alimentaire: Une Economie de la Qualité*. Paris, France: National Institute for Agronomic Research–Economica.

Oster, S. M. 1994. *Modern Competitive Analysis*, 2d ed. Oxford, England: Oxford University Press.

Ouchi, W. G. 1979. "A Conceptual Framework for the Design of Organizational Control Mechanisms." *Management Science* 25:833–48.

Porter, M. E. 1985. *Competitive Advantage: Creating and Sustaining Superior Performance*. New York, N.Y.: Free Press.

———. 1991. "Towards a Dynamic Theory of Strategy." *Strategic Management Journal* 12:95–117.

Reve, T. 1990. "The Firm as a Nexus of Internal and External Contracts." *The Firm as a Nexus of Treaties*, ed. M. Aoki, B. Gustafsson, and O. E. Williamson, pp. 133–61. London, England: Sage Publications.

Ring, P. S., and A. H. Van De Ven. 1992. "Structuring Cooperative Relationships Between Organizations." *Strategic Management Journal* 13:483–98.

————. 1994. "Developmental Processes of Cooperative Interorganizational Relationships." *Academy of Management Review* 19:90–118.

Riordan, M. H. 1990. "What Is Vertical Integration?" *The Firm as a Nexus of Treaties*, ed. M. Aoki, B. Gustafsson, and O. E. Williamson, pp. 94–111. London, England: Sage Publications.

Riordan, M. H., and O. E. Williamson. 1985. "Asset Specificity and Economic Organization." *International Journal of Industrial Organization* 3:365–78.

Rogers, R. T. 1992. *Broilers—Differentiating a Commodity.* Research Report 18, Food Marketing Policy Center, University of Connecticut, December.

Rumelt, R. P., D. E. Schendel, and D. J. Teece, eds. 1994. *Fundamental Issues in Strategy.* Boston, Mass.: Harvard Business School Press.

Sauvée, L. 1989. "Dynamique de la Concurrence et Groupes Industriels: le Cas du Secteur Avicole en France." Doctoral dissertation, Ecole Nationale Supérieure Agronomique de Rennes, France.

————. 1994. *Vertical Coordination in Agribusiness: Concepts, Theories, and Applications.* Bulletin 694, Office of Agricultural Research Programs, Purdue University, September.

Schrader, L. F. 1986. "Responses to Forces Shaping Agricultural Marketing: Contracting." *American Journal of Agricultural Economics* 68:1161–66.

Seth, A., and H. Thomas. 1994. "Theories of the Firm: Implications for Strategy Research." *Journal of Management Studies* 31:165–91.

Sheldon, I. M. 1991. "Vertical Coordination: An Overview." Paper presented at NC-194 symposium, Examining the Economic Theory Base for Vertical Coordination, Chicago, Ill., October 17–18.

Simon, H. A. 1991. "Organizations and Markets." *Journal of Economic Perspectives* 5:25–44.

Sporleder, T. L. 1992. "Managerial Economics of Vertically Coordinated Agricultural Firms." North Central Regional Research Project NC-194 Occasional Paper OP-40, Ohio State University, October.

Spulber, D. F. 1992. "Economic Analysis and Management Strategy: A Survey." *Journal of Economics and Management Strategy* 1:535–74

————. 1994. "Economic Analysis and Management Strategy: A Survey Continued." *Journal of Economics and Management Strategy* 3:355–406.

Stinchcombe, A. L. 1990. *Information and Organizations.* Berkeley, Calif.: University of California Press.

Stuckey, J., and D. White. 1993. "When and When Not to Vertically Integrate." *Sloan Management Review*, Spring, pp. 71–83.

Sylvander, B. 1992. "Les Conventions de Qualité dans le Secteur Agro-Alimentaire: Aspects Théoriques et Méthodologiques." Communication at Société Française d'Economie Rurale colloquium, Paris, France, October 26–27.

————. 1995. "Convention de Qualité, Concurrence et Coopération: Cas du Label Rouge dans la Filière Volaille." *La Grande Transformation de l'Agriculture: Lectures Conventionnalistes et Régulationnistes*, ed. G. Allaire and R. Boyer, pp. 73–96. Paris, France: National Institute for Agronomic Research–Economica.

Thorelli, H. B. 1986. "Networks: Between Markets and Hierarchies." *Strategic Management Journal* 7:37–51.

Torgerson, R. E. 1983. "Alternative Ownership and Control Mechanisms Within the Food System." *Future Frontiers in Agricultural Marketing Research*, ed. P. L. Farris, pp. 184–223. Ames, Iowa: Iowa State University Press.

Valceschini, E. 1993. "Conventions Economiques et Mutation de l'Economie Contractuelle dans le Secteur des Légumes Transformés." *Economie Rurale*, November-December, pp. 19–26.

———. 1995. "Contrats, Coordination et Institutions. Problématiques et Méthodologie de l'Economie Rurale." *La Grande Transformation de l'Agriculture: Lectures Convention-nalistes et Régulationnistes*, ed. G. Allaire and R. Boyer, pp. 241–58, Paris, France: National Institute for Agronomic Research–Economica.

Van Heck, E., and P. J. P. Zuurbier. 1989. "Towards the Explanation of the Development of Value Added Chains." Faculty of Economics, Wageningen Agricultural University.

Venkatesan, R. 1992. "Strategic Sourcing: To Make or Not to Make." *Harvard Business Review*, November-December, pp. 98–107.

Williamson, O. E. 1979. "Transaction-Cost Economics: The Governance of Contractual Relations." *Journal of Law and Economics* 22:233–61.

———. 1985. *The Economic Institutions of Capitalism: Firms, Markets, Relational Contracting*. New York, N.Y.: Free Press.

———. 1989. "Transaction Cost Economics." *Handbook of Industrial Organization*, ed. R. Schmalensee and R. D. Willig, vol. 1, pp. 135–82. Amsterdam, The Netherlands: North-Holland.

———. 1990. "A Comparison of Alternative Approaches to Economic Organization." *Journal of Institutional and Theoretical Economics* 146:61–71.

———. 1991. "Comparative Economic Organization: The Analysis of Discrete Structural Alternatives." *Administrative Science Quarterly* 36:269–96.

———. 1993a. "The Evolving Science of Organization." *Journal of Institutional and Theoretical Economics* 149:36–63.

———. 1993b. "Transaction Cost Economics and Organization Theory." *Industrial and Corporate Change* 2:107–56.

———. 1994a. "Strategizing, Economizing, and Economic Organization." *Fundamental Issues in Strategy: A Research Agenda*, ed. R. P. Rumelt, D. E. Schendel, and D. J. Teece, pp. 361–401. Boston, Mass.: Harvard Business School Press.

———. 1994b. "Visible and Invisible Governance." *American Economic Review* 84:323–26.

Williamson, O. E., and S. G. Winter, eds. 1993. *The Nature of the Firm: Origins, Evolution, and Development*. Oxford, England: Oxford University Press.

Zajac, E. J., and C. P. Olsen. 1993. "From Transaction Cost to Transactional Value Analysis: Implications for the Study of Interorganizational Strategies." *Journal of Management Studies* 30:131–45.

3 Market Structure, Vertical Integration, and Contract Coordination

JEFFREY S. ROYER

Incentives for vertical integration may arise from the existence of technological economies, transactional economies, and market imperfections (Perry 1989, pp. 187–89). Technological economies of integration are based on physical interdependencies in the production process. The usual example is the heating and handling economies that lead to integration in the production of iron and steel. Transactional economies are associated with the process of exchange instead of production. In some situations, the market may fail as an efficient means of coordinating economic activity. Consequently, a firm may be able to reduce its transaction costs by integrating. For example, in the case of a bilateral monopoly, either firm may be able to eliminate the costs of negotiating and enforcing a contract with the other through integration.

Market imperfections that may produce incentives for vertical integration include imperfect competition in addition to imperfections caused by externalities and imperfect or asymmetric information. As Perry observes (1989, p. 189), market imperfections are an important determinant of vertical integration. Vertical integration in response to technological or transactional economies can be expected to increase economic welfare. Thus the primary focus of transaction cost economics is explaining and predicting patterns of vertical integration. On the other hand, vertical integration in reaction to market imperfections may either increase or decrease welfare. Consequently, public policy questions become important.

This paper focuses exclusively on vertical integration and contract coordination arising from imperfect competition and the expected effects on output, prices, and social welfare. In particular, this paper describes several models from the industrial organization literature that may be useful in analyzing the changes in vertical relationships that have been occurring in the food system. These models, which examine vertical integration and contract coordination within various vertical market structures, including successive monopoly, successive oligopoly, and monopsony, seek to explain the conditions under which vertical integration and contract coordination are likely to occur and to predict their effects on output, prices, and the welfare of various market participants. The objectives of this paper are to explain these models, describe some of their applications, and comment on their appropriateness to studying the relationships between market structure and vertical coordination in agricultural industries. This paper is not intended to serve as an exhaustive review of the literature.

Vertical Integration of Successive Monopolies

Fixed-proportions Production Technology

The model used most frequently to illustrate the benefits of vertical integration is the model of successive monopoly under fixed-proportions production technology, which was formalized by Greenhut and Ohta (1976) for a variety of demand functions. We will follow Waterson's exposition, which incorporates a linear final product demand function.

Consider two successive monopolies. Firm A produces a single product it sells to firm B, which employs firm A's output in the production of a final product sold to consumers. Assume that firm B is subject to a fixed-proportions production technology and constant returns to scale. In other words, firm B employs firm A's output in fixed proportions to other intermediate inputs, and, for convenience, we can assume that firm B produces one unit of final product from each unit of the intermediate product it purchases from firm A. We also assume that firm A's marginal cost of producing the intermediate product is constant.

The assumption of a fixed-proportions production technology allows the model to be illustrated graphically. In addition, fixed proportions would seem appropriate for representing the technology inherent in many agricultural processing and packing industries in which the quantity of processed product is essentially invariant to the alternative production processes that might be employed. Although, within a limited range, additional capital and labor may increase the technical efficiency with which raw product is converted into processed product by reducing waste and spoilage, these factors cannot be generally substituted for raw product to increase processed product output.

The model features "arm's length" pricing by firm A, the upstream monopolist. That is, firm B, the downstream monopoly, accepts the price set by firm A as parametric and exercises no monopsony power. Firm B maximizes its profits given the price set by firm A. Firm A maximizes its profits given firm B's derived demand for the intermediate product.

Firm B's profit function can be written

$$\pi_B = p_B q - p_A q - kq \tag{1}$$

where p_A and p_B are respectively the prices firm B pays for the intermediate product and receives for the final product, q is quantity, and k is the constant marginal cost of producing the final product, exclusive of p_A. Differentiating (1) with respect to quantity yields the first-order condition:

$$\frac{d\pi_B}{dq} = \left(p_B + q \frac{dp_B}{dq} \right) - p_A - k = 0, \tag{2}$$

which can be rewritten

$$p_B \left(1 - \frac{1}{\eta_B} \right) = p_A + k \tag{3}$$

where η_B represents the own-price elasticity of demand facing firm B in the final product market and the left-hand side is equivalent to firm B's marginal revenue MR_B. In other words, the downstream monopolist maximizes its profits by setting its marginal revenue equal to the sum of the price of the intermediate product set by the upstream monopolist and the marginal cost k. Solving (3) for p_A, we can derive firm B's inverse factor demand for the intermediate product:

$$p_A = MR_B - k. \tag{4}$$

Firm A's profit function can be written

$$\pi_A = p_A q - cq \tag{5}$$

where c is the constant marginal cost of producing the intermediate product. Differentiating (5) with respect to quantity yields the first-order condition:

$$\frac{d\pi_A}{dq} = \left(p_A + q \frac{dp_A}{dq} \right) - c = 0, \tag{6}$$

which can be rewritten

$$p_A \left(1 - \frac{1}{\eta_A} \right) = c \tag{7}$$

where η_A represents the elasticity of the derived demand function and the left-hand side is equivalent to firm A's marginal revenue MR_A.

Substituting the inverse factor demand function for the intermediate product (4) into firm A's profit function (5), the latter can be rewritten

$$\pi_A = MR_B q - (c+k)q. \tag{8}$$

Thus firm A's first-order condition can be rewritten

$$\frac{d\pi_A}{dq} = \frac{d(MR_B q)}{dq} - c - k = 0. \tag{9}$$

The term $d(MR_B q)/dq$ represents the curve "marginal" to the marginal revenue curve MR_B, i.e., it holds the same relationship to the marginal revenue curve as the marginal revenue curve holds to the demand curve. The upstream monopolist, firm A, maximizes its profits by setting the curve marginal to firm B's marginal revenue curve equal to the sum of the marginal costs c and k.

The price and output solutions for the successive monopoly model are illustrated in Figure 3.1, where MMR_B represents the curve marginal to the

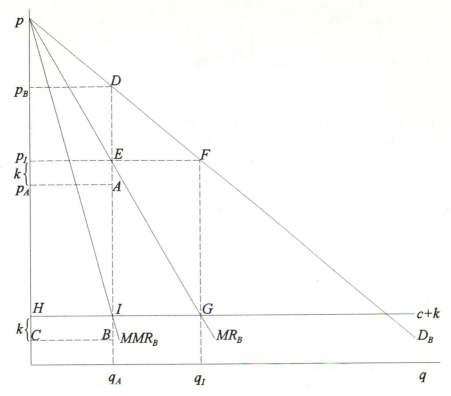

Figure 3.1 Vertical integration of successive monopolies

marginal revenue curve MR_B. The output of the upstream monopolist is q_A, determined by the intersection of the MMR_B and $c+k$ curves at point I. The price the upstream monopolist receives for the intermediate product is p_A, which is equivalent to $MR_B - k$. The upstream monopolist's profits are equal to $(p_A - c)q_A$, represented by the area $p_A ABC$. The price received by the downstream monopolist for the final product is p_B, and its profits are equal to $(p_B - p_A - k)q_A$, represented by the area $p_B DEp_I$.

If firms A and B were to integrate, the integrated firm would maximize combined profits π_{AB}:

$$\pi_{AB} = \pi_A + \pi_B = p_B q - (c+k)q, \tag{10}$$

and its first-order condition would be

$$\frac{d\pi_{AB}}{dq} = \left(p_B + q\frac{dp_B}{dq}\right) - c - k = 0. \tag{11}$$

The integrated firm maximizes its profits by setting its marginal revenue in the final product market equal to the sum of the marginal costs c and k.

In Figure 3.1, the integrated firm's output is q_I, determined by the intersection of MR_B and $c+k$ at point G. Integration eliminates the double marginalization that existed by internalizing the externalities between the two firms that resulted from both firms individually maximizing their individual profits without taking into account the incremental profits of the other. As a result of integration, output of the final product increases from q_A to q_I and the final product price falls from p_B to p_I. Consequently, consumers are better off than before. Also, the profits of the integrated firm, which are $(p_I - c - k)q_I$ as represented by the area $p_I FGH$, are greater than the combined profits of the two firms before integration. Total economic welfare is greater than before, as evidenced by the net welfare gain represented by the area $DFGI$.

Similar results hold for vertical structures characterized by bilateral monopoly or by monopsony when the downstream firm is subject to a fixed-proportions production technology. Vertical integration of the upstream and downstream firms can be expected to increase the firms' combined profits and to expand output, thereby improving social welfare. These results hold both when the downstream monopsonist sells its output in a competitive market and when it is a "monemporist," a firm that is a monopsonist in the input market and a monopolist in its output market. In contrast, vertical integration of two firms in competitive stages or the merger of either an upstream or downstream monopoly with a competitive firm in the other stage will not affect output, prices, or welfare.[1]

Variable-proportions Production Technology

It should be noted that the welfare-enhancing or neutral effects of vertical integration may be conditional on the assumption that the downstream firm is subject to a fixed-proportions production technology and they cannot be generalized to situations in which the possibility exists for substitution between the monopolized input and a competitively supplied input at the downstream stage.

If an upstream monopolist integrates forward into a downstream industry, it may produce efficiency gains through the elimination of input choice distortions due to monopoly. In determining the proportion of each input to employ, the integrated firm's perceived cost for the monopolized input will be the input's true marginal cost instead of the higher monopoly price that existed before integration. Consequently, as a result of more efficient input choices and lower costs, the integrated firm may increase its output and improve social welfare.

On the other hand, the monopoly power of the upstream monopolist may have been contained by the substitution possibilities between the monopolized and competitive inputs that existed prior to integration. By integrating forward, the upstream monopolist gains control over input use at the downstream stage and may be able to expand its monopoly power, resulting in further restriction of output and a diminution of social welfare.

The net effect of integration on social welfare will depend on the relative importance of these two effects—the increased efficiency of input use and the increased control over input choices—and, in the case of successive monopoly, the elimination of double marginalization. Numerous analytic and simulation studies of these effects have been conducted, using the Cobb-Douglas or the constant-elasticity-of-substitution (CES) functions to represent the production technology at the downstream stage.[2] These analyses demonstrate that the net effect of integration on social welfare depends on at least four factors: (1) the importance of the monopolized input in the downstream production process, (2) the elasticity of substitution between the monopolized input and other inputs, (3) the market structure of the downstream industry prior to integration, and (4) the elasticity of demand for the downstream product. Vertical integration by an upstream monopoly can lead to an increase in the price of the downstream product if the elasticity of substitution is greater than or equal to one or exceeds the elasticity of demand for the downstream product in absolute value. A price increase is somewhat more likely if the monopolized input is relatively unimportant relative to other inputs, i.e., its share of total input payments is small,[3] and the downstream industry was relatively competitive prior to integration. Similar factors explain the likelihood of a net efficiency loss due to integration.

Vertical Integration within Successive Oligopolies

Greenhut and Ohta (1979) expanded their analysis of successive monopoly by constructing a model of successive oligopoly under fixed-proportions production technology, constant marginal costs, and linear demand. They demonstrated that vertical integration by a subset of firms increased industry output and decreased the final product price. Although the profits of the integrated firms increased, overall industry profits decreased, reversing the results of successive monopoly models, in which vertical integration is beneficial to the merging monopolists as well as consumers. Nevertheless, their results support the conclusion that vertical integration is socially desirable. Abiru built a successive oligopoly model based on variable-proportions technology, which he used to isolate the pure effect of vertical integration from the effect of horizontal merger. He concluded that the pure integration effect results in an unambiguous decrease in the final product price as well as increases in industry output and consumer welfare.

Recently, Wu conducted an extensive analysis of oligopolies and vertical integration, including a two-stage successive oligopoly structure similar to that of Greenhut and Ohta (1979). Like Greenhut and Ohta, Wu assumed fixed-proportions technology, constant marginal costs, and linear demand. Following Abiru, Wu assumed an identical number of upstream and down-stream firms to avoid confusing the effects of vertical and horizontal mergers.

Wu's model (pp. 81–86) consists initially of a two-stage successive oligopoly in which n identical upstream firms produce an intermediate good used by n identical downstream firms in the production of a final product sold to consumers. Both the upstream and downstream stages are characterized by Cournot competition, i.e., each firm sets its output by assuming that the output of the other firms in the same stage is fixed. Firms in both stages operate at constant marginal costs, and the downstream firms are subject to fixed-proportions production technology. Specifically, it is assumed that production of one unit of final product requires one unit of the intermediate good. The downstream firms exercise no market power in the intermediate good market, i.e., they accept the price of the intermediate good as given. Consumer demand for the final product is assumed to take a linear form.

Vertical integration is introduced into the model by assuming that k pairs of upstream and downstream firms combine to form k vertically integrated firms that operate in both stages. Each of these vertically integrated firms manufactures the final product and provides itself with the intermediate good internally while the remaining $n - k$ downstream firms continue to rely on the intermediate good market.

The vertically integrated and nonintegrated downstream firms face the following inverse final product demand function:

$$p = a - b\left(\sum_{i=1}^{k} v_i + \sum_{i=k+1}^{n} q_i\right) \qquad a>0,\ b>0 \qquad (12)$$

where v_i represents the quantity of final product produced by the ith integrated firm and q_I represents the quantity produced by the ith nonintegrated downstream firm.

The profit function of ith integrated firm is

$$\pi_i^v = (p-c)v_i \qquad i=1,\ 2,\ \ldots,\ k. \qquad (13)$$

Substituting (12) into (13), the first-order condition for the ith integrated firm is

$$\frac{d\pi_i^v}{dv_i} = a - b\left(\sum_{j=1}^{k} v_j + \sum_{j=k+1}^{n} q_j\right) - bv_i - c = 0 \qquad i=1,\ 2,\ \ldots,\ k. \qquad (14)$$

Aggregating (14) over the k integrated firms and dividing by the number of firms, we obtain

$$a - b\frac{(k+1)}{k}\sum_{i=1}^{k} v_i - b\sum_{i=k+1}^{n} q_i - c = 0, \qquad (15)$$

which, when solved for $\sum v_i$, will produce the reaction function for the k vertically integrated firms:

$$\sum_{i=1}^{k} v_i = \frac{k}{(k+1)}\left(S - \sum_{i=k+1}^{n} x_i\right) \qquad (16)$$

where $S=(a-c)/b$.

Turning to the nonintegrated downstream firms, the profit function for the ith downstream firm is

$$\pi_i^d = (p - w)q_i \qquad i = k+1, \ k+2, \ \ldots, \ n \qquad (17)$$

where w is the price the downstream firms pay for the intermediate good.[4] Substituting (12) into (17), the first-order condition for the ith nonintegrated downstream firm is

$$\frac{d\pi_i^d}{dq_i} = a - b\left(\sum_{j=1}^{k} v_j + \sum_{j=k+1}^{n} q_j \right) - bq_i - w = 0 \qquad i = k+1, \ k+2, \ \ldots, \ n. \quad (18)$$

Aggregating (18) over the $n-k$ downstream firms, dividing by the number of firms, and solving for w, we obtain the inverse derived demand function for the intermediate good:

$$w = a - b\sum_{i=1}^{k} v_i - b\frac{(n-k+1)}{(n-k)} \sum_{i=k+1}^{n} q_i. \qquad (19)$$

The profit function of the ith nonintegrated upstream firm is

$$\pi_i^u = (w - c)x_i \qquad i = k+1, \ k+2, \ \ldots, \ n \qquad (20)$$

where x_i is the quantity of the intermediate good produced by the ith upstream firm. Substituting (19) into (20) and recalling that $q_i = x_i$, the first-order condition for the ith upstream firm is

$$\frac{d\pi_i^u}{dx_i} = a - b\sum_{j=1}^{k} v_j - b\frac{(n-k+1)}{(n-k)} \sum_{j=k+1}^{n} x_j$$

$$\qquad (21)$$

$$-b\frac{(n-k+1)}{(n-k)}x_i - c = 0 \qquad i = k+1, \ k+2, \ \ldots, \ n.$$

Aggregating (21) over the $n-k$ upstream firms and dividing by the number of firms, we obtain

$$a-b\sum_{i=1}^{k}v_i-b\frac{(n-k+1)^2}{(n-k)^2}\sum_{i=k+1}^{n}x_i-c=0, \tag{22}$$

which, when solved for $\sum x_i$ (which equals $\sum q_i$), yields the reaction function for the $n-k$ nonintegrated upstream firms:

$$\sum_{i=k+1}^{n}x_i=\frac{(n-k)^2}{(n-k+1)^2}\left(S-\sum_{i=1}^{k}v_i\right). \tag{23}$$

Solving the reaction functions (16) and (23) simultaneously, we derive the equilibrium outputs of the integrated and nonintegrated firms, which are

$$\sum_{i=1}^{k}v_i=\frac{k(2n-2k+1)S}{(k+1)(n-k+1)^2-k(n-k)^2} \tag{24}$$

and

$$\sum_{i=k+1}^{n}x_i=\frac{(n-k)^2S}{(k+1)(n-k+1)^2-k(n-k)^2} \tag{25}$$

respectively. Summing (24) and (25), total output is

$$Q=\frac{[k(n-k+1)^2-(k-1)(n-k)^2]S}{(k+1)(n-k+1)^2-k(n-k)^2}. \tag{26}$$

To determine the effect of vertical integration on the equilibrium output and the final product price, we can differentiate (26) with respect to the number of vertically integrated firms:

$$\frac{\partial Q}{\partial k}=\frac{2(n-k)(n-k+1)S}{(k+1)(n-k+1)^2-k(n-k)^2}>0. \tag{27}$$

The effect of increased vertical integration on output is expected to be positive, implying that the final product price will decrease.

The incentive for a pair of nonintegrated upstream and downstream firms to integrate can be determined by comparing their combined profits before and after integration (Wu, pp. 96–98). Assume that there currently are $k-1$ integrated firms and $n-k+1$ nonintegrated pairs of firms that rely on market transactions for exchanging the intermediate good. The combined profits of the kth pair of nonintegrated firms is

$$\pi_k^N = \pi_k^d + \pi_k^u = (p-w)q_k + (w-c)x_k. \tag{28}$$

Substituting p from (12) and w from (19) into (28) and determining $\sum v_i$, $\sum q_i$, and q_k from (24) and (25), we can restate (28) as

$$\pi_k^N = \frac{(n-k+1)(2n-2k+3)T}{[k(n-k+2)^2 - (k-1)(n-k+1)^2]^2} \tag{29}$$

where $T=(a-c)^2/b$.

The profits of the kth integrated firm are

$$\pi_k^I = (p-c)v_k. \tag{30}$$

Determining v_k from (24), (30) can be restated as

$$\pi_k^I = \frac{(2n-2k+1)^2 T}{[(n-k+1)^2(k+1) - (n-k)^2 k]^2}. \tag{31}$$

Comparing the numerical values of (29) and (31) for various combinations of n and k given T, Wu (p. 97) demonstrated that $\pi_k^I - \pi_k^N > 0$ for all n and k. Thus, regardless of the total number of firms and the number of integrated firms, a nonintegrated pair of upstream and downstream firms always has an incentive to integrate. Furthermore, in a successive Cournot oligopoly with linear demand, fixed-proportions production technology, and constant marginal costs, total vertical integration of the structure represents a Nash equilibrium.

Forward Integration by Farmer Cooperatives

Farmer cooperatives are an important element in many agricultural markets, particularly with respect to first-stage marketing activities involving raw agricultural commodities. In Royer and Bhuyan (1994, 1995), the incentives cooperatives may have for integrating forward into processing activities and the expected effects of cooperative forward integration on output, prices, and social welfare are examined.

Single Assembler and Single Processor

The two-stage model of successive monopoly discussed earlier is extended in Royer and Bhuyan (1995) to a three-stage model that includes agricultural producers, a single assembler, and a single processor. Producers sell a single raw product to the assembler, which markets the assembled raw product to the processor. The processor manufactures a processed product it sells to consumers. It is assumed the assembler faces an upward-sloping linear raw product supply curve and that its per-unit cost of assembling the raw product is constant. The processor faces a downward-sloping linear processed product demand curve, and its per-unit processing cost is constant. The processor is also subject to a fixed-proportions production technology, producing one unit of processed product from each unit of raw product. The analysis is conducted for both assembler dominance (monopoly) and processor dominance (monopsony) in the assembled raw product market.

The analysis focuses on forward integration by the assembler through acquisition of the processor. The assembler is alternately assumed to be a cooperative and, for comparison purposes, a noncooperative firm. Furthermore, the cooperative analysis is conducted under two alternative behavioral assumptions. Under the first, the cooperative maximizes the total profits of its producer-members, including patronage refunds, by setting the quantity of raw product it handles. Under the second, the cooperative does not or cannot set the quantity of raw product it handles. Instead, it accepts whatever quantity of output producers choose to market. This latter assumption conforms to the classic Helmberger and Hoos model of a marketing cooperative, in which the objective of the cooperative is to maximize the raw product price for the quantity set by producers. In the Helmberger and Hoos model, equilibrium occurs where the cooperative breaks even because its surplus is exhausted by payments to producers. It frequently has been argued that cooperatives will be unsuccessful in restricting producer output to lower levels because the receipt of patronage refunds provides producers an incentive to expand output until average net returns equal the supply price.[5]

In the model, cooperative assemblers act like competitive firms in the raw product market whereas noncooperative assemblers exercise monopsony power. Cooperative assemblers that do not restrict producer output behave like competitive firms in the assembled and processed product markets whereas noncooperative assemblers and cooperative assemblers that restrict producer output exercise monopoly power. Consequently, both producers and consumers are better off when the assembler is a cooperative instead of a noncooperative firm. Producers are generally better off when the assembler is a cooperative that restricts output whereas consumers are generally better off when the assembler is a cooperative that does not restrict output.[6] Social welfare is the greatest when the assembler is a cooperative that does not restrict output.[7]

Producers and consumers benefit from forward integration by the assembler regardless of whether the assembler is a cooperative or a noncooperative firm and whether it restricts producer output if it is a cooperative. However, the incentive to integrate depends on the assembler and whether it restricts output. Although both noncooperative assemblers and cooperative assemblers that restrict output may have an incentive to integrate forward into processing activities, this incentive may not exist for cooperatives that do not or cannot restrict output.

Several Assemblers and Several Processors

Analysis of cooperative incentives for forward integration and the effects of cooperative forward integration is applied to a three-stage vertical structure that includes several assemblers and several processors in Royer and Bhuyan (1994). In that model, producers sell a single raw product to assemblers, which market the assembled raw product to processors. The processors manufacture a processed product they sell to consumers. Initially, there are k pairs of integrated assemblers and processors, $n-k$ nonintegrated assemblers, and $n-k$ nonintegrated processors. A single nonintegrated cooperative competes among the assemblers. At first, the cooperative assembler is not integrated. The analysis focuses on the incentive this cooperative has to integrate forward into processing and the effects its integration would have on output, prices, and welfare.

The model, which is based on Wu's model of a two-stage successive oligopoly, includes assumptions similar to those in Royer and Bhuyan (1995).

Assemblers are assumed to face upward-sloping linear supply functions, and processors are assumed to face a downward-sloping linear demand function. In addition, processors are subject to a fixed-proportions production technology under which one unit of processed product is produced from each unit of raw product. The per-unit costs of assembling and processing the raw product are both assumed to be constant. Both the assembly and processing stages are characterized by Cournot competition among the firms. In the assembled raw product market, assemblers and processors are alternately assumed to exercise market power.

Simulation results based on the model indicate that integration by a cooperative assembler produces a greater industry output, a lower processed product price, and increased consumer surplus. The cooperative's output and the price it pays for the raw product increase. Thus the welfare of cooperative members is enhanced at the expense of the other producers, assemblers, and processors, whose outputs and profits decline.

If the cooperative assembler restricts producer output to optimal levels, it has an incentive to integrate at all levels of n and k although this incentive is less than for a noncooperative assembler. In addition, the net welfare gain from integration by a cooperative assembler that restricts output is frequently less than the gain from integration by a noncooperative assembler. For a given level of n, the net welfare gain from integration is less for the cooperative assembler when the level of existing integration is low. As the level of existing integration increases, the net welfare gain from integration is greater for a cooperative.

A cooperative assembler that does not restrict producer output has an incentive to integrate at many levels of n and k. In fact, when n and k are large, the integration incentives for cooperatives that do not restrict output exceed those for noncooperative assemblers and cooperatives that restrict output. Consistent with the results reported in Royer and Bhuyan (1995) for a single assembler and processor, a cooperative that does not restrict output does not have an incentive to integrate in markets in which there are few firms. The net welfare gain from integration by a cooperative that does not restrict output is negative for many levels of n and k.[8] This represents an exception to the general conclusion that, under fixed-proportions production technology, vertical integration by firms in successive monopolies and oligopolies increases economic welfare unless it is used to effect the foreclosure of downstream firms from an essential source of supply (Wu, p. 15).

Backward Integration by a Monopsony

In some agricultural markets, there are concerns about the effects on farmers of backward integration into production by processors and packers. Perry (1978) presents a model of a monopsony that examines the monopsonist's incentive to integrate and the conditions under which integration will occur. Although Perry's model considers partial integration by the monopsonist, we follow Blair and Kaserman (pp. 114–20) in demonstrating the basic profit incentive of a monopsonist to integrate backward and the effects of backward integration on output and prices by using a simplified model that does not include partial integration. In this model, which is based on Blair and Kaserman's exposition, we consider only complete integration, by which the monopsonist integrates by acquiring all of the production capacity of its input suppliers.

In the model, the downstream firm is assumed to face a perfectly competitive market for its output but is a monopsonist in the purchase of input x. The supply curve of input x is upward sloping because production of the input is assumed to require some limited resource, i.e., x is characterized by Ricardian increasing costs. Although the industry producing x is assumed to be competitive and to price its output at industry marginal cost, there is no long-run entry that will drive the price downward to industry average cost. Consequently, rents can continue to exist at the upstream stage.

The monopsonist can vary its employment of x, the monopsonized input, which is used to produce q, the final product output, which is sold at a constant price p. The monopsonist's production function, $q=q(x)$, is assumed to be continuous and twice differentiable with $dq/dx>0$ and $d^2q/dx^2<0$, and the monopsonist faces an upward-sloping inverse supply function $r=r(x)$. The total industry costs of producing the monopsonized input are represented by $C(x)$, where $dC/dx>0$ and $d^2C/dx^2>0$.

The nonintegrated monopsonist's profit function can be written

$$\pi_N = \int_0^x p \frac{dq}{dx} dx - r(x)x. \tag{32}$$

The profit function of the input industry is

$$\pi_S = rx - C(x). \tag{33}$$

In the absence of integration, profit maximization by individual input suppliers, each of which considers r a constant, results in an input supply price that is equal to the marginal cost of producing x:

$$r = \frac{dC}{dx}, \tag{34}$$

which is the monopsonist's inverse supply function, obtained by maximizing (33). Substituting (34) into the monopsonist's profit function (32), the latter can be rewritten

$$\pi_N = \int_0^x p\frac{dq}{dx}dx - \frac{dC}{dx}x. \tag{35}$$

Differentiating (35) with respect to x, we derive the first-order condition for the monopsonist:

$$p\frac{dq}{dx} = \frac{dC}{dx} + x\frac{d^2C}{dx^2}, \tag{36}$$

which implicitly defines x_N^*, the optimal level of x for the monopsonist to employ. Substituting x_N^* into (35), the monopsonist's maximized profits without integration are

$$\pi_N^* = \int_0^{x_N^*} p\frac{dq}{dx}dx - \frac{dC}{dx}\bigg|_{x_N^*} x_N^* \tag{37}$$

where $dC/dx|x_N^*$ represents the upstream industry's marginal cost of producing x evaluated at x_N^*.

If the monopsonist were to integrate backward completely into the production of x, its profit function would be

$$\pi_I = \int_0^x p\frac{dq}{dx}dx - C(x). \tag{38}$$

Maximization of (38) produces the first-order condition:

$$p\frac{dq}{dx} = \frac{dC}{dx}, \tag{39}$$

which implicitly defines x_I^*, the optimal level of x under complete vertical integration. Comparing (36) and (39), we see that $x_I^* > x_N^*$ because dq/dx must be declining. Employment of the input at level x_I^* duplicates the competitive solution because the marginal cost of input x equals the value of its marginal product in the downstream industry.

Substituting x_I^* into (38), the integrated firm's maximized profits are

$$\pi_I^* = \int_0^{x_I^*} p\frac{dq}{dx}dx - C(x_I^*). \tag{40}$$

The monopsonist will improve its profits by integrating if $\pi_I^* - \pi_N^* > 0$. From (37) and (40), we find that

$$\pi_I^* - \pi_N^* = \int_{x_N^*}^{x_I^*} p\frac{dq}{dx}dx - C(x_I^*) + \frac{dC}{dx}\bigg|_{x_N^*} x_N^*, \tag{41}$$

which indeed is positive. Thus, ignoring the costs of acquiring the upstream firms for now, we can conclude that complete backward integration by the monopsonist will always increase the firm's profits.

This result is demonstrated graphically in Figure 3.2. In the figure, the upstream industry's average cost of producing x is represented by $AC_x = C(x)/x$. Above AC_x is the industry's marginal cost curve, which under competition corresponds to the industry supply curve, $S_x = dC/dx$. Above S_x is the monopsonist's marginal factor cost curve, $MFC_x = dC/dx + x(d^2C/dx^2)$, which represents the marginal cost to the nonintegrated monopsonist of increasing its employ-

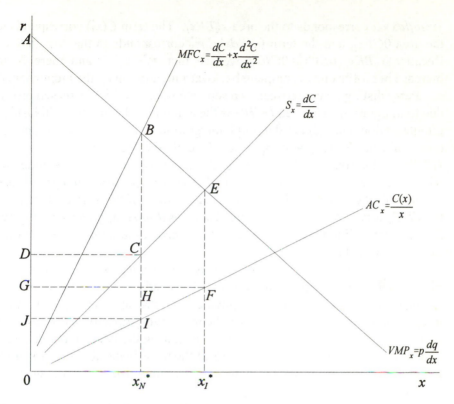

Figure 3.2 Backward integration by a monopsony

ment of x. The graph also shows the downward-sloping curve representing the value of the marginal product, $VMP_x=p(dq/dx)$.

Without integration, the monopsonist will employ x at level x_N^*, determined by the intersection of VMP_x and MFC_x at point B, according to its first-order condition (36). The monopsonist's total revenue, which corresponds to $\int p(dq/dx)dx$ in (37), is represented by the area ABx_N^*0. Its total cost is rx_N^*, which is represented by the area DCx_N^*0. Thus the monopsonist's profits are equal to the area $ABCD$.

With integration, the firm will increase its use of x to x_I^*, determined by the intersection of VMP_x and dC/dx at point E, according to the first-order condition (39). The firm's total revenue is AEx_I^*0, and its total cost is GFx_I^*0. Consequently, its profits are equal to the area $AEFG$.

The increase in profits resulting from vertical integration is represented by the area $DCBEFG$, which corresponds to the right-hand side of (41). The term

$\int p(dq/dx)dx$ corresponds to the area $x_N^* BEx_I^*$. The term $C(x_I^*)$ corresponds to the area $0GFx_I^*$, and the term $(dC/dx|x_N^*)x_N^*$ corresponds to the area $0DCx_N^*$. Because $x_N^* BEx_I^* + 0DCx_N^* > 0GFx_I^*$, we see that $\pi_I^* - \pi_N^* > 0$ and there is an increase in profits due to complete backward integration by the monopsonist.

Perry distinguishes between two separate sources of the increased profits due to integration. The area $DCHG$ is the amount of the upstream industry's preintegration rents captured through integration by the monopsonist and is a result of what Perry (1978, pp. 568–69) calls the "rent effect." The area $HBEF$ results from the elimination of the efficiency loss from the underemployment of the monopsonized input in the absence of vertical integration and is due to the "efficiency effect." The relative sizes of these areas depend on the VMP_x curve. As it becomes more elastic (as d^2q/dx^2 approaches zero), the area corresponding to the efficiency effect increases and that corresponding to the rent effect decreases.

Notwithstanding the increased profits due to integration, the monopsonist's decision to integrate backward will depend on the net benefits from vertical integration, which are equivalent to the increased profits from integration less the costs of acquiring the production capacity in the upstream industry. Under competition, the cost of acquiring the firms in the upstream industry will equal the combined profits of the firms in the absence of vertical integration. By substituting (34) into (33), the maximized profits of the input supply industry are

$$\pi_S^* = \frac{dC}{dx}\bigg|_{x_N^*} x_N^* - C(x_N^*). \tag{42}$$

Consequently, from (41) and (42), the net benefits of complete backward integration are

$$\pi_I^* - \pi_N^* - \pi_S^* = \int_{x_N^*}^{x_I^*} p\frac{dq}{dx}dx - C(x_I^*) + C(x_N^*), \tag{43}$$

which can be positive or negative because $C(x_I^*) > C(x_N^*)$.

In Figure 3.2, the first term on the right-hand side of (43), $\int p(dq/dx)dx$, is represented by the area $x_N^* BEx_I^*$. The second term $C(x_I^*)$ is represented by the area $0GFx_I^*$, and the third term $C(x_N^*)$ is represented by the area $0JIx_N^*$. Thus the net benefits from integration are $x_N^* BEx_I^* - 0GFx_I^* + 0JIx_N^*$ or *BEFH-GHIJ*. Because the difference between these two areas cannot be determined a priori, the incentive for the monopsonist to integrate completely will depend on the upstream industry cost function $C(x)$ and the monopsonist's VMP_x curve, the latter of which depends on the production function and the demand curve for the final product.

By considering partial integration, Perry demonstrated that increased backward integration by the monopsonist will generally produce an increase in employment of the input, resulting in increased output and a lower final product price for consumers. Social welfare will be improved, but the price received by the remaining independent suppliers will decrease. Perry also showed that for several reasonable specifications of the acquisition costs, the monopsonist will have an incentive to integrate backward, at least partially.

The optimal degree of integration, as defined by the proportion of upstream firms acquired, depends on the acquisition costs. If the monopsonist is allowed to acquire additional suppliers repeatedly, in small increments of the total suppliers, at rents that prevail at the time of each acquisition, it will always have an incentive to integrate further, leading it to complete integration. Likewise, if through some credible threat, the monopsonist can acquire suppliers at a cost that is less than the rents they are receiving, it will have an incentive to integrate completely. On the other hand, if the cost of acquisition is the initial rent received by suppliers, the optimal degree of integration may be something less than complete integration.

Azzam and Wellman applied Perry's model to an examination of the expected effects of increased backward integration by packers in the slaughter hog industry. Assuming constant elasticity forms for the derived demand for hogs and the hog supply function, they simulated the effects of increasing the degree of vertical integration by a monopsonistic packer on hog slaughter and variables related to independent producers for a range of elasticities of demand and supply. Their results demonstrate that increased integration can be expected to increase overall pork production and lower consumer prices while decreasing hog production by independent producers and lowering both the price they receive for hogs and their net earnings.

Vertical Coordination through Supply Contracts

Related to concerns about backward integration are concerns about the effects on farmers of the increased use of production contracts by processors and packers. Wu (pp. 63–66) has attempted to analyze the economic impacts of coordinating output in a two-stage vertical market structure through the use of supply contracts. In that model, which is structurally similar to his vertical integration model, each upstream firm supplies the intermediate good to a particular downstream firm under an exclusive supply contract. There is a market for contracts and, at equilibrium, each upstream firm signs a supply contract with one downstream firm. Although Wu indicates that the transfer prices paid by downstream firms for the intermediate good may differ among firms because they are set by individual suppliers and buyers, the prices that result from the model are the same because of the assumption of identical firms and the distribution of market power between the firms bound by a supply contract.

In the model, downstream firms engage in Cournot competition among themselves in the final product market. Each individual upstream firm sets its price for the intermediate good given the derived demand function of the downstream firm with which it is contractually bound. Cournot competition does not exist in the upstream industry. Instead, each upstream firm acts essentially as a monopolist, and there is only indirect Cournot competition from the downstream industry.

Consequently, the equilibrium output under a vertical structure based on exclusive supply contracts is less than the output of structures based on market transactions or vertical integration. In addition, the output of a vertical structure based on supply contracts is more sensitive to additional firms than the other structures. As a result, Wu suggests that vertical relations should be considered in addition to horizontal market structure in formulating public policies toward imperfect markets and that intervention to increase the competitiveness of an imperfect market will produce the greatest returns in vertical structures characterized by exclusive contractual relations.

To determine the incentives firms may have for entering exclusive supply contracts, Wu compared the profits of the kth upstream and downstream firms under an exclusive supply contract with their respective profits under market transactions in a mixed model consisting initially of $k-1$ pairs of firms that are bound together by supply contracts and $n-k+1$ upstream firms and $n-k+1$ downstream firms that rely on market transactions for exchanging the intermediate good (pp. 87–92). Under rules of individual and group rationality, for a pair of firms to establish an exclusive supply contract, the profits of each or both firms would have to be greater under supply contracts than under market transactions.

By agreeing to be bound by an exclusive supply contract, individual firms withdraw from the oligopolistic relationship between upstream and downstream firms that rely on market transactions for exchanging the intermediate good and enter an exclusive monopolistic relationship. A firm that relies on market transactions for the intermediate good can switch freely among competing suppliers. This competition among upstream suppliers reduces their market power and lowers the marginal costs of the downstream firms. When two firms establish an exclusive supply contract, the downstream firm can no longer turn to alternative suppliers for its inputs. Switching costs and the asymmetrically distributed market power increase the downstream firm's marginal cost.

Not surprisingly then, Wu's simulations indicate that the profits of the *k*th downstream firm are always greater when it relies on market transactions for supply of the intermediate good than when it is bound by an exclusive supply contract. The profits of the *k*th upstream firm also are greater under market transactions than under a supply contract except when the horizontal market structure is highly concentrated or when the number of firms relying on market transactions is small. In no case were the combined profits of the *k*th upstream and downstream firms higher under a supply contract, thus ruling out the possibility of the upstream firm offering the downstream firm a lump-sum payment to enter into an exclusive contractual relationship.

Wu's approach to analyzing the relationship between market structure and supply contracts may provide a useful point of departure for analyzing the impact of production contracts on raw product markets for agricultural commodities although his assumptions about the distribution of market power between upstream and downstream firms would seem to be inappropriate for the relationships between most agricultural producers and packers or processors. Nevertheless, Wu's analysis suggests two points worth considering. First, even though his analysis is based on the assumption of upstream market power, the general absence of a profit incentive for upstream and downstream firms to enter exclusive supply contracts suggests that market structure considerations may be inadequate by themselves to explain the existence of production contracts in agricultural raw product markets. Second, Wu's conclusion that output is more restricted under supply contracts than under other means of exchange suggests that it would be misleading to use models of vertical integration as proxies for contract coordination in assessing the expected impacts of contracts on output and prices.

Conclusions

The models described in this paper should be useful in analyzing those changes in vertical relationships occurring in the food system that are attributable to imperfect competition. In addition to helping explain the conditions under which vertical integration and contract coordination are likely to occur, these models are useful in predicting the effects of vertical coordination on output, prices, and the welfare of various market participants. Of course, these models are not appropriate for analyzing the changes in vertical relationships that occur because of transactional economies.

A review of these models demonstrates that no generalizations can be made about the effects of vertical coordination without taking into account market structure and the means of coordination. Although vertical integration usually results in increased output, lower consumer prices, and greater social welfare, situations exist in which integration can diminish overall welfare. Furthermore, the effect of integration on the welfare of particular market participants can depend on the form of integration. Whereas agricultural producers may benefit from the vertical integration of downstream firms as the result of increased sales and raw product prices, backward integration by processors and packers can bring about lower sales and prices for independent producers. Finally, overall economic welfare can depend on the form of vertical coordination. Whereas vertical integration usually increases social welfare through greater output and lower prices, there is evidence that contract coordination can reduce output and increase prices.

Notes

1 For a thorough analysis of the relationships between vertical and horizontal mergers and successive and mutually related market power under fixed-proportions production technology and various assumptions of monopoly, monopsony, and perfect competition, see Warren-Boulton, pp. 51–61.

2 See Scherer and Ross, pp. 522–27, for a succinct discussion of this topic and list of references.

3 This result stems from the greater significance of extending the monopolist's control over input use to the other inputs.

4 For a downstream firm, the marginal cost of manufacturing the final product is w, the price of the intermediate good x. Represent the firm's fixed-proportion production function as $q = \alpha(x)$ where α is a constant coefficient of production. If we set $\alpha=1$ and rescale such that $q=x$, the marginal cost will equal w (Wu, pp. 34–35).

5 Under the second assumption, when the cooperative accepts whatever quantity of raw product producers choose to market, there is assembler dominance only in the sense that

the processor is a price taker. The price of the assembled raw product is determined, not by the assembler, but by the quantity supplied by producers.
6   There is an exception under processor dominance, where the output is set by the processor and the level is not subject to the objective of the cooperative or the behavior of its producer-members. As a result, the cooperative solutions are identical.
7   This particular result depends on the assumptions about costs and processed product demand. As LeVay (p. 107–8) observes, a cooperative with unrestricted output will produce beyond the social optimum when marginal cost exceeds average cost.
8   This result apparently is caused by a shift in raw product production from independent producers to cooperative members, who produce at a higher marginal cost.

References

Abiru, M. 1988. "Vertical Integration, Variable Proportions and Successive Oligopolies." *Journal of Industrial Economics* 36:315–25.
Azzam, A. M., and A. C. Wellman. 1992. *Packer Integration into Hog Production: Current Status and Likely Impacts of Increased Vertical Control on Hog Prices and Quantities.* Research Bulletin 315-F, Agricultural Research Division, Institute of Agricultural and Natural Resources, University of Nebraska–Lincoln, June.
Blair, R. D., and D. L. Kaserman. 1983. *Law and Economics of Vertical Integration and Control.* New York, N.Y.: Academic Press.
Greenhut, M. L., and H. Ohta. 1976. "Related Market Conditions and Interindustrial Mergers." *American Economic Review* 66:267–77.
———. 1979. "Vertical Integration of Successive Oligopolists." *American Economic Review* 69:137–41.
Helmberger, P., and S. Hoos. 1962. "Cooperative Enterprise and Organization Theory." *Journal of Farm Economics* 44:275–90.
LeVay, C. 1983. "Some Problems of Agricultural Marketing Co-operatives' Price/Output Determination in Imperfect Competition." *Canadian Journal of Agricultural Economics* 31:105–10.
Perry, M. K. 1978. "Vertical Integration: The Monopsony Case." *American Economic Review* 68:561–70.
———. 1989. "Vertical Integration: Determinants and Effects." *Handbook of Industrial Organization,* ed. R. Schmalensee and R. D. Willig, vol. 1, pp. 183–255. Amsterdam, The Netherlands: North-Holland.
Royer, J. S., and S. Bhuyan. 1994. "Vertical Integration by Farmer Cooperatives: Incentives, Impacts, and Public Policy." Paper presented at NE-165/WRCC-72 research conference, Interactions between Public Policies and Private Strategies in the Food Industries, Montréal, Québec, Canada, June 27–28.
———. 1995. "Forward Integration by Farmer Cooperatives: Comparative Incentives and Impacts." *Journal of Cooperatives* 10:33–48.
Scherer, F. M., and D. Ross. 1990. *Industrial Market Structure and Economic Performance,* 3d ed. Boston, Mass.: Houghton Mifflin Co.
Warren-Boulton, F. R. 1978. *Vertical Control of Markets: Business and Labor Practices.* Cambridge, Mass.: Ballinger Publishing Co.

Waterson, M. 1984. *Economic Theory of the Industry.* Cambridge, England: Cambridge University Press.

Wu, C. 1992. *Strategic Aspects of Oligopolistic Vertical Integration.* Amsterdam, The Netherlands: North-Holland.

4 Quantifying Vertical Coordination: Refinement of the Frank-Henderson Vertical Coordination Index

DENNIS R. HENDERSON and STUART D. FRANK

The purpose of this paper is to advance a refinement in our 1992 vertical coordination index (Frank and Henderson) that, we submit, has the potential to improve the accuracy of empirical measurements by substituting a term that is observable for one that was subjectively estimated in our earlier work. We do so from a belief that the concept of vertical coordination can be specified in a manner that is analytically useful, i.e., vertical coordination can be treated as a variable or parameter in analytical models focusing on factors motivating vertical arrangements other than spot markets and/or their economic consequences. This effort is the spirit of Sporleder's call twenty years ago that ". . . requisite to quantitatively testing hypotheses concerning vertical integration is design of an acceptable quantitative vertical integration measure" (p. 13).

The paper is organized as follows: The first section clarifies our concept of vertical coordination as a continuum of vertical governance structures, variable in the extent to which one party of a vertical exchange prescribes the behavioral pattern of another. The second section revisits our original formulation of the vertical coordination index and places it relative to other measures of vertical integration. The third section examines how the concept of principal-agent may be used as a basis for respecifying one of the terms of our original formulation in a manner that allows replacement of subjective estimation with empirical observation. Our final comments regard some considerations for empirical application.

Vertical Coordination as Governance Structures

The agriculture-food (agro-food) sector can be conceptualized, inter alia, as a system of vertically interrelated stages. These stages are tied together through a variety of activities and institutions, ranging from the sale of intermediate goods via arm's length transactions in spot markets, through a variety of informal and formal contractual agreements, to consolidation of two or more stages under the common management of a single firm, i.e., vertical integration.

The simplest type of vertical system is one in which an unprocessed agricultural commodity is sold from the farm gate at price p_F to a food processing firm; this firm adds value to the commodity and sells a processed food product at price p_W to a food retailer that, in turn, sells it to consumers at price p_R. This is an example of vertical coordination through spot-market transactions. In a timeless world of perfectly functioning markets, spot transactions between the different stages would likely be the coordination practice of choice. The papers in this conference, however, give testimony to the existence of a plethora of more complex exchange arrangements.

Williamson has described such arrangements as the ". . . governance structure of transactions" (1979, p. 234), further defining governance structures as the "institutional matrix within which transactions are negotiated and executed" (p. 239). When viewed as a means by which the output of an upstream entity is transposed into an input for a downstream entity, governance structures can be arranged or ordered hierarchically. This ordering is based on the premise that contracts are not the same as spot markets, i.e., contracts are more tightly governed than are spot market transactions; they are more specific in tying together the behavior of upstream and downstream firms. It also presumes distinctions between contracts; different contracts imply unique governance structures.

We argued earlier (1992) that governance structures can be arrayed on a continuum ranging from spot transactions at one extreme to vertical integration at the other. We used the term "administered coordination" to characterize the changes along this continuum. In essence, the extent to which one party to the exchange administers, directs, or controls the behavior of the other party ranges from none to complete. At the spot-market extreme, both the upstream and downstream agents act independently; they deal at "arm's length" and rely entirely on the market outcome (in terms of, e.g., price, quantity, and quality exchanged). At the vertical integration extreme, one party is employer of the other; interdependence is complete in the sense that the employer (or principal) directs, or *administers*, the behavior of the employee (or agent).

Arrayed in between these extremes are contracts that provide for some degree of control by one party (a principal) over another, vertically related party (an agent). The degree of control varies, depending upon the nature of the contract. Informal marketing agreements, for example, may specify only a few terms of exchange (e.g., time of delivery, selection of commodity by quality, price premium) whereas classical contracts provide a set of legal rules with formal documents and self-liquidating transactions; neoclassical contracts involve longer-term arrangements that do not cover all contingencies but include resolution structures such as arbitration and pricing tournaments. Specific to the agricultural marketing literature, Mighell and Jones described three general types of contracts: (1) market specification, (2) production management, and (3) resource providing, that follow a progression (hierarchy) of increasing control by one party.

As we discuss in somewhat more detail in the next section, it is this range of control that is a key component of our vertical coordination index; a component that distinguishes the vertical coordination index from other measures of vertical coordination that have appeared in the industrial organization literature. It is on the measurement of control that our effort in the third section focuses; therein we put forth what we believe to be a substantial contribution to the systematic quantification of this concept.

Measures of Vertical Coordination

Most of the attempts to quantify vertical coordination have focused on vertical integration (see, for example, Joskow; Monteverde and Teece). Measures of vertical integration include the *Vertical Ratio* (Rumelt) and the *ratio of value added to sales* (Adelman). Both have limitations. The former, defined as the share of a firm's total product that is part of a vertical chain within the firm, requires a breakout of a firm's total production by product line, data typically not included in annual reports or other publicly available sources. The latter, while data friendly, is subject to both profits bias and primary-industry bias (i.e., a firm's position in the value-adding chain). Profits bias results from cyclical variation in profits that influence the ratio of value-added to sales over time within the same firm, thus distorting time-series measurements. It can also result from conglomerate (e.g., vertically unrelated) integration. Primary-industry bias stems from high value-added-to-sales ratios in primary, compared to secondary, stages of production, thus distorting cross-sectional comparisons.

Maddigan developed a measure of vertical integration that is more data-friendly than the Vertical Ratio and blunts the profits and primary industry biases of the value-added-to-sales ratio. Her vertical industry connections (VIC) index incorporates vertical interdependencies drawn from input-output matrices: input-output coefficients are combined with a specification of vertically related industries within which a given firm operates. As such,

Maddigan's VIC index captures all upstream and downstream product linkages for a firm but is not influenced by either conglomerate integration or a firm's position within the processing-distribution chain.

Maddigan's formulation, however, is also subject to measurement limitations. It includes only industries in which a firm holds a 100 percent equity position, thus capturing neither what Blois has labeled vertical quasi integration (control through partial ownership), nor the array of vertical contract possibilities. Further, it is limited in application to the level of industry disaggregation for which input-output coefficients are available, and it cannot discriminate between firms that operate in identical sets of industries.

Few attempts have been made to systematically arrange various types of governance structures on a scale of control. Gatignon and Anderson, in a study of the determinants of the degree of control exercised by multinational corporations over vertically interdependent foreign subsidiaries, classified control on the basis of equity shares held by the parent firm: wholly owned subsidiaries, dominant partnerships, balanced partnerships, and minority holdings. These were scaled from high control (wholly owned) to low control (minority partnerships), thus encompassing both vertical integration and quasi integration. While Gatignon and Anderson applied this classification scheme to international ties, conceptually it is equally applicable in a domestic context.

One appeal of the Gatignon and Anderson scaling is that it can be calculated from generally available firm-level data. Equating equity share with degree of control, however, seems arbitrary; the degree of control a parent actually exercises over a minority-held subsidiary, for example, may vary from nearly total to practically none. Further, it ignores contracts. Thus their approach can best be characterized as a partial specification of vertical control.

Nonetheless, Gatignon and Anderson demonstrated analytical richness with their measure. In econometric analysis, they found that the incidence of wholly owned subsidiaries (vertical integration) was related to a number of variables used as proxies for transaction costs. However, they found no significant differences associated with other categories of vertical control (e.g., dominant partnerships, minority holdings). Thus their measure appears to be most useful for distinguishing vertical integration from contractual forms of vertical control.

In our earlier analysis of vertical ties used by U.S. food manufacturers for procuring commodity inputs, we developed the vertical coordination (VC) index by adding a vector of control to Maddigan's VIC index. The control vector is styled after that of Gatignon and Anderson but incorporates a hierarchy of contract-like vertical governance structures. Adding the control vector eliminates the restriction of the VIC index to the case of vertical integration.

The VC index utilizes the Leontief framework input-output matrix **X**, where each x_{ij} is the optimal value of industry I's output used as an input by industry j. The input-output matrix is manipulated to create industry k's upstream and downstream linkage matrices, **C** and **D**. Matrices **C** and **D** capture an industry's inter-industry connections. Each element c_{ij} of matrix **C** represents the share of net output of industry j ($j = k$) that is supplied by industry I. Each element d_{ij} of matrix **D** represents the share of net output of industry I ($I = k$) that is supplied to industry j.

Matrices **E** and **F** capture the control associated with an industry's vertical exchange arrangements. In matrix **E**, each element e_{ij} represents the extent of control influenced by industry j over upstream industry I. Similarly, each element f_{ij} in matrix **F** represents industry I's control of downstream industry j. Equation (1) defines matrices **E** and **F**:

$$e_{ij} \text{ and } f_{ij} = \sum_{g=1}^{s} \sum_{h=1}^{t} L_{gh} \, O_{gh} \, N_{gh} \tag{1}$$

where: g = number of products produced in each industry, $g = 1, \ldots, s$;
$\quad\quad\;\; h$ = type of exchange arrangement, $h = 1, \ldots, t$;
$\quad\quad\;\; L$ = for e_{ij}, product g's share of industry j's inputs and,
$\quad\quad\quad\quad$ for f_{ij}, product g's share of industry I's outputs;
$\quad\quad\;\; O$ = assigned value of consolidated control; and
$\quad\quad\;\; N$ = share exchanged by each type of exchange arrangement.

Each governance structure, or exchange arrangement, was assigned an assumed (subjective) value representing extent of consolidated control (argument O).

To quantify the vertical tie, the generalized formulation of the VC index for industry k is expressed as:

$$VC_k = 1 - \left[1 \bigg/ \prod_{i=1}^{n} (C^i)^p (D_i)^p (E^i)^p (F_i)^p \right] \tag{2}$$

where: C^i = column I of industry k's upstream input-output matrix (**C**),
$\quad\quad\;\; D_i$ = row I of industry k's downstream input-output matrix (**D**),

E^i = column I of industry k's upstream vertical control matrix (**E**),
F_i = row I of industry k's downstream vertical control matrix (**F**),
p = vector scalar product, and
n = number of industries with which industry k is interdependent.

Focusing attention on argument O in equation 1, the true functional form for the control relationship was not known. Therefore, to express vertical control in our specification, farm commodity acquisitions by food manufacturers were partitioned into five discrete categories of exchange arrangements, as defined by Mighell and Jones: spot markets, market specification contracts, production management contracts, resource-providing contracts, and vertical integration (Frank and Henderson, Table 1, p. 945). The value for consolidated control (argument O) assigned to each type of exchange arrangement ranged from zero for spot markets to 100 percent for vertical integration.

Within this 0–1 range, three functional forms for argument O were examined: (1) increasing marginal rate of control, where the share of control transferred increases at an increasing rate for each successive exchange arrangement, spot market through contracts to integration; (2) constant marginal rate, where control transfer increases at a constant rate; and (3) decreasing marginal rate, where control transfer increases at a decreasing rate. For example, the assigned values for the decreasing marginal rate of control were: spot market, 0; market specification contract, 0.5; production management contract, 0.8; resource providing contract, 0.9; and integration, 1.0.

All three functional forms were tested. Findings revealed that the most robust results were associated with a decreasing marginal rate of control, i.e., the amount of direct control by one party over another in the vertical chain increases at a decreasing rate, moving from the spot-market extreme. This appears to be consistent with Williamson (1975) and Coase, both of whom maintained that firms internalize transactions (vertically integrate) up to the point at which (decreasing) marginal benefits equal (increasing) marginal costs associated with direct control. This suggests that the first unit of control transferred from one firm to another provides greater benefits than the second, ad infinitum. Even so, these measures of control transfer were assumed; they are devoid of empirical content.

Our use of discrete categories for the control relationship forced the measurement into a set of specific, noncontinuous values. In reality, however, it is likely that there are numerous exchange arrangements currently classified as production management contracts that vary in the degree of control by one party over another. Thus forcing a control continuum into discrete categories introduces the possibility of bias. In our initial approach, similar exchange arrangements in different industries were assigned the same value of control even though structural and institutional differences may exist.

Our original estimated values for upstream VC indices for the U.S. food manufacturing industries, using 1982 data, are shown in Table 4.1. Index values ranged from 0 for industries that procure virtually no input from U.S. farms (e.g., coffee roasters) to nearly 1 for industries with highly specialized farm commodity inputs and a high incidence of production management contracts (e.g., pickles, canned, and dehydrated fruits and vegetables). The mean index value across all industries is 0.47. We interpret this to imply that, on average, vertical interdependencies between U.S. farms and food manufacturers are roughly at the midpoint on a continuum from no upstream control by the latter over the former, i.e., fully independent farms, to the point at which farmers behave as employees. With a standard deviation of 0.355, there is considerable variability across industries.

Even though our earlier specification of the VC index has a "soft" measure of vertical control and is subject to the same level-of-industry disaggregation and firm-level discrimination limitations as is Maddigan's VIC index, it represents a step toward a scaled measure of vertical coordination that is consistent with a hierarchical concept of control. Applied at the four-digit U.S. SIC industry level, it proved to be useful in econometric studies of both determinants (Frank and Henderson) and performance implications (Henderson and Frank). We interpret those findings as support for the view that conceptualizing vertical coordination in a context of hierarchical control conveys useful empirical information.

Vertical Coordination as Principal-Agent

Governance structures can also be considered as a form of principal-agent (Ross). Katz, for example, has shown that vertical contracts are a type of principal-agent relationship in which a given principal may have multiple agents, and agents of multiple principals may compete among themselves. Such a structure is often observed in the agro-food sector.

One characteristic of a principal-agent relationship is that the principal engages in optimizing behavior, then induces the agent to behave accordingly through the use of an incentive payment (or penalty) scheme. This gives rise to a vertical contract that provides for some form of a nonlinear payment schedule. The payment or compensation scheme typically follows the general form of a two-part tariff that is an ad valorem or per-unit payment plus a set, or lump-sum, fee, the latter associated with effort[1] put forth by the agent.

Table 4.1 Upstream VC indices for U.S. food manufacturing industries, 1982

Industry	VC	Industry	VC
Ice cream and frozen deserts	0.999	Refined sugar	0.499
Frozen specialties	0.999	Animal feeds	0.423
Canned specialties	0.999	Soybean oil mill products	0.416
Pickles, sauces, and salad dressings	0.979	Other vegetable oil mill products	0.386
Macaroni and spaghetti	0.952	Sausages and other prepared meats	0.335
Canned fruits and vegetables	0.945	Pet food	0.276
Dehydrated fruit, vegetables, and soup	0.899	Malt beverages	0.267
Bread, cake, and related products	0.823	Rice mill products	0.165
Frozen fruits and vegetables	0.822	Cotton seed mill products	0.155
Cereal breakfast foods	0.812	Wet corn mill products	0.126
Creamery butter	0.796	Flour mill products	0.121

Processed egg products	0.771	Shortening and cooking oils	0.110
Cheese	0.737	Preserved seafoods	0.039
Confectionery products	0.664	Soft drinks	0.033
Condensed and evaporated milk	0.611	Fresh fish	0.033
Dressed poultry	0.565	Chocolate and cocoa products	0.012
Fluid milk	0.543	Animal fats and oils	0.009
Fresh meats	0.528	Distilled liquor	0.002
Wine and brandy	0.516	Roasted coffee	0.000

Source: Frank.

A common form of contract is one that sets compensation $y = pq + s$, where p is a per-unit (linear) price, q is quantity, and s is the nonlinear portion of the payment, i.e., s is not directly proportional to q. The lump-sum element, s, may be an incentive payment tied to effort by the agent that is desirable from the principal's perspective, for example, agent behavior upstream that allows the principal to carry out optimal downstream market strategy. Or it may be a penalty tied to the lack of agent effort. The fixed portion of the payment can be either positive (e.g., a franchise fee paid to a food service provisioner by a restaurateur) or negative (e.g., a slotting fee paid by a food manufacturer to a grocery retailer). It may be paid before delivery (e.g., an incentive paid by a food manufacturer to a farmer for adopting a specific cultural practice) or after delivery (e.g., a reward to a livestock grower by a meat processor for above-average lean-to-fat ratio).

The rationale for two-part tariffs are well developed (see Katz, for example). In general, incentives derive from complex transactions in which a single, uniform price cannot assure an efficient exchange. Examples include:

Moral hazard—where effort by the agent cannot be directly observed by the principal, an incentive payment can be used to prevent agent shirking. Sheldon, for example, has demonstrated that a combination of piece-rate (uniform pricing) and fixed fee is necessary to induce a risk-averse agent to exercise effort that has a probability (p) greater than 0 but less than 1 (i.e., $0 < p < 1$) of resulting in a desirable outcome.

Risk sharing—where, in the presence of uncertainty and mutual risk aversion, a linear or uniform price shifts the entire burden of risk to the agent. Under such conditions, Shavell has shown that, with uniform pricing, the agent will supply or acquire a suboptimally low quantity (i.e., put forth low effort). The principal can induce a Pareto-better outcome by offering a fixed payment to (partially) compensate the agent for the possibility of a poor event that adversely affects joint (principal and agent) earnings accruing to agent effort.

Opportunism—where the agent makes an investment that has value only in a specific principal-agent relationship, the principal may reopen bargaining over price once the sunk (idiosyncratic) investment has been made. Hence, in the case of linear pricing, underinvestment results as the agent limits the extent to which s/he is locked in (i.e., is a hostage). As developed by Williamson (1983), a fixed payment creates a relation-specific investment by the principal, thus making the principal and agent mutual hostages.

Unequal information—where the principal knows the value of agent effort but the agent does not, Katz has shown that an offer of a uniform price by the principal will be interpreted by the agent as an admission by the principal of low (or no) value associated with agent effort; effort is not forthcoming. The addition of a fixed payment conveys information on the value of effort to the agent, thus motivating such effort.

Double marginalization—where in the presence of successive stages of market power, a fixed fee can be used by one party to capture a portion of rents earned by the second party in return for joint profit-maximizing marginal cost pricing by the first party. This case was first presented by Spengler as rationale for vertical integration and has since been shown to be applicable to cases of nonlinear contracts (McCorriston; Shaffer).

Many situations can be envisioned in the agro-food sector that generate these types of incentives for nonlinear payment schemes. Between agricultural producers and food manufacturers, for example, the case of performance incentives tied to such things as harvest or marketing date, rate-of-gain, or quality attributes are well known, as is the case of retail promotion or shelving allowances between food manufacturers and retailers. However, for our purposes the salient characteristic is not the incentive for, but the existence of, a two-part compensation scheme for a given transaction, i.e., *s* (lump sum) plus *pq* (price per unit).

We contend that the relative size of the fixed component of a nonlinear payment carries intelligence regarding the extent to which the principal's ability to maximize profits rests on specific behavior by an agent. Thus it provides a measure of the extent to which the principal finds it of interest to control the agent's behavior. With a spot market transaction, the entire payment is ad valorem (uniform price); this implies no direct control by a principal over an agent. Essentially, both are independent agents, dealing at "arm's length." With vertical integration, the entire payment is lump sum; the agent receives a salary or wage not tied to output quality or quantity sold.

Returning to the array of vertical governance structures on a continuum of control, principal-agent theory leads to an intriguing possibility—that of measuring control by a principal over an agent based on the share of total compensation accounted for by a nonlinear (or fixed) payment. Conveniently, this places spot-market transactions and vertical integration at the polar ends. Movement from the spot-transaction extreme, as captured by an increasing fixed (s) share of total compensation, which at least in concept is observable, reflects increasing control by a principal in the vertical chain over upstream and/or downstream agents.

Based upon this reasoning, we put forward reformulated **E** and **F** matrices for the VC index, as follows:

$$e_{ij} \text{ and } f_{ij} = [\sum_{g=1}^{n} |s| \;] \, / \, [\sum_{g=1}^{n} y \;] \qquad (3)$$

where: g = number of products produced and transferred between industries I and j;

s = value of lump-sum, or incentive, payment from industry j to industry I; and

y = total compensation from industry j to industry I.

Importantly, the variables in this argument (equation 3) are both continuous and empirically observable, thus overcoming limitations in our original formulation that potentially weakened its accuracy as an empirical measure of vertical control. With this formulation, the measure of control of agent by principal ranges from 0 to 1; 0 when there is no lump-sum component (i.e., s = 0, s/y = 0) and 1 when all reimbursement is lump sum (i.e., $y = s$, $s/y = 1$).

In this formulation, y represents an upstream payment and is always positive. However, s may be either positive (i.e., an upstream payment; $y > pq$) or negative (i.e., a downstream payment; $y < pq$). We suggest that the sign on s can be used as a means of identifying which parties are principals and which are agents. In the case of a positive s, that is, an upstream payment, the downstream firm is reimbursing the upstream entity for effort (e.g., a food manufacturer paying a quality premium to a producer); thus the former is the principal. In the case of a negative s, that is, a downstream payment, the upstream firm is reimbursing the downstream entity for effort (e.g., a food manufacturer paying a shelving fee to a retailer); the upstream firm is the principal.

Empirical Considerations

In our initial stages of planning, we hoped to reestimate upstream VC values for U.S. food manufacturing industries using the reformulated **E** and **F** matrices and to compare those to our original estimations. Unfortunately, we are not able to deliver on this intent. Empirical realities intervened.

By this we mean that, even though, in concept, s is observable, we could not easily make such observations from readily available secondary data. In short, little effort has been made to collect or report data on nonlinear payments made in the agro-food sector. We have occasional and random observations. For example, Bacon, Halbrendt, and Gempesaw suggest that more than 90 percent of all broiler chickens in the United States are grown under some type of a two-part reimbursement schedule; Knoeber suggests that about half of the payment by broiler processors to growers of 634 flocks over a two-year period took the general form of s (incentive payments); Rhodes and Grimes report that nearly 60 percent of the large producers of slaughter hogs were reimbursed on an incentive payment basis.

Indeed, there appears to be a presumption embodied in nearly all publicly available reports that income is exclusively the product of price and quantity. This seems to be carried to the point that statistical reports treat any one of the three variables, p, q, or y, as fact when the other two can be observed. Obviously, this is absurd given both casual observation of, and seemingly rational expectations for, the presence of s. Aside from our call for data related to s for the purposes—some would consider arcane—of quantifying vertical coordination, one is left wondering how much error is introduced into generally accepted statistics, such as estimates of farm income, that are derived from an equation that is missing a nonlinear component.

Note

1   Effort is used herein to represent all aspects of agent performance, such as producing the desired quality and delivery at the appropriate time.

References

Adelman, M. A. 1955. "Concept and Statistical Measurement of Vertical Integration." *Business Concentration and Price Policy*, ed. G. J. Stigler, pp. 281–330. Princeton, N.J.: Princeton University Press.

Bacon, J. R., C. K. Halbrendt, and C. M. Gempesaw. 1990. *A Survey of Production and Economic Trends: Contract Broiler Growout Production.* Bulletin 489, Agricultural Experiment Station, University of Delaware, November.

Blois, K. J. 1972. "Vertical Quasi-Integration." *Journal of Industrial Economics* 20:253–72.

Coase, R. H. 1952. "The Nature of the Firm." *Readings in Price Theory*, ed. K. E. Boulding and G. J. Stigler, pp. 331–51. Chicago, Ill.: Richard D. Irwin.

Frank, S. D. 1990. "The Structure and Performance of the U.S. Food Manufacturing Industries: Measuring and Analyzing Vertical Coordination." Ph.D. dissertation, Ohio State University.

Frank, S. D., and D. R. Henderson. 1992. "Transaction Costs as Determinants of Vertical Coordination in the U.S. Food Industries." *American Journal of Agricultural Economics* 74:941–50.

Gatignon, H., and E. Anderson. 1987. *The Multinational Corporation's Degree of Control Over Foreign Subsidiaries: An Empirical Test of a Transaction Cost Explanation.* Report 87–103. Cambridge, Mass: Marketing Science Institute, October.

Henderson, D. R., and S. D. Frank. 1990. "Industrial Organization and Export Competitiveness of U.S. Food Manufacturers." North Central Regional Research Project NC-194 Occasional Paper OP-4, Ohio State University, March.

Joskow, P. L. 1988. "Asset Specificity and the Structure of Vertical Relationships: Empirical Evidence." *Journal of Law, Economics and Organization* 4:95–117.

Katz, M. L. 1989. "Vertical Contractual Relations." *Handbook of Industrial Organization*, ed. R. Schmalensee and R. D. Willig, vol. 1, pp. 655–721. Amsterdam, The Netherlands: North-Holland.

Knoeber, C. R. 1989. "A Real Game of Chicken: Contracts, Tournaments, and the Production of Broilers." *Journal of Law, Economics and Organization* 5:271–92.

McCorriston, S. 1994. "Economics of Vertical Market Competition." Paper presented at conference, Economics of Innovation—The Case of Food Industry, Piacenza, Italy, June 10–11.

Maddigan, R. J. 1981. "The Measurement of Vertical Integration." *Review of Economics and Statistics* 63:328–35.

Mighell, R. L., and L. A. Jones. 1963. *Vertical Coordination in Agriculture.* Washington, D.C.: U.S. Department of Agriculture, Economic Research Service, Agricultural Economic Report 19, February.

Monteverde, K., and D. J. Teece. 1982. "Appropriable Rents and Quasi-Vertical Integration." *Journal of Law and Economics* 25:321–28.

Rhodes, V. J., and G. Grimes. N.d. "Structure of U.S. Hog Production: A 1992 Survey." Department of Agricultural Economics, University of Missouri–Columbia.

Ross, S. 1973. "The Economic Theory of Agency: The Principal's Problem." *American Economic Review* 63:134–39.

Rumelt, R. P. 1974. *Strategy, Structure, and Economic Performance.* Cambridge, Mass.: Harvard University Press.

Shaffer, G. 1991. "Capturing Strategic Rent: Full-Line Forcing, Brand Discounts, Aggregate Rebates, and Maximum Resale Price Maintenance." *Journal of Industrial Economics* 39:557–75.

Shavell, S. 1979. "Risk Sharing and Incentives in the Principal and Agent Relationship." *Bell Journal of Economics* 10:55–73.

Sheldon, I. M. 1995. "Contracting, Imperfect Information and the Food System." *Public Policy in Foreign and Domestic Market Development*, ed. D. I. Padberg, pp. 41–54. Food and Agricultural Marketing Consortium 95-1, Texas A&M University.

Spengler, J. 1950. "Vertical Integration and Anti-Trust Policy." *Journal of Political Economy* 81:347–52.

Sporleder, T. L. 1975. "Algorithms for Vertical Integration Indices." North Central Regional Research Project NC-117 Working Paper WP-3, University of Wisconsin–Madison, October.

Williamson, O. E. 1975. *Markets and Hierarchies: Analysis and Antitrust Implications.* New York, N.Y.: Free Press.

———. 1979. "Transaction Cost Economics: The Governance of Contractual Relations." *Journal of Law and Economics* 22:233–62.

———. 1983. "Credible Commitments: Using Hostages to Support Exchange." *American Economic Review* 73:519–40.

PART II
CONTRACTS, GRADING, AND THE MARKETING CHANNEL

5 Contractual Arrangements at the Farm Gate

GARTH JOHN HOLLOWAY

This paper investigates two-part pricing in farmer first-handler markets. Its primary purpose is to motivate the study of principal-agent contracts in the marketing and distribution of farm commodities. Despite a growing number of applications in the production literature, there have been relatively few applications of this theory to the study of marketing contracts. Recent applications in agricultural settings study the consequences of alternative crop-sharing arrangements. Considering the prevalence of this organizational structure, this focus is not surprising.

Three features of the landlord-tenant relationship lend itself to principal-agent theory. The first is the sole ownership of the resource base by one of the parties. The second is the availability of surplus labor. The third is a comparative advantage by the contracted party in the performance of activities mandated by the contract.

Several features of this problem are relevant to marketing farm commodities. In the author's experience, they are particularly relevant to marketing problems facing primary producers in the New Zealand export sector. There, farmers have ownership of a resource, but not a comparative advantage in its sale. Regulators have long been aware of this issue and have viewed it as one of the principal concerns in New Zealand agriculture. They have responded by legislating cooperative and single-desk selling in an effort to mitigate two features of the problem. One is the perceived weakness of atomistic competition in foreign markets; the other is the price risk inherent in terminal markets.

Following the removal of support payments and intervention in other sectors of the New Zealand economy, there has emerged a growing number of organizations whose sole jurisdiction is the sale of farm commodities. Correspondingly, farmers have enjoyed access to a variety of alternative marketing arrangements for their commodities. In the absence of insurance and futures markets, these arrangements have acted as conduits for the amelioration of risks associated with the sale, rather than the production of, farm commodities. Generally speaking, the forms of contracts offered differ in a number of important ways, but they also share many similarities.

In the New Zealand situation, the prevalent commodity—both in terms of the number of farmers supplying the product and the total value of exports—is lamb. Historically, transactions have been enacted through the only institution that was available until recently—the auction market. Ownership of the product was transferred at the time the transaction occurred, thus the farmer's involvement in the post-harvest phase of operations was limited. Increasingly, export companies have become involved in the production of the primary commodity, offering incentives to farmers to produce meat of a particular quality and consistency. Simultaneously, farmers have become more involved in the downstream activities of the export companies. Many of the smaller export organizations selling specialty products are now completely farmer-owned. In a number of others, in which vertical integration has not occurred, farmers are paid a fixed amount at the time the product leaves the farm and are amended a residual tied to the price received in the terminal market.

This marketing situation parallels the marketing situation for many specialty crops such as tree commodities and specialty grass seeds. In these cases, the commodity requires little processing prior to final consumption. Farmers have elected to contract the activities involved in selecting appropriate outlets and distributing the product. These types of situations differ in an important way from the situation arising in meat exporting. In particular, it is usually the farmer who dictates the terms of the contract, the timing of supply, and many other details associated with the distribution of the commodity. However, in this case too, farmers are usually guaranteed a fixed payment at the time the product leaves the farm, with a residual paid subsequent to sale in the terminal market.

A third situation arises in many developing countries in which production and marketing are tied to some form of credit arrangement. Reimbursement of a loan may occur in cash or in kind and may be made contingent on the revelation of output. In some situations, the lending agency and the farmer contract to share the costs of the farm production and the marketing stages of the distribution process (e.g., Fabella). An interesting example of this form of contract occurs in broiler production in the southeastern United States.

Each of these organizational forms shares a number of important similarities. The central, underlying feature is that they involve substantial price risk. A contract that allows both parties to agree on a fixed wage at the time the product leaves the farm removes part of the uncertainty facing farmers at the time planting decisions are made. It also allows marketers the possibility of orchestrating marketing plans with greater precision than they otherwise would be able to. Clearly, both the extent and nature of the risks across the parties differ across contracts, but little attention has been granted these contracts in the agricultural economics literature. Contracts of these forms lend themselves to investigation through principal-agent theory. Like the landlord-tenant situation, the risk-reducing and risk-monitoring features of the problem play an important role in the design of an efficient contract. However, unlike that example, the nature of "ownership" of the productive asset remains with the farmer. Consequently, when downstream activities are at issue, it is more natural—and more appropriate—to consider the farmer as the principal and the marketer as agent. This important feature of the problem has been neglected in the literature to date.

My purpose in the remainder of this paper is to lay out the essential features of principal-agent theory applied to the design of efficient marketing contracts. I focus on the implications of three alternative contracts. Although the overarching feature of downstream activities is that they involve substantial risk, a good deal can be ascertained prior to introducing uncertainty. Therefore, the problem at hand is couched in the context of a deterministic model of choice in which the binding relationship between the two parties is the sale of the farm product in a downstream market. A fairly general model is presented and, subsequently, simplified. Three sets of efficient contracts are derived. Extensions are discussed.

Agents, Technologies, and Markets

Consider the terminal market for a specific commodity. Aggregate consumption in the amount, y, occurs. This activity is affected by two parameters. One is the price paid for the product, which we term p, and the other is the level of money income, which we term ε. Accordingly, consumption activities generate the inverse demand relation

$$p = D(y | \varepsilon). \tag{1}$$

In this specification we acknowledge that the parameter ε is exogenous to consumption decisions. It will prove convenient for later discussion if we retain this general specification. Subsequently, however, we may wish to consider situations in which the price p is exogenous and, accordingly, situations in which there may be multiple terminal markets. The supposition that there is but one terminal market is consistent with conventional food-industry theory (Gardner).

About the relation in (1), we will make the usual assumptions, namely that the relationship between quantity and price is nonpositive and that the relationship between income and price is nonnegative. It will prove convenient for later reference if we note, as follows:

ASSUMPTION 1 (Quantity Effects). $\partial D(\cdot)/\partial y \leq 0$.

ASSUMPTION 2 (Income Effects). $\partial D(\cdot)/\partial \varepsilon \geq 0$.

In the marketing sector there are N individuals indexed $\{i\ i=1, \ldots, N\}$, which we call "firms." Each selects a quantity of a variable input, $\{x_i\ i=1, \ldots, N\}$, and distributes the product in the terminal market. This marketing activity may be productive in the sense that the good that is readied for market and the good made available for consumption may be different physical commodities. Let $\{y_i\ i=1, \ldots, N\}$ denote the set of marketed commodities, and let $\{f_i(\cdot)\ i=1, \ldots, N\}$ denote the set of productive activities. Then

$$y = \sum_{i=1}^{N} y_i \qquad (2)$$

denotes the relationship between aggregate and individual marketings of the product and

$$y_i \leq f_i(x_i | \tau_i) \qquad i=1, \ldots, N \qquad (3)$$

denote the set of marketing activities, wherein the parameters $\{\tau_i\ i=1, \ldots, N\}$ represent a set of exogenous technological innovations. About the functions $\{f_i(\cdot)\ i=1, \ldots, N\}$, we make the usual assumptions, namely that for all $x_i \geq 0$ and $i=1, \ldots, N$:

ASSUMPTION 3 (Monotonicity). $\partial f_i(\cdot)/\partial x_i = 0$.

ASSUMPTION 4 (Concavity). $\partial^2 f_i(\cdot)/\partial x_i^2 < 0$.

ASSUMPTION 5 (Essentiality). $f_i(0) = 0$.

ASSUMPTION 6 (Boundedness). $\lim_{x_i \to x_i^*} \partial f_i(\cdot)/\partial x_i = 0$.

ASSUMPTION 7 (Innovation). $\partial f_i(\cdot)/\partial \tau_i > 0$.

These assumptions imply the usual restrictions on returns to the variable factor, namely that they diminish with increased intensity of use, that the factor is essential for production, and that there is some maximum amount attainable by each enterprise. In addition, technological innovations are assumed to lead to expansions in output. The issue of whether the innovation is factor augmenting has received considerable attention (e.g., Muth; Freebairn, Davis, and Edwards; Alston and Scobie; Holloway). But it is rather moot in the present investigation. This is by virtue of the single-factor assumption. For this reason, a few comments are in order.

The single-input assumption is unreasonable and inconsistent with the conventional framework (Gardner) in which a second, nonfarm input is assumed. Its justification is purely the desire to keep the model to a tractable level. In the conventional setting, the primary focus of marketing is its employment as a productive conduit between the farm and retail sectors of the distribution channel. In this paper, the focus is the effects of alternative contract forms on the efficiency of resource allocation. As we shall see, a thorough treatment of this issue quickly becomes complex, and the added realism engendered by the inclusion of an additional marketing input is not justified by the analytical cost it incurs.

The set of variable factors employed in marketing, the set $\{x_i, i=1, \ldots, N\}$, is the result of another set of activities. Collectively we call them "farming." Each farmer enters into a contract with one of the marketing agents, who contracts to supply the product to the downstream market. Though not apparent at present, it will become obvious that the number of farmers relative to the number of marketing agents has an important implication for equilibrium in the system. Although it is possible for a farmer to contract with more than one agent, it is conjectured—and validated, at least partially from the author's own experience—that the converse situation is more prevalent. For this reason and, once again, the desire to keep things tractable, we will assume that farmers select one, and only one, agent with whom to contract. Therefore, we group farmers according to the agents with whom they contract. It may help if we think of the agents themselves as being distinguished by location and thus the contracting parties as those individuals existing within a given region. This interpretation, while unnecessary for the work considered subsequently, may prove useful for one other reason. When considering departures from the nonstochastic model studies below, contracts may be correlated within regions.

Let $\{x_j \ j=1, \ldots, M\}$ denote the quantities supplied by the primary producers, whom we index $\{j=1, \ldots, M\}$, so that

$$x_i = \sum_{j=1}^{M_j} x_j \qquad i=1, \ldots, N \qquad (4)$$

denotes the aggregate levels of the input contracted by each agent. Thus $M=\sum M_j$. Assume that each agent offers a single contract, by which each of the farmers who have selected that agent agree to abide. Then there are, in total, $N \le M$ such contracts. However, the possibility exists that there is only one contract that dominates the market. For simplicity, we will consider this possibility as the starting point for the investigation below.

To complete the specification of the model, we note that farm production is a costly activity and that some of those costs depend on factors determined outside of the system itself. Accordingly, let $\{c_j(x_j|v_j) j=1, \ldots, M\}$ denote the costs of producing the commodity, where $\{v_j \ j=1, \ldots, M\}$ denotes a set of exogenous shocks, for example, a set of variable factor prices.

As we did above, let us make some assumptions about the technology in farming. In particular, let us assume that for all $x_j \ge 0$ and $j=1, \ldots, M$:

ASSUMPTION 8 (Monotonicity). $\partial c_j(\cdot)/\partial x_j \ge 0$.

ASSUMPTION 9 (Convexity). $\partial^2 c_j(\cdot)/\partial x_j^2 \ge 0$.

ASSUMPTION 10 (Fixity). $c_j(0) > 0$.

ASSUMPTION 11 (Boundedness). $\lim_{x_j \to x_j^*} \partial c_j(\cdot)/\partial x_j = \infty$

ASSUMPTION 12 (Innovation). $\partial c_j(\cdot)/\partial v_j > 0$.

These assumptions together ensure that marginal costs slope upward and are convex, that fixed costs exist, that production may be efficiently organized by allocating the product among a number of alternative suppliers, and that the exogenous factor in farming leads to cost increases.

Contracts

Let $\{s_{ij}(\,\cdot\,)\ i=1, \ldots, N; j=1, \ldots, M\}$ denote the set of contracts offered. In general, each contract will contain provisions for quality, timeliness, and other features of performance, but we restrict attention to three features, possibly four: (1) an agreed-upon per-unit payment for each quantity of the commodity supplied; (2) a share of the output revenues received from sale in the terminal market; (3) a share of the costs incurred in the supply of the primary product; and, possibly, (4) a fixed fee decoupled from both the downstream and the upstream activities. For this purpose, we introduce some additional notation. Let $\{\omega_{ij}\ i=1, \ldots, N; j=1, \ldots, M\}$ denote the set of agreed-upon wages, $\{\alpha_{ij}\ i=1, \ldots, N; j=1, \ldots, M\}$ denote the set of revenue shares, $\{\beta_{ij}\ i=1, \ldots, N; j=1, \ldots, M\}$ denote the set of cost shares, and $\{\kappa_{ij}\ i=1, \ldots, N; j=1, \ldots, M\}$ denote the set of fixed fees. Although it need not be the case, we restrict attention to positive wages and true shares so that each contract contains the set of joint restrictions $\omega_{ij} > 0$, $0 \le \alpha_{ij} \le 1$, and $0 \le \beta_{ij} \le 1$. In contrast, because it is decoupled from production activities, the fixed fee may take either positive or negative values. In the first case, we view the payment as a transfer from marketers to farmers, and conversely when negative.

Using the notation presented in the previous section, the set of farmer first-handler contracts is completely specified by the set of payment schedules:

$$s_{ij}(\,\cdot\,) \equiv \omega_{ij} x_j + \alpha_{ij} p y_i + \beta_{ij} c_j(x_j | v_j) + \kappa_{ij} \qquad i=1, \ldots, N; j=1, \ldots, M. \quad (5)$$

Thus it is clear that each contract may differ in an important way across the various suppliers. However, for further simplicity we will assume that the contract terms $\{\omega_{ij}, \alpha_{ij}, \beta_{ij}, \kappa_{ij}\}$ are constant across each agent $\{i\ i=1, \ldots, N\}$. In other words, the potential number of contract types is $N \times M$, but we restrict attention to only N of these, namely $\{s_i(\,\cdot\,)\ i=1, \ldots, N\}$.

Conduct

Given the schedules $\{s_i(\,\cdot\,)\ i=1, \ldots, N\}$, marketing agents make input decisions over the set of variable factors $\{x_i\ i=1, \ldots, N\}$ and farmers make output decisions over the output levels $\{x_j\ j=1, \ldots, M\}$. To make things tractable, we will assume initially that the marketers perceive no market power in the terminal market. Whether they have the ability to do so is altogether another matter. Nevertheless, it will complicate things unduly if we divert our attentions to oligopoly. Therefore, in the usual manner, let $\{\hat{\theta}_i, i=1, \ldots, N\}$ define the set of perceived abilities to influence the outcome in the terminal market, where $\{\hat{\theta}_i \equiv (\partial \psi_i(\cdot)/\partial y_i)(y_i/\psi_i(\cdot))\ i=1, \ldots, N\}$ and the functions $\{\psi_i(\cdot)\ i=1, \ldots, N\}$ denote the *conjectural variations*. In the usual way, we can define the domains of the beliefs $\{\hat{\theta}_i \in [0, 1]\ i=1, \ldots, N\}$, where the value one represents monopoly and the origin denotes competition, and assume that for each agent, $i=1, \ldots, N$:

ASSUMPTION 13 (Price Taking). $\hat{\theta}_i = 0$.

This assumption, it should be noted, is perhaps more restrictive than the others we have used thus far. In the absence of uncertainty, the presence of market power in the terminal market may help explain the empirically relevant fact that primary producers often pool through a common agent when allocating the product. With this assumption at hand, we can characterize the allocations as the simultaneous solutions to

$$\text{Problem 1:} \quad \left\{ \begin{array}{l} \underset{x_i}{\text{Max}}\ \upsilon_i(\cdot) \equiv pf_i(x_i|\tau_i) - s_i(\cdot) \quad\quad i=1, \ldots, N. \end{array} \right. \quad (6)$$

The solution to this problem is a first-order condition that sets the marginal value product of the input in the terminal market to the perceived costs, as conditioned by the contract. Specifically, the conditions

$$p\frac{\partial f_i(\cdot)}{\partial x_i} - \frac{\partial s_i(\cdot)}{\partial x_i} \equiv \phi_i(x_i|\omega_i, \alpha_i, \beta_i, \phi_i) = 0 \quad\quad i=1, \ldots, N \quad (7)$$

are implied.

In an analogous manner, we can depict the allocations selected by each of the farmers. These are the solutions to

$$\text{Problem 2:} \quad \left\{ \begin{array}{l} \underset{x_j}{\text{Max}}\ \pi_j(\cdot) \equiv s_j(\cdot) - c_j(x_j|v_j) \quad\quad j=1, \ldots, M, \end{array} \right. \quad (8)$$

namely, a set of first-order conditions:

$$\frac{\partial s_i(\cdot)}{\partial x_j} - \frac{\partial c_j(\cdot)}{\partial x_j} \equiv \phi_j(x_j | \omega_j, \alpha_i, \beta_i, \kappa_i) = 0 \qquad j=1, \ldots, M \qquad (9)$$

that yield supply responses conditioned by the terms of the contract.

Equilibrium

In the usual way, we can count equations and unknowns and characterize an equilibrium as the solution to a given number of equations. At this point, a problem arises. To illustrate, let us assume momentarily that, at the time that the contracts are signed, they consist of simply the agreed-upon set of farm-gate prices $\{\omega_i \ i=1, \ldots, N\}$. Further, let us assume that the parties involved agree to set these prices at "the going rate," where this rate is determined as the rate that clears the market. Under these circumstances, an equilibrium is defined for a total of $3N+M+2$ endogenous variables. These are the price and quantity in the terminal market, p and y; the N outputs produced by each of the agents, $\{y_i \ i=1, \ldots, N\}$; the N inputs required to produce these outputs, $\{x_i \ i=1, \ldots, N\}$; the M outputs produced by each of the farm-commodity suppliers, $\{x_j \ j=1, \ldots, M\}$; and the N wages $\{\omega_i \ i=1, \ldots, N\}$ that the contracted parties agree to uphold. The equations determining these values are, respectively, the inverse demand relation, (1); the aggregation condition, (2); the N production functions specified in (3); the N output-distribution conditions in (4); the N input demand conditions defined by (7); and the M supply relations defined by (9). This system is the same as the conventional model of price determination in food marketing.

Suppose, instead of agreeing to a wage rate determined by laissez faire, that the wage and contract parameters are now negotiated. The system is now underidentified. In particular, it is so specified by a measure N representing the set of additional contract parameters. In general, the terms of the contract lead to an identification problem. This problem is significant for two reasons. The first is that it represents the main departure from conventional theory. The second is that it leads us to consider an issue that places the farm-gate problem in a more realistic light. The issue is the matter of who dictates the terms of the contract.

Who Dictates Terms?

Inevitably, the terms of the contract are dictated by the contracting party with the greater bargaining power. This issue is mostly ignored in the principal-agent literature. However, it is exceedingly important in many agricultural settings because farmers may have limited bargaining power. In the landlord-tenant problem it is often argued (e.g., Taslim; Braverman and Stiglitz) that the landlord has access to an abundant supply of labor and may force terms of the contract more strongly than could be achieved otherwise. Frequently, these issues are cast against the backdrop of a developing economy in which significant unemployment may exist. In the presence of excess labor, it is then argued that the landlord dictates terms because he has ownership of the resource base necessary to produce the product.

In the marketing context considered here, the situation may be reversed. Often the farmer, or a farm group, has control of the product and retains ownership of it until it is sold in the terminal market. Such a situation suggests that it may be more appropriate to assume that the terms of the contract are dictated from the supply side rather than the demand side. Whether this is actually the case, we leave open to conjecture, but reflection leads to insights about the formation of the terms in the contract. In some situations, exporting companies clearly dictate terms. They offer a set of common contracts that bid for supply among producers. There, the relative bargaining power between the parties is clear. The case that the export agency dictates terms can be made even stronger in situations in which they enact penalties for low-quality product. In New Zealand agriculture, for example, this approach has been pursued—relatively effectively it appears—in both export lamb raising and export dairy production. In the first case, lower premiums have been paid for over-fat stock and, in the second, a set of tariffs is imposed whenever contaminated milk enters the processing chain. This situation contrasts sharply with the situation in other sectors, for example, the horticultural industry in which it appears the primary producer often dictates terms. In the analysis below, we consider the latter situation.

Contract Design under Certainty

The provision of information and its asymmetry between the contracting parties are central to the efficiency of contract design. However, much insight can be gained from investigating the situation under certainty. Assume that the farmer, as principal, sets the terms of the contract. The problem confronting each principal is to select the parameters of the contract in such a way that they maximize farmer returns. The key constraint is that the contract must ensure an adequate return to the agent. In the certainty context considered here, the constraint that binds the farmer's actions is a profit constraint. Usually, a zero-profit condition is implied in the conventional model by invoking the assumption of constant returns to scale in marketing. Here we analyze the profit constraint explicitly.

As usual, insight is gained by restricting attention to representative-agent settings. Therefore, let $x^* \equiv x(\omega, \alpha, \beta, \kappa)$ denote the input level of the farm commodity when the marketing agent faces a contract with terms $(\omega, \alpha, \beta, \kappa)$. This condition comprises the solution to equation (9), but it is now expressed assuming that there is a single agent and a single supplier. Monopolistic-cum-monopsonistic concerns are ignored. Also, since the information structure is complete, the farmer is assumed to know this equation and the particular way in which the agent will adjust his demand for the factor, given any change in the terms of the contract. In this regard, there are three computations that the farmer must complete before he selects the parameters of the contract. Specifically, he must compute from equation (7) the implicit derivatives

$$\frac{\partial x}{\partial \alpha} = \frac{p \partial f(\cdot)/\partial x}{\Phi} \tag{10}$$

$$\frac{\partial x}{\partial \beta} = \frac{\partial c(\cdot)/\partial x}{\Phi} \tag{11}$$

$$\frac{\partial x}{\partial \omega} = \frac{1}{\Phi} \tag{12}$$

where $\Phi \equiv \partial^2 \pi(\cdot)/\partial x^2$ is the second-order condition corresponding to Problem 1. A fourth computation, namely $\partial x/\partial \kappa = 0$, is implied by the fact that the fixed fee κ does not appear in the first-order condition. Therefore, the farmer knows that increases in each of the parameters α, β, and ω lead to reductions in demand for the factor and that the level of the fixed fee has no influence.

Two-part Pricing and the Principal's Problem

Given the information above, the farmer's problem is to select the terms $\{\omega, \alpha, \beta, \kappa\}$ in (5) to solve

$$
\text{Problem 3:} \quad
\begin{cases}
Max \ \pi(x^*) \equiv s(x^*) - c(x^*) \\[2mm]
sto \ \upsilon(\omega, \alpha, \beta, \kappa) \geq \gamma
\end{cases}
\quad i=1, \ldots, N, \quad (13)
$$

where $\upsilon(\omega, \alpha, \beta, \kappa)$ is the maximized value of the agent's objective function and γ denotes some target level of profit. Under complete information, this value is likely zero, but this is not the case in general.

To simplify things further, let us assume that the farmer restricts attention to two-part pricing arrangements, each of which involves a fixed per-unit wage and one of the alternative instruments. We consider each contract in turn, beginning with the wage rate combined with a fixed fee.

ω-κ Contracts

In a contract involving a fixed per-unit payment on the level of the product supplied and the negotiation of a fixed fee, the farmer computes isoprofit combinations in the ω-κ plane. These are simply relative changes that are permitted by the participation constraint, which appears in Problem 3. Assuming that this constraint is binding, we can write the parameter κ as an implicit function of the wage $\kappa(\omega)$ and compute from the agent's value function

$$
\frac{\partial \kappa(\cdot)}{\partial \omega} = -x^*. \tag{14}
$$

With this condition at hand, the maximization in Problem 3 is simplified considerably. The first-order condition is

$$
\frac{\partial \pi(\cdot)}{\partial \omega} \equiv x^* + \left(\omega - \frac{\partial c(\cdot)}{\partial x} \right) \frac{\partial x^*(\cdot)}{\partial \omega} + \frac{\partial \kappa(\cdot)}{\partial \omega} \tag{15}
$$

where the derivative $\partial x^*(\cdot)/\partial\omega$ implies a "Slutsky" relation defined with respect to two effects. The first is the *direct* effect of the change in the wage on the demand for the input; the second is the *indirect* effect realized through (14). Setting (15) equal to zero and using (14), the first-order condition implies that the contracted wage rate be set equal to the value of marginal costs. This should not surprise. Problem 3 sets out a set of efficient terms, and there is complete information. Hence the ω-κ contract traces out points along the Pareto-efficient frontier.

Finding the optimal level at which to set the fee κ is now simply a matter of retracing the steps back through equation (14). The efficient action—at least from the principal's viewpoint—is to set the fee so that the participation constraint just binds. Accordingly, a ω-κ contract equilibrium in p, y, x, ω, and κ is defined by the five equations:

$$p=D(y) \tag{16}$$

$$y=f(x) \tag{17}$$

$$\omega=p\frac{\partial f(\cdot)}{\partial x} \tag{18}$$

$$\omega=\frac{\partial c(\cdot)}{\partial x} \tag{19}$$

$$\upsilon=pf(\cdot)-\omega x-\kappa. \tag{20}$$

Figure 5.1 depicts the equilibrium.

ω-α Contracts

A contract regime in which the farmer negotiates a share of the agent's revenue can be analyzed in a similar manner to the one above. Equation (14) is replaced by the condition

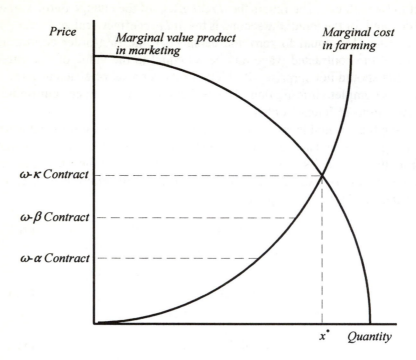

Figure 5.1 The allocative consequences of alternative regimes

$$\frac{\partial \alpha(\cdot)}{\partial \omega} = \frac{-x^*}{pf(\cdot)}, \tag{21}$$

and the first-order conditions imply

$$\frac{\partial \pi(\cdot)}{\partial \omega} \equiv x^* + \left(\omega + \alpha p \frac{\partial f(\cdot)}{\partial x^*} - \frac{\partial c(\cdot)}{\partial x^*} \right) \frac{\partial x^*(\cdot)}{\partial \omega} + pf(\cdot) \frac{\partial \alpha(\cdot)}{\partial \omega}. \tag{22}$$

Consequently, the equations characterizing equilibrium in the ω-α regime are

$$p = D(y) \tag{23}$$

$$y = f(x) \tag{24}$$

$$\omega = (1-\alpha)p\frac{\partial f(\cdot)}{\partial x} \tag{25}$$

$$\omega = \frac{\partial c(\cdot)}{\partial x} - \alpha p\frac{\partial f(\cdot)}{\partial x} \tag{26}$$

$$\upsilon = (1-\alpha)pf(\cdot) - \omega x. \tag{27}$$

Equations (25) and (26) combine to illustrate an important feature: Although the equilibrium implies the same level of output as that prevailing under the ω-κ contract—as it should, for both are efficient—the distribution of the price is different. In particular, the real wage in the ω-α regime is lower than the wage in the ω-κ regime. Figure 5.1 depicts the equilibrium.

ω-β Contracts

When farmers secure a commitment by marketers to share in the costs of farm production, the relationship between the real wage and the share of costs contracted is given by

$$\frac{\partial \beta(\cdot)}{\partial \omega} = \frac{-x^*}{c(\cdot)}. \tag{28}$$

The first-order condition is

$$\frac{\partial \pi(\cdot)}{\partial \omega} \equiv x^* + \left(\omega - (1-\beta)\frac{\partial c(\cdot)}{\partial x^*}\right)\frac{\partial x^*(\cdot)}{\partial \omega} + c(\cdot)\frac{\partial \beta(\cdot)}{\partial \omega}, \tag{29}$$

and the equations characterizing equilibrium are

$$p = D(y),$$

(30)

$$y = f(x)$$

(31)

$$\omega = p\frac{\partial f(\cdot)}{\partial x} - \beta\frac{\partial c(\cdot)}{\partial x}$$

(32)

$$\omega = (1-\beta)\frac{\partial c(\cdot)}{\partial x}$$

(33)

$$\upsilon = pf(\cdot) - \omega x - \beta c(\cdot).$$

(34)

Once again, the real wage is lower in this regime than it is under the ω-κ contract, but, in general, the wage may be lower or higher than under the ω-α contract. The relative differences depend on the relative shares of costs and revenues contracted. In particular, the wage in the ω-α regime is lower or higher than the wage in the ω-β regime as the revenue share α is respectively higher or lower than the cost share β. Figure 5.1 depicts the equilibrium.

Comparative Statics

Short of deriving reduced-form expressions for each of the endogenous variables, some insight can be gained by examining their qualitative responses to certain shocks within the various systems. These systems are recursive. In particular, the two first-order conditions can be combined and incorporated with the production function in marketing and the demand equation in the terminal market to generate a system in the three endogenous variables x^*, y^*, and p^*. Subsequently, the qualitative responses of each of the contract parameters can be evaluated.

We consider responses to three specific effects, namely a demand shift caused by parameter ε, a technological innovation in marketing caused by parameter τ, and a shift in the costs of supplying the farm commodity through parameter υ.

Let tildes denote proportional changes. That is, for some variable of interest, say v, define $\tilde{v} \equiv \Delta v / v$ as its proportional change. The qualitative effects of the equilibrium can be determined from the system

$$
\begin{pmatrix} 1 & -\xi & \\ & 1 & -\eta \\ 1 & & \eta-\delta \end{pmatrix} \begin{pmatrix} \tilde{p} \\ \tilde{y} \\ \tilde{x} \end{pmatrix} = \begin{pmatrix} 1 & & \\ & 1 & \\ -1 & & 1 \end{pmatrix} \begin{pmatrix} \tilde{\varepsilon} \\ \tilde{\tau} \\ \tilde{v} \end{pmatrix},
\tag{35}
$$

where $\xi \in (-\infty, 0]$ represents the price flexibility in the terminal market, $\eta \in (0, 1)$ denotes the returns to the variable input in the marketing sector, and $\delta \in (1, +\infty)$ is the cost elasticity pertaining to the farm commodity cost function. With these definitions at hand, some predictable results can be formalized: Innovations in the terminal market cause price to rise and lead to simultaneous expansions in quantities traded; technological innovations cause output to rise, cause price to fall, and lead to increases in factor employment when demand is elastic; farm cost innovations raise price and contract quantities.

From the last two equations in the ω-κ equilibrium, we can determine the responsiveness of the terms of the contract parameters to each of the exogenous effects. The equilibrium wage responds positively to demand and cost innovations. It responds positively to technological innovations if demand is elastic, and negatively otherwise. The level of the fixed fee κ responds positively to innovations in the terminal market but has an ambiguous sign in the other situations.

In the ω-α regime, demand shifts lower the wage rate but increase the revenue share. Cost shifts increase the wage rate and cause the revenue share to rise or fall depending on the elasticity of demand. Technological innovations in marketing have an ambiguous effect on the wage rate and cause the revenue share to rise when demand is inelastic and fall when it is elastic.

In the ω-β regime, innovations in the terminal market raise the equilibrium level of the fixed wage but leave the equilibrium value of the cost-share parameter unchanged. Technological innovations raise the wage when demand is elastic but contract it otherwise, leaving the cost-share parameter unaffected. Farm cost shifts lead to ambiguous movements in both of the contract parameters.

Extensions

The study of marketing arrangements in a principal-agent setting leads to several predictable results. These predictions are not unlike those of the conventional, price-taking model. However, the setting formalized here is, perhaps, a more realistic depiction of the way actual marketing systems work. In view of this importance and the desire to further embellish the realism of the present model, several directions for further research appear fruitful. One lies in relaxing the representative-agents assumption; another lies in moving the analysis toward nonstochastic environments. Relaxing the complete-markets assumption by allowing for uncertainty in the terminal market seems a natural next step. The analysis of such a system in either the mean-variance or expected-utility frameworks offers additional analytical challenges for which the present investigation provides a useful starting point. It remains to be seen whether the added realism implied by uncertainty is capable of overturning results from the conventional, price-taking model.

References

Alston, J. M., and G. M. Scobie. 1983. "Distribution of Research Gains in Multistage Production Systems: Comment." *American Journal of Agricultural Economics* 65:353–56.

Braverman, A., and J. E. Stiglitz. 1986. "Cost-Sharing Arrangements Under Sharecropping: Moral Hazard, Incentive Flexibility, and Risk." *American Journal of Agricultural Economics* 68:642–52.

Fabella, R. V. 1992. "Price Uncertainty and Trader-Farmer Linkage." *Journal of Public Economics* 47:391–99.

Freebairn, J. W., J. S. Davis, and G. W. Edwards. 1983. "Distribution of Research Gains in Multistage Production Systems: Reply." *American Journal of Agricultural Economics* 65:357–59.

Gardner, B. L. 1975. "The Farm-Retail Price Spread in a Competitive Food Industry." *American Journal of Agricultural Economics* 57:399–409.

Holloway, G. J. 1989. "Distribution of Research Gains in Multistage Production Processes: Further Results." *American Journal of Agricultural Economics* 71:338–43.

Muth, R. F. 1964. "The Derived Demand for a Productive Factor and the Industry Supply Curve." *Oxford Economic Papers* 16:221–34.

Taslim, M. A. 1989. "Short-Term Leasing, Resource Allocation, and Crop-Share Tenancy." *American Journal of Agricultural Economics* 72:785–90.

6 Grower Response to Broiler Production Contract Design

TOMISLAV VUKINA and WILLIAM E. FOSTER[1]

The U.S. broiler industry is almost entirely vertically coordinated by production contracts or, to a lesser extent, by processor-owned broiler farms. Today there are about twenty companies, commonly called integrators, that control virtually all the market (Brown). Approximately 90 percent of U.S. broilers are produced by contract growers. Judged by their prevalence, contracts have proven to be a successful mode of organizing broiler production. They have benefited farmers by offering opportunities to earn income with relatively low capital requirements, by alleviating cash flow problems typically plaguing small farms, and by allowing enterprise diversification on the farm. The major efficiency gain from contracts probably is the reallocation of risk from the farmers to integrators who have means to act upon uncertain outcomes.[2] Broiler contracts also have their critics, largely originating from the growers' own ranks, who complain about gains from contract arrangements being largely appropriated by integrators while growers receive only small, or even negative, returns from contract production.

The existing controversy can be reduced to a standard principal-agent problem. Production contracts are designed to provide growers with appropriate incentives to manage their broiler farms in a way that will maximize integrators' returns while simultaneously significantly rewarding growers to keep the existing growers in business and attract new ones. Growers then attempt to maximize their net returns within the constraints of the contract. Assuming a perfect incentives mechanism or costless monitoring and enforcement, profit-maximizing growers would also maximize the integrators' profit. To the extent that the two outcomes differ, room for welfare improvement potentially exists either through rearrangement of incentives (i.e., contract redesign) or through more efficient monitoring and enforcement.

The disparity between grower management practices and management practices prescribed by the integrator has long been recognized by agricultural engineers and poultry scientists. The divergence between the strategy that maximizes returns to the grower and the one that maximizes returns to the integrator was first identified by Timmons and Gates, and Gates and Timmons. Using a simulation approach, they found that the contractual arrangement between grower and integrator influences the optimal housing environment and may, in fact, decrease economic returns for one party at the expense of the other. In subsequent work, Aho and Timmons found that, depending on the contract specifications, chicken house temperature settings that maximize returns to the grower can be greatly different from those that maximize returns to the integrator. They also found that fine tuning contract specifications can result in temperatures selected by the grower that more closely approximate the integrator optimum. In all these studies monitoring and enforcement costs have been largely ignored.

The objective of this paper is to model the grower's decision-making process and to gauge the sensitivity of the decision rules to changes in the contract parameters. The underlying hypothesis is that the adequate manipulation of production contract parameters may result in efficiency improvement. Econometric estimation of the cost functions and behavioral relationships is done using the combination of settlement cost and farm-level data from one broiler contract grow-out farm in North Carolina. The results seem to suggest that switching part of the utility costs from the grower to the integrator may result in a mutual welfare gain.

Broiler Production Contracts

Production contracts are legal agreements between an integrator company and a producer (farmer) that bind the producer to specific production practices. Broiler contracts vary from company to company, but all of them have two common features. One is the division of responsibility for providing inputs, the other is the method used to determine grower compensation (Knoeber). Both features have been subject to modifications over time and are still undergoing changes.

The grower provides land and housing facilities, utilities (electricity and water), and labor. Operating expenses such as repairs and maintenance, chicken house clean-up cost, and manure and dead birds disposal are also the responsibility of the grower. The integrator company provides chicks, feed, medication, and the services of field men. Typically, the company also owns and operates hatcheries, feed mills, and a processing plant and provides transportation of feed and live birds. Items such as fuel or litter can be the responsibility of either the integrator or the grower, or can be shared.

The decision about the volume of production, i.e., the rotation of flocks on a given farm, is determined by the integrator as is the size (capacity) of the technological unit (chicken house). Today, most integrators require chicken houses be built according to strict technical specifications regarding construction and equipment. New houses are typically well-insulated units 40 feet by 500 feet in size, with highly automated feeders, drinkers, and heating and cooling devices. Chicks of certain genetic characteristics are also provided by the integrator as is the feed mix (feed formula).

Most broiler contracts have a fairly similar structure characterized by the three types of farmer remuneration schemes: (1) the performance payment, (2) the minimum guaranteed payment, and (3) the disaster payment. The performance payment is based on the fixed base payment per pound of live meat produced, and the variable bonus payment is based on the grower's relative performance (sometimes called the prime-cost rating). The bonus payment is determined as a percentage of the difference between the average settlement costs of all growers that belong to the integrator's particular profit center whose flocks were harvested in the same week's period and a producer's individual settlement costs. Settlement costs are obtained by adding chick, feed, medication, and other customary flock costs and dividing by total pounds of live poultry produced. For below-average settlement costs (above-average performance), the grower receives a positive bonus, and for above-average settlement costs, he receives a negative bonus. A grower with settlement costs substantially above the average (typically this threshold is set at 1.25 cents) will be excluded from the calculation of the average. As a result, other growers are not rewarded when one grower performs badly. Similarly, costs substantially below average also are typically excluded from the average.

The total revenue (R) to the grower is the sum of the base and bonus payments multiplied by the live pounds of poultry moved from the grower's farm:

$$R_{it} = (b_t + B_{it})q_{it} \tag{1}$$

where i denotes the ith grower, t denotes tth flock, b_t denotes the base payment per live pound, B_{it} is the bonus payment per live pound, and q_{it} is the number of pounds of live poultry moved. The current broiler production technology typically allows for grow-out of six flocks during a year. Algebraically, the bonus payment to the *i*th grower for the *t*th flock can be expressed as a fraction of his prime-cost rating:

$$B_{it} = \beta\left[\frac{1}{n}\sum_{j=1}^{n}\frac{c_{jt}}{q_{jt}} - \frac{c_{it}}{q_{it}}\right] = \beta\left[\frac{1}{n}\sum_{j\neq i}\frac{c_{jt}}{q_{jt}} - \frac{n-1}{n}\frac{c_{it}}{q_{it}}\right] \quad j=1, 2, \ldots, n \quad (2)$$

where *n* represents the total number of growers within the profit center, c_{it}/q_{it} is the settlement cost previously defined, and β is a bonus factor (usually 50 or 75 percent). Expressions (1) and (2) can be combined to give the performance payment-based revenue function of the *i*th grower's *t*th flock:

$$R_{it} = \left[b_t + \beta\left(A_t^- - \frac{n-1}{n}\frac{c_{it}}{q_{it}}\right)\right]q_{it} \quad (3)$$

where A_t^- is the *t*th flock average settlement cost for the entire group of growers excluding the individual settlement cost of the grower under consideration.

If the producer's revenue based on the performance payment is smaller than some minimum guaranteed revenue, the minimum payment formula will be applied. In the event of a disaster such as fire, flood, or hail storm involving a loss of the entire flock or a fraction of the flock, the grower will be compensated based on the disaster payment. With the majority of integrators, neither the minimum guaranteed payment schedule nor the disaster payment apply in cases of gross negligence. One such example would be the loss of a substantial portion of the flock (e.g., more than 2 percent) as the result of a lack of oxygen or heat exhaustion when the outside temperature is below 95° F.

Minimum guaranteed payment and the disaster payment schemes differ substantially among different integrators and are not the object of analysis in this paper. Both schemes are designed to secure sufficient payments to prevent a grower from defaulting on the chicken houses mortgage. The remainder of the paper is based on the assumption that conditions for the implementation of a minimum or a disaster payment mechanism never occur.

Formulation of the Problem

The contract between the grower and the integrator is designed with the intention of providing growers incentives to manage the poultry farm in a manner that will maximize returns to the integrator. To minimize unit cost of production, integrators require prescribed management practices to be adopted by the growers. In order to avoid costly monitoring of the growers' management practices, most integrators have introduced relative performance-based bonus payments as a standard part of the overall remuneration schemes. The grower attempts to maximize net returns within the constraints of the contract.

Some evidence from the poultry science literature (e.g., Aho and Timmons) suggests that the existing contractual arrangements are the source of the divergence between the management strategy that maximizes net returns to the grower and that of the integrator. If this is true, then there is a possibility for manipulating contract specifications to reduce the divergence between the two individually optimal strategies. However, as long as one grower willingly signed the proposed contract, expected returns from the contractual arrangement were at least equal to, if not greater than, his reservation wage. But observing such contracts does not necessarily preclude the possibility of other contract specifications through which the welfare position of one party may be improved without deteriorating the welfare position of another party.

The objective of this paper is to simulate the sensitivity of grower's decision rules to specific changes in contract parameters in order to find out whether such an improvement is admissible. We start the analysis by formulating a grower's static profit maximization problem. Within the static framework, decisions are made on a per-flock basis, and individual flock decisions are mutually independent. In the dynamic framework, a grower would maximize the present value of all future net revenues with terminal time presumably determined by his retirement. Since the frequency of flock rotations is decided by the integrator (the integrator's problem resembles the forestry optimal rotation models), and hence is exogenous to the grower, the dynamic framework appears to add little to the understanding of the grower's problem.

The most important cost of broiler production is feed, accounting for approximately two-thirds of the live-weight costs. Ownership of feed is retained by the integrator, and all contracts provide some type of feed efficiency bonus or penalty to motivate efficiency and prevent pilferage. Feed constitutes the single largest component of the integrator's cost. Other components of the so-called chargeable flock costs (i.e., settlement costs) are the costs of chicks and medication.

The bulk of growers' costs comprises labor and utilities (electricity and fuel). Smaller items of growers' costs include repairs and maintenance costs, and manure and mortality disposal costs. If the grower decides to expend more labor input by taking better care of the chickens, this should, ceteris paribus, increase the total pounds of live meat produced, positively impact his relative performance, and, consequently, increase the payment per pound. Another control variable at the grower's disposal is the selection of appropriate broiler house temperature throughout the life of the broilers. Setting the in-house temperatures should respond to the dynamic environmental requirements of birds growing to the market weight under a wide range of climatic conditions and variety of housing types. Since both inputs are scarce, whatever the grower perceives as the optimal use of labor and utilities will depend on his or her respective opportunity costs, determined by, among other things, the farm enterprise portfolio, grower's socioeconomic characteristics, and specific contract design (i.e., the distribution of production costs responsibilities). An important difference between labor and utilities costs is that the first is typically a noncash expense because most growers tend to work alone or employ family labor, while the electricity bill is often the single largest operating cash expense of the grower, and, as such, could assume an exaggerated importance in the grower's optimization strategy.

Using the performance payment formula (3), with subscripts suppressed for convenience, the grower's static profit maximization problem can be formulated as

$$
\underset{q,u}{Max}\ \pi\ =\ \left[b\ +\ \beta\left(A^{-} -\frac{c(q,u)+\lambda p_u u}{q} \right) \right]q\ -\ g(q,u,w)\ -\ (1-\lambda)p_u u \quad (4)
$$

where $c(q,u)$ is the integrator's cost associated with an individual grower (i.e., settlement cost), $g(q,u,w)$ is the grower's cost, u and p_U are the utilities input and price, and w is the wage rate. The number of growers contracting with one integrator is assumed fairly large so that the $(n-1)/n$ term from expression (3) is assumed to be close to unity. Settlement cost is determined by the level of output and the grower's inputs and is obtained by summing up feed and other chargeable flock costs (chicks and medication) delivered to the grower's farm. The grower's cost is a function of output, utilities, and the prevailing wage rate, and is obtained by summing up small operating expenses (repairs and maintenance) and labor expenses, where the number of hours worked is assumed constant for a given capacity. The specification of the grower's profit function in (4) allows for the portion (λ) of the utility cost to be a part of the settlement cost. For example, if $\lambda=0$, the entire electricity bill is borne by the grower (the current typical case); if $\lambda=1$, the electricity cost becomes a part of the settlement costs.

The necessary conditions for the problem (4) are

$$\frac{\partial \pi}{\partial q} = b + \beta A^- - \beta \frac{\partial c(q,u)}{\partial q} - \frac{\partial g(q,u,w)}{\partial q} = 0 \tag{5}$$

$$\frac{\partial \pi}{\partial u} = -\beta \frac{\partial c(q,u)}{\partial u} - \frac{\partial g(q,u,w)}{\partial u} - p_u[\lambda(\beta-1)+1] = 0. \tag{6}$$

Optimal volume of production from the grower's perspective is determined by the point at which the sum of the marginal settlement cost (adjusted by the bonus factor β) and the own marginal cost equals the sum of the group average settlement cost, adjusted for the bonus factor, and the base payment. In order to achieve maximum profits, the grower employs utilities to the point at which the sum of adjusted marginal settlement cost (with respect to utilities) and own marginal cost equals factor price. The sufficient conditions for profit maximization in (4) require the matrix of second derivatives of the profit function to be negative definite.

The first-order conditions (5) and (6) can be solved for the choice functions in terms of prices and contract specification parameters:

$$q^* = q(A^-,b,\beta,\lambda,w,p_u)$$
$$u^* = u(A^-,b,\beta,\lambda,w,p_u). \tag{7}$$

Assuming that it is possible to solve the system (7) for q^* and u^*, it becomes meaningful to evaluate signs of the partial derivatives comprising the comparative statics of the profit-maximizing model. However, one has to keep in mind that changes in prices and contract parameters will also affect other growers within the group whose average settlement costs are represented by A^-. In order to solve this apparent problem, we assume that a change in a contract parameter will affect all growers competing for the bonus payment within the same group equally, so that the relative position of an individual grower vis-à-vis the entire group before and after the change will remain the same. Analytically, the above assumption reduces to augmenting the system (7) by a third equation maintaining the relationship between the individual grower's settlement costs and the average settlement cost of the remaining growers in the group fixed. The new system to be solved for the optimal values of q, u, and A has the following form:

$$q^* = q(b, \beta, \lambda, w, p_u)$$

$$u^* = u(b, \beta, \lambda, w, p_u)$$

$$\frac{c^*}{q^*} = \delta A^*$$

(8)

where δ measures an average settlement cost differential between an individual grower and the group. If the performance of the individual grower (averaged over a certain number of flocks) is below the group average (i.e., the settlement cost per unit of output is above the group average), δ will be greater than 1, and vice versa. Rather than evaluating the signs of the comparative statics, the grower's response to changes in contract specifications will be simulated by solving the system of equations in (7) and (8) for different values of contract parameters.

Estimation of the Cost Functions

The empirical analysis based on the presented analytical model is performed using the combination of settlement cost and farm-level data from one broiler contract grow-out farm in North Carolina. The data on individual grower's settlement costs, pounds of live meat produced, and the bonus payment calculation (percentage of the spread between average settlement cost for the whole group of growers and the individual settlement cost) are available from flock settlement sheets. Growers generally maintain the historical records of flock settlements from the start of their poultry contract growing operations. Problems, however, arise with every attempt to collect the grower's own cost data. Separate records on labor inputs going into the broiler growing operation typically do not exist because of many enterprises on the farm sharing either paid or unpaid labor. Smaller expenses, such as repair and maintenance costs, are rarely available as well. The situation is generally better with the utility bills. Most of the newer chicken houses have separate electric meters that enable accurate monitoring of the electricity consumption.

The data set assembled for the purposes of this study reflects a representative North Carolina broiler contract growing enterprise. The farmer has four chicken houses with a total average capacity of 104,000 birds and grows chickens for one of the largest companies in the country. Aside from broilers, there are other enterprises on the farm such as corn, soybeans, tobacco, and sweet potatoes. The data set covers the period between January 1, 1988, and April 6, 1994. In that period, the farmer grew thirty-six broiler flocks. The settlement costs, the electricity consumption and costs, and the repair, maintenance, and other small operating costs data are available for the entire period.

Electricity is used for lights and ventilation and is the grower's single largest operating cash expense related to the broiler business. Fuel cost is part of the settlement cost. Monthly electricity bills were converted into electricity consumption and cost per flock using the number of occupancy days for each flock. A similar approach was used to convert monthly figures for repair, maintenance, and other operating expenses into per-flock dollar amounts. Observations on labor input were not available. Data points were constructed by assuming a constant labor requirement of two hours per day per chicken house, considered to be an industry average by most integrators. Since our grower has four chicken houses, the labor requirements translate into eight hours a day for each occupancy day during the life of the flock. The price of labor was obtained from the Employment Security Commission of North Carolina. The quarterly statewide data on average weekly wage per employee in the Agricultural Production–Livestock sector (SIC code 02) was converted into an average hourly wage rate based on the forty-hour work week. Total labor expenses were obtained by multiplying the number of occupancy days by eight and by the wage rate. The only other piece of information used was the average monthly temperature measured at the meteorological station closest to the farm under consideration. Using the number of occupancy days in different months, the monthly temperature averages were transformed into average temperatures for each of the thirty-six flocks. The average temperatures for thirty-six flocks were then averaged again, and the absolute temperature deviations from that historical mean were calculated for each flock.[3]

Allowing for flexibility in the functional form, the total settlement cost (obtained by summing up chicks, feed, medication, and other customary flock costs) was specified as a translog function of output (pounds of live poultry moved from the grower's farm) and utilities (normalized electricity usage). The electricity consumption was normalized by the absolute temperature deviations so that the variable represented kwh of electricity used per degree Fahrenheit deviation from the historical mean temperature. Grower's own cost (calculated as a sum of small operating expenses and labor expenses) was specified as a translog function of output, utilities, and the wage rate. The two cost functions were separately estimated using OLS, and the significance of all cross- and higher-order terms was jointly tested. In both cases, the tests failed to reject the null hypothesis that those parameters are jointly zero.

With all cross- and higher-order terms insignificantly different from zero, the translog specification reduces to the Cobb-Douglas functional form. The new model parameters were obtained by estimating the system of four equations—two cost functions (settlement cost and grower's own cost) and two first-order conditions—using 3SLS. The Cobb-Douglas cost functions represent technological relationships while the system of first-order conditions represents a set of behavioral relationships. Multiplying (5) and (6) by q/cg and u/cg, respectively, and introducing the following notation: $P=(b+\beta A)$, $\alpha_q=(\partial c/\partial q)(q/c)$, $\alpha_u=(\partial c/\partial u)(u/c)$, $\gamma_q=(\partial g/\partial q)(q/g)$, and $\gamma_u=(\partial g/\partial u)(u/g)$, the first-order conditions can be rewritten in elasticity forms:

$$\frac{Pq}{cg} = \alpha_q \frac{\beta}{g} + \gamma_q \frac{1}{c} \tag{9}$$

$$-\frac{P_u u}{cg} = \alpha_u \frac{\beta}{g} + \gamma_u \frac{1}{c}. \tag{10}$$

Equations (9) and (10) can be divided by either β/g or $1/c$, providing the opportunity to econometrically estimate four different linear relationships. Which ones to use is an empirical question and was determined by the goodness of fit.

The system of four equations actually estimated is of the following form:

$$\log c = \log\alpha_0 + \alpha_q \log q + \alpha_u \log(\frac{u}{\tau}) + \alpha_t \log t + \epsilon_1$$

$$\log g = \log\gamma_0 + \gamma_q \log q + \gamma_u \log(\frac{u}{\tau}) + \gamma_w \log w + \gamma_t \log t + \epsilon_2$$

$$\frac{Pq}{g} = \gamma_q + \alpha_q \frac{\beta c}{g} + \epsilon_3 \tag{11}$$

$$-\frac{p_u u}{\beta c} = \alpha_u + \gamma_u \frac{g}{\beta c} + \epsilon_4$$

where t is a time variable denoting the flock number, τ is the absolute deviation from the average temperature, and other variables are previously defined. The estimated system parameters were tested to see whether technological parameters differ significantly from the corresponding behavioral parameters for profit maximization. Testing the null hypotheses about the equality of the corresponding parameters individually resulted in a failure to reject the null for γ_q and α_u, and the rejection of the null for α_q and γ_u. The null hypothesis that corresponding parameters are jointly identical was rejected. Nevertheless, system (11) was reestimated while imposing cross-equation restrictions on parameters. The estimated parameters of the cost functions from the restricted model presented in Table 6.1 satisfy the second-order conditions for profit maximization.[4] Almost all parameters are highly significant and have expected signs. Both settlement and grower's own costs are increasing functions of production volume and decreasing functions of electricity consumption. From the grower's perspective, the increase in bonus payment and the decrease in other own costs can be achieved with increased electricity expenditures. It is important to note the different sign of the time variable in settlement cost (α_t) and grower's own cost function (γ_t). The results indicate that as the number of flocks grown increases, the total settlement cost decreases and the grower's own increases. Both results seem to be intuitively correct. With more flocks grown, the grower becomes more skilled, and the feed conversion ratio of his birds improves. Contrary to that, with the progression of time, the facilities deteriorate, which increases the cost of repair and maintenance.

Table 6.1 3SLS estimates of the grower's model parameters

Coefficient	Estimate	t-Statistic
$\log \alpha_0$	−3.5787	−11.25
α_q	1.2166	64.47
α_u	−0.013773	−5.504
α_t	−0.11693	−3.376
$\log \gamma_0$	−1.51	−0.4674
γ_q	0.61628	2.413
γ_u	−0.078557	−2.623
γ_w	0.32666	1.298
γ_t	0.4454	2.699

Simulation Results

Given the cost functions estimates, the solution to the system of first-order conditions for profit maximization is analytically intractable. The individual first-order conditions include the sums of two Cobb-Douglas functions for which a closed-form solution does not exist. Therefore, the system was solved using numerical algorithms.[5] We explored two scenarios. In the first scenario, the value of the group average settlement cost A^- was fixed at the sample mean and the system of equations in (7) was solved for optimal choices of u and q. The maximum profit of $10,180.94 was obtained by selecting $q^* = 458,388$ lbs. of live meat and $u^* = 16,061$ kwh of electricity. In the second scenario, we allowed the group average settlement cost to vary freely, fixing the relative position of the individual grower vis-à-vis the entire group. Historically (thirty-six flocks average), the performance of our grower is below the group average performance, i.e., his settlement costs are above the group average by approximately 2 percent (δ=1.021). The system of equations in (8) was solved for optimal choices of q, u, and A and the following set of results was obtained: $\pi^* = 9,464.53$, $q^* = 434,470$ lbs., $u^* = 15,224$ kwh, and $A^* = 0.26$/lb. In both cases, the optimal values are within one standard deviation from the sample mean values.[6]

In the analysis that follows, the welfare position of a grower is represented by his profit function, as specified in (4). Since all elements necessary to describe the profit function of an integrator are not available, we must resort to an approximation of the integrator's ultimate objectives. Being part of the completely vertically integrated industry, aside from broiler grow-out enterprise, broiler companies also own and operate broiler breeder flocks, hatcheries, feed mills, processing facilities, and transportation and marketing departments. The only observable segment of the vertically integrated chain of activities comprising broiler production is the one in which integrator's activities intersect with growers' actions and decisions. Therefore, we describe the integrator's objective as one of minimizing the settlement costs (i.e., chicks, feed, medication, and other customary flock costs per pound of live poultry produced). Alternatively, an integrator's objective may be defined as minimizing the sum of settlement costs and payments made out to growers for their services rendered per pound of poultry produced. While pursuing the first goal is almost entirely technologically determined, the second goal may involve constraints such as nourishing a good relationship with growers and maintaining a positive image with the community at large.

Having an analytical framework based on observed behavior of how growers make decisions conditional upon contract stipulations allows simulation of alternative designs. Given the estimated technical production relationships and the associated optimal grower decision rules, an optimal contract design could be determined by searching over possible contract parameter values. The foci of our analysis are the three contract parameters: the base payment b, the bonus factor β, and the utilities cost allocation factor λ. The results are summarized in Tables 6.2–6.4, and Figures 6.1–6.3.

Searching over possible values for the base payment parameter b shows that increasing base payment creates larger profits for the grower, but also larger per pound integrator's costs (Pareto incomparable results). Allowing for the group response generates more rapid response as one moves away from the mean observed value of b (3.66 cents per pound) compared to the scenario with the individual grower's response only. The rates of change indicate that the change in the base payment generates more rapid response in grower's profit than in integrator's per-unit cost. However, this can be misleading because of the relative magnitudes of the integrator's total costs and grower's profit. For example, allowing all growers to adapt to changes simultaneously, the increase in the base payment from 3.65 cents per pound to 3.70 cents per pound increases profit to our grower by $1,107 while total costs to the integrator increase by $13,020. On the other hand, the integrator gained close

Table 6.2 Base payment comparative statics simulation

b	q*	u*	A*	c*/q*	R/lb.	Int. cost	Profit
Case 1:	Allowing for the grower's response only:						
0.0350	434817	15237		0.2638	0.0349	0.2987	9482.05
0.0355	442221	15495		0.2647	0.0350	0.2997	9700.56
0.0360	449719	15757		0.2656	0.0350	0.3006	9922.79
0.0365	457310	16023		0.2665	0.0351	0.3016	10148.77
0.0370	464996	16293		0.2674	0.0351	0.3025	10378.56
0.0375	472776	16566		0.2683	0.0352	0.3035	10612.21
0.0380	480654	16843		0.2692	0.0352	0.3044	10849.75
Case 2:	Allowing for the group response:						
0.0350	301654	10655	0.2420	0.2449	0.0336	0.2785	5584.73
0.0355	458287	15883	0.2636	0.2666	0.0340	0.3006	9690.29
0.0360	458287	15883	0.2636	0.2666	0.0345	0.3011	9919.43
0.0365	458287	15883	0.2636	0.2666	0.0350	0.3016	10148.57
0.0370	494244	17322	0.2673	0.2707	0.0353	0.3060	11255.75
0.0375	567415	19923	0.2749	0.2784	0.0357	0.3141	13522.40
0.0380	644049	22685	0.2820	0.2856	0.0362	0.3218	15976.34

to 36,000 live pounds of chicken meat. Since the total revenue obtained for these broilers is unknown as are the other components of the integrator's costs, the conclusion as to whether an increase in the base payment can qualify as a contract-improving design remains ambiguous. Simulation also seems to indicate that decreasing the base payment away from its actual value has an offsetting effect on the welfare position of the two parties. The decline in grower's profit almost exactly matches the decline in integrator's total cost, with almost no change in the production volume.

Experimenting with different values of the bonus factor generated the results presented in Table 6.3 and Figure 6.2. Searches were conducted over only a fairly narrow range of β values. Moving further away from the actual

Table 6.3 Bonus factor comparative statics simulation

β	q^*	u^*	A^*	c^*/q^*	R/lb.	Int. cost	Profit
Case 1: Allowing for the grower's response only:							
0.475	481850	16311		0.2695	0.0338	0.3033	10230.27
0.480	476868	16256		0.2689	0.0341	0.3029	10217.49
0.485	472037	16204		0.2683	0.0343	0.3026	10206.23
0.490	467351	16154		0.2677	0.0346	0.3023	10196.42
0.495	462803	16106		0.2672	0.0348	0.3020	10188.01
0.500	458388	16061		0.2666	0.0351	0.3017	10180.94
0.505	454100	16018		0.2661	0.0353	0.3014	10175.16
0.510	449934	15976		0.2656	0.0356	0.3011	10170.62
0.515	445885	15937		0.2651	0.0358	0.3009	10167.27
0.520	441948	15899		0.2646	0.0361	0.3006	10165.07
Case 2: Allowing for the group response:							
0.475	673360	22890	0.2847	0.2884	0.0348	0.3232	15956.63
0.480	619108	21160	0.2799	0.2835	0.0349	0.3183	14461.73
0.485	568304	19534	0.2750	0.2786	0.0349	0.3134	13071.50
0.490	520654	18005	0.2702	0.2736	0.0349	0.3085	11777.19
0.495	475876	16562	0.2653	0.2687	0.0349	0.3036	10570.54
0.500	434470	15224	0.2604	0.2637	0.0349	0.2986	9464.53
0.505	458287	15883	0.2636	0.2666	0.0350	0.3017	10173.96
0.510	458287	15883	0.2636	0.2666	0.0350	0.3017	10167.05
0.515	458287	15883	0.2636	0.2666	0.0350	0.3017	10160.13
0.520	458287	15883	0.2636	0.2666	0.0350	0.3016	10153.21

value of β = 0.5 generates optimal values for q and u outside the technologically feasible region, and, in the case of full adjustment, the scenario causes serious numerical problems. The results seem to indicate that increasing the

Table 6.4 Utilities allocation factor comparative statics simulation

λ	q^*	u^*	A^*	c^*/q^*	R/lb.	Int. cost	Profit
Case 1: Allowing for the grower's response only:							
-1.0	442177	10468		0.2661	0.0362	0.3023	9697.54
-0.8	444909	11259		0.2662	0.0360	0.3022	9779.03
-0.6	447855	12175		0.2663	0.0359	0.3021	9866.90
-0.4	451052	13249		0.2664	0.0356	0.3020	9962.23
-0.2	454543	14523		0.2665	0.0354	0.3019	10066.33
0.0	458388	16061		0.2666	0.0351	0.3017	10180.94
0.2	462663	17951		0.2667	0.0347	0.3015	10308.35
0.4	467472	20328		0.2669	0.0343	0.3012	10451.67
0.6	472964	23406		0.2670	0.0337	0.3008	10615.29
0.8	479358	27544		0.2672	0.0330	0.3003	10805.70
1.0	486994	33393		0.2674	0.0321	0.2995	11033.04
Case 2: Allowing for the group response:							
-1.0	382351	9069	0.2551	0.2584	0.0358	0.2942	7950.67
-0.8	391264	9915	0.2561	0.2593	0.0357	0.2950	8206.95
-0.6	400745	10905	0.2571	0.2604	0.0355	0.2959	8480.97
-0.4	410891	12077	0.2581	0.2614	0.0354	0.2968	8775.73
-0.2	421824	13482	0.2592	0.2625	0.0352	0.2976	9095.00
0.0	434470	15224	0.2604	0.2637	0.0349	0.2986	9464.53
0.2	446716	17332	0.2615	0.2649	0.0346	0.2995	9828.14
0.4	461159	20053	0.2628	0.2661	0.0342	0.3004	10257.16
0.6	477415	23628	0.2642	0.2675	0.0338	0.3013	10743.02
0.8	496056	28514	0.2657	0.2691	0.0331	0.3022	11303.82
1.0	517972	35549	0.2674	0.2708	0.0323	0.3031	11967.75

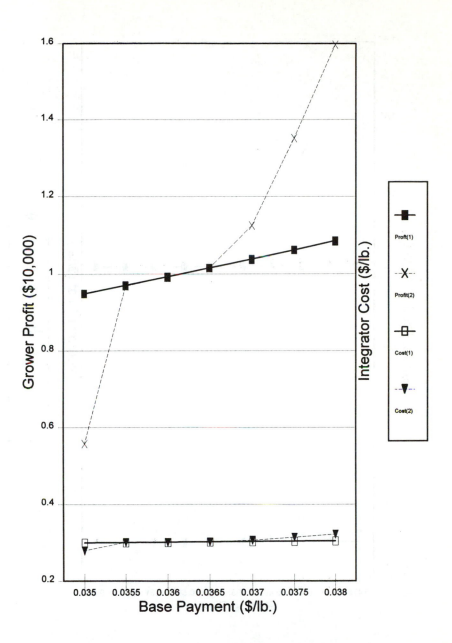

Figure 6.1 Base payment simulation results

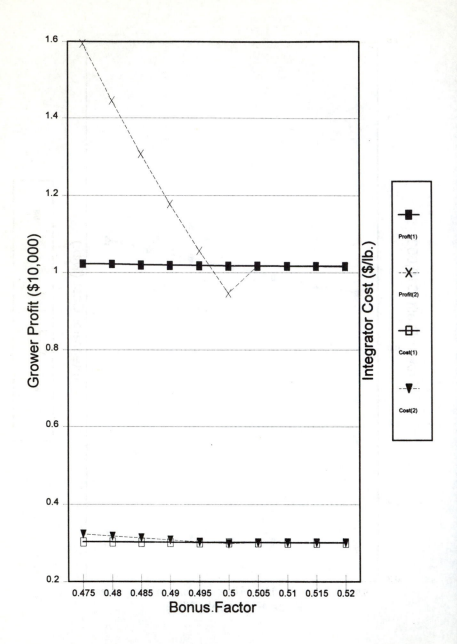

Figure 6.2 Bonus factor simulation results

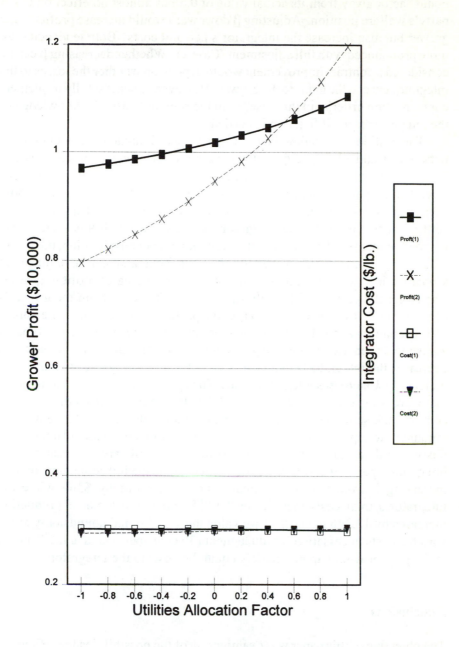

Figure 6.3 Utilities allocation factor simulation results

bonus factor away from its actual value of 0.5 has almost no effect on either party's welfare position. Adjusting β downward would increase profits to the grower but also increase the integrator's per-unit costs. Both tendencies are more pronounced with full adjustment (Case 2). Whether decreasing β can be considered a contract improvement would depend on whether the losses to the integrator exceed the gains to the grower. However, to successfully implement compensation criteria, in this case, as in the previous case, the knowledge of the integrator's profit function is needed.

The utilities allocation factor impact was simulated for values of λ between -1 and $+1$. Specifying the negative values for λ reallocates part of the existing settlement cost from integrator to grower, and positive values for λ reallocates part of the utilities bill from the grower to the integrator. Both scenarios are meaningful due to the fact that fuel cost is a part of the settlement cost borne by the integrator and the electricity bill is a part of the grower's expenses. For the particular contract under consideration, the actual value of λ is zero. Under both full adjustment and partial adjustment scenarios, increasing the utilities allocation factor increases profit to grower. The larger the portion of the utilities costs switched over from the grower's cost into the settlement cost, the larger the profits for the grower. The impact of a change in λ on the integrator's per-unit cost depends on the type of adjustment scenario. Under the partial adjustment scenario, the increase in λ decreases the integrator's unit cost. Under the full adjustment scenario, the increase in λ increases integrator costs. The obtained results seem to indicate that increasing λ, i.e., switching part of the electricity cost from the grower's cost into the settlement cost, may constitute a Pareto move. There are two arguments to support this claim. First, the partial adjustment model unambiguously signals a Pareto improvement (grower's profits are increasing while integrator's per-unit cost is decreasing). Second, in the full adjustment model, increasing λ from 0 to 0.2 increases grower's profit by \$364 while the integrator's total costs increase by \$4,058 and the volume of production increases by 12,246 pounds. If we value these additional pounds only at the variable costs necessary to produce them (30 cents per pound[7]), the benefits to the grower would approximately equal the costs to the integrator.

Conclusions

The objective of this paper was examination of the possibilities for efficiency gains from redesigning contracts, taking into consideration individual grower's behavioral responses. Poultry grow-out contract design has evolved over time in response to market variations and institutional innovations in order to increase total returns available to both integrators and growers. Contract refinements are aimed at better coordinating integrator and grower actions and harmonizing the two parties' criteria for making input decisions. The evolution of contracts as well as the simultaneous existence of different specifications make us believe that even the most recent contracts may be redesigned in order to improve the overall welfare.

Using the analytical framework based on observed behavior of how growers make decisions conditional upon contract specifications, alternative contract designs were simulated by searching over possible contract parameter values. The foci of our analysis were three contract parameters: the base payment b, the bonus factor β, and the utilities cost allocation factor λ. In the first two cases, the simulation generated Pareto-incomparable results. The lack of data necessary to recover the integrator's profit function prevented us from using a compensation criterion to see whether the party that gains can theoretically compensate the party that loses. In searching over possible values of the utilities costs allocation factor, it seems that switching part of the electricity cost from the grower's cost into the settlement cost may result in a mutual welfare gain.

The possibilities for future research in this area are numerous. First, the entire analysis in this paper was conducted using data from only one farm. Identifying broiler companies willing to cooperate to begin the process of accurate farm-level data collection is an important task. Having data for a reasonable number of growers and possibly several different integrators with different contract specifications would lend more credibility to the estimation and simulation results. Second, the model in this paper is static while, in fact, the broiler grow-out is characterized by two types of dynamic processes. One is the inter-flock decision-making process that brings into play additional complications such as, for example, the minimum guaranteed payment scheme. The second is the intra-flock dynamics determined by the time-dependent production technology. The metabolism of birds is changing with age and so is the feed conversion ratio. As the result of that, more precise results might be obtained by casting the problem into a dynamic programming framework. Third, weather plays an important factor in broiler production. Birds are very susceptible to heat, which brings a stochastic component into the analysis. Finally, more research and data are needed to formulate the integrator's side of the problem more accurately.

Notes

This paper was previously published as "Efficiency Gains in Broiler Production Through Contract Parameter Fine Tuning" in *Poultry Science*, 75(1996):1351–58, and is used here by permission of the editor-in-chief.

1   The authors would like to thank Wally Thurman, Chuck Knoeber, and other participants of the Agricultural Economics Workshop at North Carolina State University for helpful comments and suggestions. Any remaining errors are the responsibility of the authors.
2   When compared with independent producers, contract growers derive significant benefits from risk shifting. There are two sources of risks shifted from growers to integrators: (1) the common part of the production risk and (2) inputs and output price risk (for more details, see Knoeber and Thurman).
3   The entire data set is available from the authors upon request.
4   Based on the estimation of the Cobb-Douglas settlement and growers' own cost functions, without decision rules (9) and (10), one cannot reject the constant-returns-to-scale technology hypothesis.
5   The solution was obtained using the Gauss-Newton method using the "fsolve" routine available in the MATLAB Optimization Toolbox software.
6   The mean values of profit and decision variables (with standard deviations in parentheses) are: $\pi = 10{,}227$ (2,096); $q = 458{,}287$ (30,976); $u = 15{,}883$ (3,044); and $A = \$0.26$ (0.02).
7   This number is obtained as the sample mean of the average settlement cost for the entire group (\$0.26 per pound) plus the sample mean of the per-pound payment to the grower (\$0.04 per pound).

References

Aho, P. W., and M. B. Timmons. 1988. "Disparate Grower and Integrator Optimum Growout Temperatures." *Poultry Science* 67:534–37.

Brown, R. H. 1994. "Processors Try New Approaches with Poultry Growers." *Feedstuffs*, December 12, pp. 19 and 27.

Gates R. S., and M. B. Timmons. 1986. "Real-Time Economic Optimization of Broiler Production." Paper presented at American Society of Agricultural Engineers winter meeting, Chicago Ill., December 16–19.

Knoeber, C. R. 1989. "A Real Game of Chicken: Contracts, Tournaments, and the Production of Broilers." *Journal of Law, Economics and Organization* 5:271–92.

Knoeber, C. R., and W. N. Thurman. 1995. "Don't Count Your Chickens . . .: Risk and Risk Shifting in the Broiler Industry." *American Journal of Agricultural Economics* 77:486–96.

Timmons, M. B., and R. S. Gates. 1986. "Economic Optimization of Broiler Production." *Transactions of the American Society of Agricultural Engineers* 29:1373–78, 84.

7 The Effect of Ownership on Contract Structure, Costs, and Quality: The Case of the U.S. Beet Sugar Industry

JEANINE KOENIG BALBACH[1]

Until the advance of transaction cost economics, nonstandard forms of economic relationships such as vertical integration and cooperatives generally had only monopoly explanations (e.g., leverage, price discrimination, or entry barriers). Under transaction cost economics, these nonstandard forms can often be interpreted as having efficiency purposes.

This paper provides empirical evidence from the U.S. beet sugar industry to support the transaction cost economics hypothesis that vertical integration can serve efficiency purposes. In the beet sugar industry, efficiency gains can be attributed to a change in the ownership of the processing company.

Of the nine beet sugar processing companies, three are grower-owned cooperatives. In the 1970s, the cooperative processors developed a more complex form of beet purchase contract, the extractable-sugar contract. Under this contract, each grower is paid for the actual amount of recoverable sugar he delivers. This contract differs from previous contracts in that a more precise measurement is made of the quality of each grower's sugar beets. In addition to measuring sugar content, the cooperative processors also measure the impurity level of each grower's sugar beets. Only the three cooperative processors use the extractable-sugar contract.

The extractable-sugar contract contains incentives for growers to supply higher-quality sugar beets. In this paper, I show that under the extractable-sugar contract, growers supplied 12 percent more sugar per ton of beets processed. In contrast, for processors who retained the old type of contract, growers did not supply beets with a higher amount of sugar per ton.

Integrated ownership of the supply of sugar beets and the sugar processing company is needed to use this new form of beet purchase contract. Processors have an incentive to underreport quality and keep more returns for themselves. The costs of monitoring the processor's quality measurements are too high in

155

a traditional, investor-owned firm for the extractable-sugar contract to be useful. Vertical integration of the processing company by the growers reduces these monitoring and measurement costs. As owners of the company, the growers presumably have greater trust in the quality measurements being made by their own employees.

There is an extensive theoretical literature in economics on contracting, vertical integration, agency problems, measurement, and information. However the amount of empirical work systematically looking at contracts is small. This type of empirical research is needed to provide a basis for structuring economic models. There is no way to know what will actually happen with regard to contracting unless the costs and benefits of various contracts and ownership arrangements are known. This study of contracts and ownership in the U.S. beet sugar processing industry provides such evidence.

The paper is organized as follows. A brief overview of transaction cost economics is followed by the history of vertical integration in the U.S. beet sugar industry. Next, I discuss sugar beet quality and beet purchase contracts. This is followed by the empirical results of vertical integration. Next I present an overview of the contracts currently used by the noncooperative processing companies, then the quality measurements for noncooperative processors. This is followed by a discussion of the relationship between processing company ownership and contract type. The final section concludes.

Transaction Cost Economics

Coase first identified the key to the transaction cost theory: "There is a cost of using the price mechanism [market]." Firms are established to minimize these transaction costs of exchange. If it is more expensive for a firm to acquire an input in the market than to produce it itself, the firm will vertically integrate into production of the input.

Williamson expanded on Coase's idea. He considered the main purpose of vertical integration to be "economizing on transaction costs." Williamson identified transaction costs of two types: ex ante and ex post. Ex ante costs include the costs of drafting, negotiating, and safeguarding an agreement. Ex post costs are those costs incurred when agreements become misaligned, such as the cost of resolving disputes. Transaction cost economics examines how trading parties organize or govern an exchange in order to minimize these transaction costs.

Transactions differ in four aspects: (1) the presence of relationship-specific investments, (2) the uncertainty about other parties' actions, (3) the frequency with which the transactions occur, and (4) the complexity of the exchange arrangement. The choice of the appropriate governance structure for an exchange depends on these characteristics of the relationship. Transaction cost economics recognizes the first, asset specificity, as the most important aspect in distinguishing relationships between buyers and sellers.

Williamson defines relationship-specific investments or "specific assets" as "durable investments that are undertaken in support of particular transactions, the opportunity cost of which investments is much lower in best alternative uses or by alternative users should the original transaction be prematurely terminated." Williamson identifies four types of asset specificity: (1) site specificity, (2) physical asset specificity, (3) human asset specificity, and (4) dedicated assets. Site specificity refers to successive stages of production that are located near each other to minimize inventory and transportation costs. A specific physical asset is one whose function is specific to production of the item being exchanged (e.g., specialized dies used to produce a component). Specific human assets arise from "learning-by-doing." Investments in dedicated assets are investments in generalized production capacity made for the sole purpose of supplying a certain customer.

Vertical integration is a form of governance structure. Vertical integration can lead to lower transaction costs. The presence of relationship-specific investments raises the cost of creating safeguards to protect against the expropriation of quasi rents. Klein, Crawford, and Alchian recognized this potential for post-contractual opportunistic behavior in the presence of specific assets. Once a contract is signed and a specific investment is made, it is possible that one party to the contract will renege on the agreement. Their central hypothesis is that "as assets become more specific and more appropriable, quasi rents are created, the costs of contracting will generally increase more than the cost of vertical integration." Vertical integration can reduce the hold-up problem that may arise with specific assets.

Uncertainty about the future or the other party's actions leads to higher transaction costs. Uncertainty of future events increases drafting and negotiating costs. It is too costly for trading parties to cover all possible contingencies in their contract. Uncertainty about, or unobservability of, a party's actions may lead to strategic behavior on that party's part. He may inflate reported costs or underreport revenues in order to keep a larger share for himself. This potential for strategic behavior, in the presence of uncertainty or asymmetric information, raises the measurement and monitoring costs in a transaction. The complexity of the transaction also increases these same costs of drafting, negotiating, measurement, and monitoring. Vertical integration and internalization of an exchange can reduce or eliminate these costs.

Much of the empirical work in transaction cost economics focuses on the "make-or-buy" decision or the choice to vertically integrate (Monteverde and Teece; Masten; Masten, Meehan and Snyder). Other empirical work has examined contractual arrangements. Joskow's (1985, 1987, 1988) series of papers on coal contracts identifies the presence of transaction-specific investments as important in determining contract duration and the structure of the payment mechanism.

In agricultural economics, much attention is given to cooperatives, but most of the work is theoretical. At issue is why people join cooperatives and what advantages or disadvantages cooperatives have (Sexton; Craig and Pencavel). Little connection has been made between the cooperative literature and transaction cost economics, but a cooperative is a form of vertical integration. Cooperatives are organizations owned by the individuals who do business with them. These owners are the workers, customers, or suppliers of the cooperative. Cooperatives are not a textbook example of vertical integration in which two or more successive stages in production are brought under common ownership and management. In cooperatives, one stage of the production process (e.g., the growing stage) is not controlled by one owner or ownership group. Each grower makes his own decisions about how his farm firm will be run. However, there are definite elements of vertical integration in the decision to form a cooperative, and transaction cost economics can be applied to this decision.

Vertical Integration in U.S. Beet Sugar Industry

The U.S. beet sugar industry provides a natural opportunity for the examination of the organization of exchanges and vertical integration. A structural change occurred in this industry with the formation of grower-owned processing cooperatives in the 1970s. These cooperatives compete today with traditional, investor-owned firms.

In the beet sugar industry, the relationship between the growers and the processors is key. Contracts have always been used to govern the exchange of sugar beets from the grower to the processor. Contracts are used due to the nature of sugar beets. Sugar beets are perishable and expensive to transport.

Thus processors use contracts to ensure an adequate supply for their factories. There are no other buyers of sugar beets than sugar processors, so growers need contracts to ensure a market for their crop before it is planted. A detailed description of the beet sugar production process may be found in Appendix I.

Of the nine companies processing beet sugar today, three are grower-owned cooperatives. See Table 7.1 for beet sugar companies as of 1995. Minn-Dak Farmers Cooperative and Southern Minnesota Beet Sugar Cooperative were established in the 1970s as cooperatives, but American Crystal Sugar was originally a corporation. The story of American Crystal Sugar is particularly interesting.

American Crystal Sugar Company was incorporated in 1899 as American Beet Sugar Company. It started processing beet sugar at factories in California and Nebraska. Between 1899 and 1973, the company also operated factories in Colorado, Iowa, Montana, Minnesota, and North Dakota.

In 1971, the contracted beet acreage in the Red River Valley of Minnesota and North Dakota was cut 20 percent by the company. Processing plants at Chaska, Minnesota, and Mason City, Iowa, were closed in 1971 and 1973, respectively. The growers knew that the other factories were not getting the maintenance they required (American Crystal Sugar Co. 1992, p. 7). In general, the company was not putting money back into the industry to allow for expansion. At this time, while the growers were earning high returns from sugar beets, processing firms were earning low returns. Because of these low returns to processing, the old American Crystal Sugar was not interested in expanding its facilities. However, sugar beets were the best cash crop for the farmers in the Red River Valley. These farmers wanted to expand their output and, therefore, wanted American Crystal Sugar to expand processing capacity.

In 1973, these conflicting interests lead 2,000 Red River Valley Sugar Beet Growers Association members to purchase American Crystal and form a cooperative. As a cooperative, the growers who supply the processing company with sugar beets also have an ownership share in the processing company. Today, American Crystal Sugar owns and operates processing facilities only in the Red River Valley.

The reorganization of American Crystal Sugar and the formation of the two other beet sugar processing cooperatives in the Red River Valley correspond with a dramatic growth in the beet sugar industry in Minnesota and North Dakota. Sugar beet production has more than quadrupled in this region. American Crystal Sugar's acreage increased from approximately 165,000 acres in 1972 to 400,000 acres in 1992.[2]

Table 7.1 1994–1995 beet sugar companies and factories

Company	City	State	Year erected	Daily slicing capacity (tons)
Imperial Holly Sugar Corporation	Brawley	Calif.	1947	7,500
	Hamilton City	Calif.	1906	3,700
	Tracy	Calif.	1917	4,800
	Sidney	Mont.	1925	5,000
	Hereford	Tex.	1964	8,000
	Torrington	Wyo.	1923	5,400
	Worland	Wyo.	1917	3,600
Speckels Sugar Company	Manteca	Calif.	1919	4,200
	Mendota	Calif.	1963	4,200
	Woodland	Calif.	1937	3,600
Western Sugar Company	Fort Morgan	Colo.	1906	4,000
	Greeley	Colo.	1902	2,500
	Billings	Mont.	1906	4,500
	Bayard	Nebr.	1917	2,550
	Mitchell	Nebr.	1920	2,500
	Scottsbluff	Nebr.	1910	4,000
	Lovell	Wyo.	1916	3,000

Company	City	State	Year	Acres
Amalgamated Sugar Company	Mini-Cassia	Idaho	1917	9,000
	Nampa	Idaho	1942	12,000
	Twin Falls	Idaho	1916	6,200
	Nyssa	Ore.	1938	9,300
Michigan Sugar Company	Caro	Mich.	1899	3,200
	Carrollton	Mich.	1902	2,850
	Croswell	Mich.	1902	3,000
	Sebewaing	Mich.	1902	4,250
(Great Lakes Sugar Company)	Fremont	Ohio	1900	3,600
Monitor Sugar Company	Bay City	Mich.	1901	8,000
American Crystal Sugar Company*	Crookston	Minn.	1954	4,500
	East Grand Forks	Minn.	1926	6,700
	Moorhead	Minn.	1948	4,400
	Drayton	N. Dak.	1965	5,400
	Hillsboro	N. Dak.	1974	4,500
Minn-Dak Farmers Cooperative*	Wahpeton	N. Dak.	1974	5,900
Southern Minnesota Beet Sugar Cooperative*	Renville	Minn.	1975	9,000

* Cooperatives.

Source: American Sugarbeet Growers Association.

The record of the sugar beet industry in regions other than the Red River Valley is very different. Table 7.2 shows the decline or demise of this industry over the past thirty years in several western states. Sugar beets are no longer grown in Arizona, Kansas, and Utah. California has experienced a large decline in this industry. From 1972 to 1992, harvested acreage and the number of tons produced declined by more than 50 percent in California and Colorado. Since 1970, twenty-seven processing facilities have closed. As Table 7.3 shows, most of these facilities were in western states.

The story of American Crystal Sugar raises several interesting questions. How could the grower-owned processing company be successful when the corporation was cutting back because of low returns to processing? Why have American Crystal and the other cooperatives continued to grow and remain very strong companies while in the past twenty-five years other beet sugar processors have filed for bankruptcy or shut down? The obvious difference is the ownership of the cooperatives—supplier-owned processing facilities. Can the success and efficiencies of these cooperatives be attributed to the vertically integrated structure?

Sugar Beet Quality and Beet Purchase Contracts

In this section, I examine the relationship between beet purchase contracts and industry efficiency. Beet sugar industry efficiency is a function of the quality of sugar beets growers supply to the processing company. Higher-quality sugar beets contain more recoverable sugar. The amount of recoverable sugar is determined by the beets' percentage sugar content and the level of impurities present in the beets.

The relationship between sugar content and recoverable sugar has always been known. In the first beet purchase contracts written in the United States, payment was based on the tons of beets delivered and their sugar content. The payment terms as described in an 1898 Henry Oxnard (founder of American Crystal) contract were "$3.25 per ton containing not less than twelve percent sugar and an additional twenty-five cents per ton for each and every additional one percent of sugar contained in beets above twelve percent."

The first major change in beet purchase contracts came at the time of World War I. The price of refined sugar rose more than 75 percent when price controls were removed. Sugar beet growers wanted a share of this sugar price increase. Payment scales were changed to be based on sugar content and the market price of sugar. In 1915, American Crystal added a provision in its contract for a fifty cent bonus per ton if the average net selling price of refined sugar received by the company equaled or exceeded 4.5 cents per pound. In 1917, the American Crystal Sugar contract was changed so payment would depend on the percentage sugar content and the average net selling price received by the company, instead of a fixed price per ton and the sugar content of beets. This type of contract is known as a "participation" contract. Growers share in a certain percentage of the company's returns from the sale of refined sugar. These percent-sugar-content contracts are still used by the traditional, investor-owned processors. An example of the payment formula under such a contract is presented in the section, "Contracts Used by Noncooperative Processors."

In the 1970s, the cooperative processors made another change in beet contracts. They developed the extractable-sugar contract. Extractable-sugar contracts measure the actual amount of recoverable sugar per ton of beets.

As mentioned previously, recoverable sugar depends on sugar content and on the level of impurities present in the beets. The focus on the impurity level is a new line of research. The impurity level and the amount of recoverable sugar are negatively correlated. The main impurities found in beets are sodium, potassium, and amino nitrogen. These impurities are called "molasses formers." Their presence prevents some sugar from crystallizing and it is "spun out" during processing into the molasses by-product. These impurities are natural elements, but the level of nitrogen in the soil influences the root uptake of sodium, potassium, and amino nitrogen. The level of nitrogen in the soil is affected by the amount of nitrogen fertilizer applied. Nitrogen fertilizer is used to increase tonnage per acre. Growers can reduce impurity levels by using stricter agronomic practices, including the reduction of nitrogen fertilizer, early planting, higher plant populations, weed control, disease and insect control, and longer crop rotations.

A formula was developed in the 1960s to calculate the percentage sugar loss to molasses. The processing company measures the amounts of the sodium, potassium, and amino nitrogen impurities present in a random sample of each grower's beets. The Carruthers Formula converts these amounts into the percentage sugar loss to molasses. On average, one pound of impurities translates into one and one-half pounds of sugar lost to molasses.[3]

Under the extractable-sugar contract, a grower is paid for the amount of sugar actually recoverable from his beets. The pounds of sugar recoverable from a ton of beets is calculated by subtracting the percentage sugar loss to molasses from the percentage sugar content and multiplying this difference by 2,000 pounds per ton. For example, beets with a 17.57 percent sugar content

Table 7.2 U.S. sugar beet crops: Area, yield, and production by state, 1972 and 1992

Area	Acres harvested (1,000 acres)		Yield per acre (short tons)		Production (1,000 short tons)		Percent of production	
	1972	1992	1972	1992	1972	1992	1972	1992
Red River Valley:								
Minnesota	111.9	370.0	14.0	18.5	1,568	6,845	5.5	23.5
North Dakota	48.2	186.9	12.5	15.5	601	2,894	2.1	9.9
Total	160.1	556.9	13.5	17.5	2,169	9,739	7.6	33.4
West:								
Arizona	13.0	0.0	23.2	0.0	302	0	1.1	0.0
California	329.0	150.0	27.5	28.2	9,037	4,230	31.8	14.5
Colorado	133.8	39.9	19.4	23.9	2,594	954	9.1	3.3
Idaho	172.7	200.0	20.5	24.5	3,542	4,900	12.5	16.8
Kansas	35.6	0.0	18.2	0.0	650	0	2.3	0.0
Montana	45.2	55.8	18.6	22.8	842	1,272	3.0	4.4
Nebraska	82.1	77.5	20.1	17.9	1,650	1,387	5.8	4.8
New Mexico[a]	0.6	–	24.7	–	16	–	0.1	–
West. North Dakota	25.7	7.8	15.8	63.3	407	494	1.4	1.7
Oregon	22.3	17.3	24.7	22.8	551	394	1.9	1.4

Texas	23.1	39.9	22.6	21.0	523	838	1.8	2.9
Utah	22.0	0.0	19.6	0.0	431	0	1.5	0.0
Washington[a]	91.6	–	25.5	–	2,337	–	8.2	–
Wyoming	57.2	69.1	20.3	20.8	1,146	1,437	4.0	4.9
Total	1,053.9	657.3	19.6	24.2	24,028	15,906	84.5	54.6
East:								
Michigan	86.6	175.0	18.9	17.7	1,638	3,098	5.8	10.6
Ohio	32.6	20.5	18.4	16.0	601	328	2.1	1.1
Total	119.2	195.5	18.8	17.5	2,239	3,426	7.9	11.8
Other[b]	–	1.8	–	40.0	–	72	–	0.2
U.S. Total	1,333.2	1,411.5	18.8	20.6	28,436	29,143	100.0	100.0

[a] 1992 included in other to avoid disclosure of individual operations.
[b] Includes New Mexico and Washington.

Source: U.S. Department of Agriculture (1975, 1994).

Table 7.3 Beet sugar processing facilities closed since 1970

State	City	Company	Year erected	Year closed	1971 daily slicing capacity (tons)
Ariz.	Chandler	Spreckels	1965	1982	4,200
Calif.	Clarksburg	Delta	1935	1993	3,000
Calif.	Betteravia	Holly	1897	1993	5,000
Calif.	Santa Ana	Holly	1909	1978	1,800
Calif.	Spreckels	Spreckels	1899	1982	6,500
Colo.	Rocky Ford	American Crystal	1901	1979	3,400
Colo.	Brighton	Great Western	1917	1977	2,200
Colo.	Eaton	Great Western	1902	1976	2,200
Colo.	Longmont	Great Western	1903	1977	3,200
Colo.	Loveland	Great Western	1901	1985	3,500
Colo.	Ovid	Great Western	1926	1985	2,800
Colo.	Sterling	Great Western	1905	1985	2,400
Colo.	Delta	Holly	1920	1977	1,800
Idaho	Idaho Falls	Utah-Idaho	1903	1979	4,400
Iowa	Mason City	American Crystal	1917	1973	2,400
Kans.	Goodland	Great Western	1968	1985	3,200

Maine	Easton	Maine Sugar Industries	1967	1970	4,000
Minn.	Chaska	American Crystal	1906	1971	2,200
Mont.	Hardin	*	*	1971	2,000
Nebr.	Gering	Great Western	1916	1985	2,200
Ohio	Ottawa	Dextra	*	1979	1,600
Ohio	Findlay	Great Western	1911	1978	1,650
Utah	Lewiston	Amalgamated	1905	1972	1,950
Utah	Garland	Utah-Idaho	1903	1979	2,700
Utah	West Jordan	Utah-Idaho	1916	1971	1,700
Wash.	Moses Lake	Utah-Idaho	1953	1979	8,500
Wash.	Toppenish	Utah-Idaho	1937	1979	3,825
Total capacity shutdown					84,325

* Not available.

and a 1.495 percent sugar loss to molasses yield 321.5 pounds of recoverable sugar per ton of beets:

$$(.1757 - .01495) \times 2,000 \text{ pounds per ton} = 321.5 \text{ pounds per ton.} \quad (1)$$

Processing and storage costs are the same for one ton of beets regardless of the impurity level of the beets. Higher-quality beets (lower impurity level and higher sugar content) yield more pounds of sugar. Therefore, cost per recovered pound of sugar declines if higher-quality beets are processed.

A major goal of the cooperative American Crystal Sugar was, as stated in the 1981 annual report, "to improve sugarbeet quality in the Red River Valley, thereby increasing the profit to the member through the production of more recoverable sugar per acre." The cooperative employed a "quality payment system" to provide "the incentive for the individual grower to adopt production practices that [would] result in more sugar and less impurities in the beet root." Therefore, as a consequence of the new incentive structure for growers (quality pay), one should observe growers supplying the company with higher-quality beets over time. American Crystal Sugar's quality payment system was first used for the 1980 crop (the 1981 fiscal year).

As a part of their quality payment system, American Crystal Sugar uses an extractable-sugar contract. In fact, only the cooperative processors use the extractable-sugar contract; the investor-owned companies use the percent-sugar-content contract. The following section demonstrates the efficiency gain resulting from adoption of the extractable-sugar contract. The section titled "Processing Company Ownership and Contract Type" presents an explanation for why only the cooperative processors use this contract.

Measures of Beet Quality and Empirical Results

The contract structure or payment mechanism affects the quality of the product delivered and, therefore, also the processing costs. The efficiency gain can be measured in several ways: (1) processing cost per refined pound of sugar, (2) sugar loss to molasses, (3) extraction rate, and (4) pounds of sugar produced per ton of beets sliced.

Processing Costs

As described in the previous section, when higher-quality beets are processed, more sugar is produced per ton of raw beets. Therefore, the processing cost per refined pound of sugar is lower. If the contract structure affects the quality of the product delivered, one should observe that the real cost of the product sold per refined pound declines starting in 1981, the first year in which American Crystal Sugar's quality payment system and the extraction-based contract were used. The results are presented in Table 7.4. Under the old contract, the mean real cost of product sold per refined pound is $0.1141. The mean for the extractable-sugar contract is $0.0994. This is a 14 percent reduction in costs. American Crystal Sugar produces, on average, 1.5 billion pounds of sugar a year. This $0.0147 reduction in the cost of product sold per refined pound translates into a total savings of $22 million per year. Therefore, the contract type produces real efficiencies in terms of processing costs.

There are better measures than processing cost per refined pound to measure quality directly. The first of these measures is sugar loss to molasses. The second is the extraction rate, and the final quality measure is pounds of sugar produced per ton of beets sliced.

Sugar Loss to Molasses

As discussed earlier, sugar loss to molasses is a result of the presence of impurities in beets that prevent some of the sugar from being extracted from a beet during processing. This portion of the sugar ends up in the molasses by-product.[4] Sugar loss to molasses is measured as a percentage. Higher-quality beets have a lower percentage sugar loss to molasses. If the extraction-based contract provides an incentive for growers to supply higher-quality beets, one should observe a declining trend in sugar loss to molasses. This data is presented in Table 7.4. Sugar loss to molasses declined from 2.22 percent in 1981 to 1.54 percent in 1993 (a 36 percent decline). Since this measure was developed for the extractable-sugar contract, it is not available for the old contracting period. However, the 36 percent reduction in sugar loss to molasses shows that the extraction-based contract did induce the growers to supply higher-quality beets.

Extraction Rate

Another direct measure of sugar beet quality is the extraction rate. Extraction is the percentage of sugar entering the factories that is actually extracted during processing. Extraction depends primarily on the sugar content, the impurity level, and the condition of the beets. Sugar beets are a fresh vegetable. After being harvested, beets burn sugar to stay alive. If the beets

Table 7.4 American Crystal Sugar Company, Red River Valley (fiscal years[a])

Summary	Real cost[b] of product sold per refined pound	Sugar loss to molasses	Extraction rate	Pounds of sugar produced per ton of beets sliced
Mean under old contract (1966–80)	$0.1141	[c]	73.92%	234
Mean under extractable sugar contract (1981–93)	$0.0994	1.79%	80.62%	263
Percentage change (old contract to new contract)	-14%	-36% (from 1981 to 1993)	0.09	0.12
Test for difference between two means	t=1.26 (not significant)	[c]	t=5.45 (significant at the .001 level)	t=2.43 (significant at the .05 level)
Standard error	0.0117	[c]	1.23	11.95

[a] Fiscal year 1966 = 1965 crop.
[b] Real cost calculated using GDP deflator.
[c] Not available.

Source: American Crystal Sugar Company.

are not processed immediately after harvest, they will lose part of their sugar content. Therefore, time between harvest and processing decreases the extraction rates.[5]

In general, the processing of higher-quality beets results in a higher extraction rate. The data in Table 7.4 show that extraction increased under the extraction-based contract, from an old contract mean of 73.92 percent to an extractable-sugar contract mean of 80.62 percent (a 9 percent increase). These means are statistically different at the .001 level.

Sugar Produced per Ton of Beets Sliced

The final direct measure of sugar beet quality is sugar produced per ton of beets sliced. Higher-quality beets yield more sugar per ton of beets sliced. This measure, as reported in Table 7.4, supports the hypothesis that the extraction-based contract provides an incentive for growers to supply higher-quality sugar beets. The old contract mean for pounds of sugar produced per ton of beets sliced is 234 pounds. The extractable-sugar contract mean is larger, 263 pounds (a 12 percent increase). These means are statistically different at the .05 level.

Contracts Used by Noncooperative Processors

The previous section demonstrates that the quality payment system and the extraction-based contracts developed by American Crystal Sugar, the cooperative beet sugar processing company, produced efficiencies for the company. This new payment system induced the growers to supply higher-quality beets that provided more sugar per ton. As a result, processing costs per pound of sugar declined.

Only the cooperative processors currently use the extractable-sugar contract. The traditional, investor-owned companies still use the percent-sugar-content contract. A question remains unanswered: Why is integrated ownership of the beet supply and the processing company needed to use this new type of payment system? If transaction cost economics is applicable to this question, then there must be some aspect of the transaction between beet growers and processors that is different for the cooperatives than for the noncooperatives. Does the degree of asset specificity differ? How does asymmetric information affect the transaction? Are the measurement, negotiating, monitoring, or enforcement costs of the extractable-sugar contract greater in the noncooperatives, causing them to adopt the lower-cost percent-sugar-content contract?

To help answer this question, I must describe the details of the contracts used by noncooperative processors. There are two types of noncooperative contracts: the eastern contract used in Michigan and Ohio and the western "sliding-scale" contract used in all other beet-growing states.

The Eastern Contract

In the eastern contract, growers and processors share revenues and costs at a fixed ratio. Growers receive 53.1 percent of the gross sales of sugar and by-products less 53.1 percent of the marketing costs. Growers also absorb 53.1 percent of the sugar losses that occur in storage. Growers are responsible for 100 percent of the growing costs. Each grower's share of these revenues and costs depends on the amount of sugar a grower delivers. This amount is determined by the percentage sugar content and the number of tons of beets a grower delivers. In turn, the processor receives 46.9 percent of the gross sales less 46.9 percent of the marketing costs and sugar losses. The processor is responsible for 100 percent of the processing costs. This arrangement has been in place for sixty to seventy-five years.

Grower payments are not directly based on impurity levels in the East, but there are incentives for the growers as a group to deliver beets with a lower impurity level. Beets with lower impurity levels will yield more sugar and, as the grower receives a part of all sugar sales, he will benefit if more sugar is produced. His individual contribution to the sugar pool is based only on percentage sugar content, so any individual effort at reducing impurity levels will not be directly rewarded. A grower could "free ride" on the efforts of other growers and benefit from lower average impurity levels even if he does not reduce his individual impurity level. Growers are not responsible for any of the processing costs, so there is no direct incentive for growers to provide beets with a lower impurity level in order to reduce processing costs per pound of refined sugar.

The Western Sliding-Scale Contract

Under the western "sliding-scale" contract, the payment per net ton of beets depends on the average net return per 100 pounds of sugar received by the processing company and the individual sugar content of a grower's beets. The net return for sugar is computed by deducting all marketing and sales expenses (including packaging, liquefying, powdering, and final product storage expenses) from the gross sales price of sugar. The grower is credited for the sugar he delivers according to the sugar content of the beets he delivers and a fixed extraction rate for the factory. For example, if a grower delivers beets with a 17 percent sugar content and the fixed extraction rate is 86 percent, then the grower is credited with delivering 292.4 pounds of sugar per ton:

$$2,000 \text{ pounds per ton} \times .17 \times .86 = 292.4 \text{ pounds.} \qquad (2)$$

In the West, growers receive 60 percent and processors 40 percent of the net sales from sugar. (The western grower's share is larger than the eastern grower's share because western growers receive no part of the revenues from the sugar by-products.) If the net return for sugar were $25 per cwt., the grower would receive fifteen cents per pound of sugar:

$$(\$25 \times .60) / 100 = 15 \text{ cents.} \qquad (3)$$

The grower delivering beets with a 17 percent sugar content would receive a payment of $43.86 per ton of beets:

$$292.4 \text{ pounds} \times .15 = \$43.86. \qquad (4)$$

The key difference in the western contract is that the extraction rate is fixed. The grower benefits if the actual factory extraction rate is less than the fixed rate in the contract. He does not have to share in the reduced revenue from the sale of less sugar. In the same way, the processor benefits if the actual extraction rate is higher than the fixed rate. The processor receives all of the increased revenue from the sale of additional sugar. Currently, the fixed extraction rate in western beet contracts is approximately 85 percent. Some growers benefit because of this; the average extraction rate for the United States over the past twenty years has been 82 percent (U.S. Department of Agriculture 1991, Table 31).

Quality Measures for Noncooperative Processors

The western contracts provide no incentives, either direct or indirect, for growers to reduce impurity levels and increase extraction rates. Thus one should expect that sugar beet quality has not improved over time as it has for the cooperative processor. It has been difficult to find the data to demonstrate this point. Several years of regional level data (corresponding with the expiration of the Sugar Act in 1974 until passage of the new program in 1981) have not been published. In this section, I present three sources of data to support my hypothesis that sugar beet quality has not improved in the West. All three sources show no change or a decline in sugar beet quality in the West, while the cooperative's quality improved.

Table 7.5 shows pounds of sugar per ton of beets increased by 8 percent for American Crystal Sugar in the Red River Valley, while the same measure declined by 8 percent in the West. Table 7.6 also shows that sugar produced per ton of beets sliced has not significantly changed over time in the West. The 1948–1979 mean is 258 pounds and the 1980–1992 mean is 259 pounds. These means are not statistically different. In Table 7.7, the data show that for the United States as a whole, pounds of sugar produced per ton of beets sliced has increased by 4 percent, while American Crystal's increase was 12 percent.[6]

Processing Company Ownership and Contract Type

Why have the noncooperative processors not adopted the extractable-sugar contract to induce growers to supply higher-quality beets? Why is integrated ownership of the supply of beets and the processing company needed to use this new type of payment system? The growers for noncooperatives do not

Table 7.5 Pounds of sugar per ton of beets (crop years)

	American Crystal (Iowa, Minnesota, and North Dakota)	The West
1948–57 mean	243[a]	281[a]
1980–92 mean	263[b]	259[c]
Percentage change	+8%	-8%

Sources: [a] U.S. Beet Sugar Association.
      [b] American Crystal Sugar Company.
      [c] U.S. Department of Agriculture (1985, 1993, 1994).

Table 7.6 The West

Summary	Pounds of sugar per ton of beets (crop years)*
1948–1973 mean	258
1981–1992 mean	259

* For the years 1981–1992, the West includes all states west of the Mississippi, excluding Minnesota and eastern North Dakota. For the years 1948–1973, the West includes Arizona, California, Idaho, Nevada, Oregon, and Washington.

Sources: U.S. Department of Agriculture (1985, 1993, 1994); U.S. Beet Sugar Association. No data published for 1974–1980.

Table 7.7 The United States

Summary	Pounds of sugar per ton of beets (crop years)
1965–1979 mean	248
1980–1990 mean	257
Percentage change (first period to second period)	0.04

Source: U.S. Department of Agriculture (1985, 1993, 1994).

directly benefit from processing cost savings as they are not owners and are not responsible for these costs. The processor should theoretically be able to write an agreement that gives the growers a portion of the processing cost savings for supplying beets with a lower impurity level. In this section, I argue that asymmetric information and the presence of specific assets affect the measurement, negotiating, monitoring, and enforcement costs. For the noncooperatives, it is too costly to adopt the extractable-sugar contract.

The extraction-based contract requires an additional measurement of beet quality, the percentage sugar loss to molasses, by the processor. Asymmetric information is a problem. Processors have an incentive to underreport quality (inflate sugar losses to molasses) and keep more returns for themselves. The costs of monitoring the processor's quality measurements are too high in a traditional, investor-owned firm for the extractable-sugar contract to be useful. Vertical integration of the processing company by the growers reduces these monitoring and measurement costs. The cooperative's board of directors is composed of sugar beet growers. These growers on the board can credibly communicate the benefits of the extractable-sugar contract to their neighbors and fellow growers. Also, as owners of the company, the cooperative growers presumably have greater trust in the quality measurements being made by their own employees.

There is a possible solution to this informational problem for the noncooperatives. A third party could perform the quality measurements. This option is not used. Growers are allowed to observe (or send a representative to observe) the measurement process, but the processing company makes the measurements.

In addition to lower transaction costs, there may be another element of a cooperative structure that is necessary for adoption of the extractable-sugar contract—the cooperative grower's ownership share of the processing company. Under the extractable-sugar contract, growers who supply low-quality beets are paid less. However, in the cooperative, these "low-quality" growers are willing to risk some of their crop returns because, as shareholders in the company, they have an additional investment to protect—their equity investment in the processing company. These growers want to ensure the continued success of their processing company and, in turn, a return to their investment and a long life for their company. Adoption of the extractable-sugar contract has lead to the success of American Crystal Sugar.

The nature of the competitive environment for a grower's land is also important in determining contract type. In the West, beet sugar processors compete with other crops for acreage. For example, in California, sugar beets are ranked nineteenth in crop returns. Because of these crop alternatives, western growers hold a strong bargaining position with processors. These growers will not accept a contract that is more complex, requires more agronomic management on their part, and would result in a loss for growers who could not reduce their impurity levels. Their refusal to sign an extraction-based contract would leave the processor without suppliers if that is the contract the processor insists upon using.

The competitive environment for land in the West also explains why there are no beet sugar processing cooperatives in the West. With a price tag of more than $100 million, these processing facilities are very expensive. The buy-out of such a facility by a cooperative requires a substantial investment by each grower. In 1973, American Crystal's growers each invested $100 per acre. For an average grower, the total investment was $10,000. Western growers have little incentive to make such a large investment to buy out a sugar processing facility when there are several alternative crops that offer higher returns. No grower wants to lock himself into growing sugar beets.

In the Red River Valley, where the cooperatives are located, sugar beets are the highest cash crop that farmers can grow. Red River Valley farmland is a site-specific asset. The value of the land, for other than growing sugar beets, is much lower, as the alternative crop values are smaller. Site specificity of the land in the Red River Valley lead to the vertical integration or buy-out of American Crystal Sugar by its growers. Formation of the cooperative ensured the continued existence of the beet sugar industry in the Red River Valley and a market for these growers' number one cash crop.

Conclusion

The empirical evidence presented here shows that vertical integration has real efficiency consequences. The cooperative beet sugar processor was able to write a contract that induced growers to supply higher-quality beets to the company. By processing higher-quality beets, the cooperative processor lowered its cost of sales. Integrated ownership of the supply of beets and the processing company reduces the transaction costs of the complex contracting that is required to achieve these productive efficiencies.

Notes

1   I owe special thanks to the following for their time and valuable insight into this industry: Doug Sillers; D. Hal Sillers; Robert Levos, James Horvath, and Dave Hilde, American Crystal Sugar Company; Calvin Jones, Holly Sugar Corporation; Robert Young, Great Lakes Sugar Beet Growers Association; and Ben Goodwin, California Beet Growers Association. I would also like to thank Lee Benham, Douglass North, Bruce Petersen, Mary Olson, Randy Nielsen, Bruce Rayton, and Mike Sykuta for helpful comments.

2   See Table 7.2.

3   See Appendix II for the exact specification of the Carruthers Formula.

4   The molasses by-product is used in pharmaceuticals, livestock feeds, and brewer's and baker's yeast. Molasses desugarization is a new technology used to extract sugar normally lost to this by-product. In 1990, Southern Minnesota Beet Sugar Cooperative was the first beet sugar company to add such a facility. American Crystal Sugar Company's molasses desugarization facility was complete in time for fiscal 1994. With this facility, American Crystal expects to produce 1.2 million additional cwt. of sugar per year at no additional on-farm costs.

5   Processing companies have developed storage technologies to help minimize the beet deterioration that occurs in storage. One such technology was developed by American Crystal Sugar in 1984 when it constructed the first covered deep-freeze storage facilities. Freezing beets stops them from burning sugar. By 1990, American Crystal's deep-freeze facilities had a capacity of 500,000 tons of beets.

6   See Table 7.4

References

American Crystal Sugar Co. 1973–1993. *Annual Report*. Moorhead, Minn.

American Sugarbeet Growers Association. 1994. *Directory 1994–1995*. Washington, D.C.

Blake, Richard W. 1967. "Grower-Processor Bargaining in the Sugarbeet Industry." Remarks made at the National Bargaining Conference, New Orleans, La., January 7.

Bonin, J. P., D. C. Jones, and L. Putterman. 1993. "Theoretical and Empirical Studies of Producer Cooperatives: Will Ever the Twain Meet?" *Journal of Economic Literature* 31:1290–1320.

Coase, R. 1937. "The Nature of the Firm." *Economica* 4:386–405.

Craig, B., and J. Pencavel. 1992. "The Behavior of Worker Cooperatives: The Plywood Companies of the Pacific Northwest." *American Economic Review* 82:1083–105.

Federal Trade Commission. 1975. "The U.S. Sugar Industry." Washington, D.C., July.

Goodwin, Ben. 1994. Personal interview with Executive Manager, California Beet Growers Association, Stockton, Calif., September 29.

Goodwin, J. W., and H. E. Drummond. 1982. *Agricultural Economics*. Reston, Va.: Reston Publishing Co.

Grossman, S. J., and O. D. Hart. 1986. "The Costs and Benefits of Ownership: A Theory of Vertical and Lateral Integration." *Journal of Political Economy* 94:691–719.

Hart, O. D. 1991. "Incomplete Contracts and the Theory of the Firm." *The Nature of the Firm: Origins, Evolution, and Development*, ed. O. E. Williamson and S. G. Winter, pp. 138–58. New York, N.Y.: Oxford University Press.

Hilde, D. 1994. Personal interview with General Agronomist, American Crystal Sugar Co., Moorhead, Minn., August 15.

Horvath, J. 1993. Personal interview with Vice President of Finance, American Crystal Sugar Co., Moorhead, Minn., August.

Jacobs, J. 1990a. "Sugarbeet Cooperatives Look to Improved Facilities, Marketing Innovations for '90s." *Farmer Cooperatives*, March, pp. 22–25.

———. 1990b. "Sugarbeet Cooperatives Major Contributors to Economies of Upper Midwest Communities." *Farmer Cooperatives*, February, pp. 4–6.

————. 1992. *Role of Sugarbeet Bargaining Associations.* Washington, D.C.: U.S. Department of Agriculture, Agricultural Cooperative Service, Research Report 108, September.

Jones, C. 1993. Personal interviews with Vice President of Agriculture, Holly Sugar Corporation, Colorado Springs, Colo., February 5.

————. 1994. Personal interviews with Vice President of Agriculture, Holly Sugar Corporation, Colorado Springs, Colo., September 28.

Joskow, P. L. 1985. "Vertical Integration and Long-Term Contracts: The Case of Coal-Burning Electric Generating Plants." *Journal of Law, Economics and Organization* 1:33–80.

————. 1987. "Contract Duration and Relationship-Specific Investments: Empirical Evidence from Coal Markets." *American Economic Review* 77:168–85.

————. 1988. "Price Adjustment in Long-Term Contracts: The Case of Coal." *Journal of Law and Economics* 31:47–83.

————. 1991. "Asset Specificity and the Structure of Vertical Relationships: Empirical Evidence." *The Nature of the Firm: Origins, Evolution, and Development*, ed. O. E. Williamson and S.G. Winter, pp. 117–37. New York, N.Y.: Oxford University Press.

Klein, B., R. G. Crawford, and A. A. Alchian. 1978. "Vertical Integration, Appropriable Rents, and the Competitive Contracting Process." *Journal of Law and Economics* 21:297–326.

Klein, P. G., and H. A. Shelanski. 1994. "Empirical Research in Transaction Cost Economics: A Survey and Assessment." Business and Public Policy Working Paper BPP-60, Center for Research in Management, Haas School of Business, University of California–Berkeley, June.

Koenig, J. R. 1996. "Vertical Integration and Contracts: Application to the U.S. Beet Sugar Industry." Ph.D. dissertation, Washington University.

Leffler, K. B., and R. R. Rucker. 1991. "Transactions Costs and the Efficient Organization of Production: A Study of Timber-Harvesting Contracts." *Journal of Political Economy* 99:1060–87.

Levos, R. 1992. Personal interview with Vice President of Agriculture, American Crystal Sugar Co., Moorhead, Minn., December.

Masten, S. 1984. "The Organization of Production: Evidence From the Aerospace Industry." *Journal of Law and Economics* 27:403–17.

Masten, S., and K. J. Crocker. 1985. "Efficient Adaptation in Long-Term Contracts: Take-or-Pay Provisions for Natural Gas." *American Economic Review* 75:1083–93.

Masten, S., J. Meehan, and E. Snyder. 1989. "Vertical Integration in the U.S. Auto Industry: A Note on the Influence of Specific Assets." *Journal of Economic Behavior and Organization* 12:265–73.

May, W. J., Jr. 1989. *The Great Western Sugarlands.* New York, N.Y.: Garland Publishing.

Minnesota Historical Society. 1985. *Guide to the Records of the American Crystal Sugar Company.* St. Paul, Minn.

Monteverde, K., and D. Teece. 1982. "Supplier Switching Costs and Vertical Integration in the Automobile Industry." *Bell Journal of Economics* 13:206–13.

Northwest Minnesota Historical Center. 1993. *A Guide to the Collections of the Red River Valley Sugar Beet Growers Association.* Moorhead, Minn.: Moorhead State University.

Rhodes, V. J. 1983. "The Large Agricultural Cooperative as a Competitor." *American Journal of Agricultural Economics* 65:1090–95.

Sexton, R. J. 1986. "The Formation of Cooperatives: A Game-Theoretic Approach with Implications for Cooperative Finance, Decision Making, and Stability." *American Journal of Agricultural Economics* 68:214–25.

Sillers, D. 1992. Personal interview, American Crystal Sugar Co., Moorhead, Minn., December.

Sillers, D. H. 1992. Personal interview, American Crystal Sugar Co., Moorhead, Minn., December.

United States Beet Sugar Association. 1959. *The Beet Sugar Story*. Washington, D.C.

U.S. Department of Agriculture. 1975. *Sugar Statistics and Related Data*, vol. 2. Washington, D.C.: Agricultural Stabilization and Conservation Service, Sugar Division, Statistical Bulletin 244.

———. 1985. *Sugar and Sweetener: Situation and Outlook Yearbook*. Washington, D.C.: Economic Research Service, Commodity Economics Division.

———. 1991. *U.S. Sugar Statistical Compendium*. Washington, D.C.: Economic Research Service, Commodity Economics Division.

———. 1993. *Sugar and Sweetener: Situation and Outlook Yearbook*. Washington, D.C.: Economic Research Service, Commodity Economics Division.

———. 1994. *Sugar and Sweetener: Situation and Outlook Yearbook*. Washington, D.C.: Economic Research Service, Commodity Economics Division.

U.S. Department of Commerce. *1987 Census of Agriculture*. Washington, D.C.: Bureau of the Census.

———. *1987 Census of Manufactures*. Washington, D.C.: Bureau of the Census.

———. *1992 Census of Agriculture*. Washington, D.C.: Bureau of the Census.

Wiggins, Steven N. 1991. "The Economics of the Firm and Contracts: A Selective Survey." *Journal of Institutional and Theoretical Economics* 14:603–61.

Williamson, O. E. 1985. *The Economic Institutions of Capitalism*. New York, N.Y.: Free Press.

Young, R. 1993. Personal interview with Executive Vice President. Great Lakes Sugar Beet Growers Association, Saginaw, Mich., March 24.

———. 1994. Personal interview with Executive Vice President. Great Lakes Sugar Beet Growers Association, Saginaw, Mich., September 15.

Appendix I

The Production of Beet Sugar

Through the process of photosynthesis, chloroplasts in the leaves of the sugar beet use the sun's energy to combine oxygen, carbon, and hydrogen to form sugar which is then stored in the root. All plants make sugar in some form. Sugar cane and sugar beet plants produce and store more sugar than other plants. It is also easy to extract the sugar from these plants. The sugar (technically sucrose) extracted from cane and beets is chemically identical. Estimated sugar production in the United States for October, 1992–September, 1993, was 4.3 million tons of beet sugar and 3.4 million tons of cane sugar. In 1987, according to the Census of Manufactures (U.S. Department of Commerce), the total value of shipments for establishments in SIC code 2063, beet sugar, was $1.8 billion.

The sugar beet root is cream colored and, on average, weighs two pounds and is a foot long. Each root contains about sixteen teaspoons of sugar. Sugar beets are only used for the production of sugar. They are not consumed by humans as are red beets.

White crystal sugar, powdered sugar, and brown sugar are produced from sugar beets and sugarcane. These products are sold to wholesalers, retailers, and food manufacturers. The by-products of sugar beets are pulp and molasses. Pulp is fed to dairy cattle. Molasses is used in pharmaceuticals, fed to livestock, and used in the production of brewer's and baker's yeast.

Sugar beets also have value as a rotation crop. The large root system fertilizes and aerates the soil to a depth of seven feet. The cultivation required in the production of the sugar beet crop is another reason for its value as a rotation crop. Sugar beets must be cultivated between the rows and between the plants in each row. This loosening of the soil improves the soil's physical condition. Weeds are destroyed while they are still young and their reseeding and spread is prevented.

Sugar beets are grown in California, Idaho, Oregon, Colorado, Minnesota, Montana, Nebraska, North Dakota, Texas, Wyoming, Michigan, and Ohio. The costs of growing beets vary in the United States from region to region. The lowest costs are in Minnesota, North Dakota, Michigan, and Ohio. The main reason for the cost differences is irrigation costs. Beets in Minnesota, North Dakota, Michigan, and Ohio are not irrigated.

The growing and harvesting of beets require some specific equipment. Planters and cultivators are not specific. They can be adapted to use with different crops. Harvesting equipment is specific. Beet growers also need several trucks for the harvest, and these trucks are not necessarily used at any other time in the year. In California, much of the harvest is done by "custom operators." Only perhaps 30 percent of the growers in California own their own harvesting equipment.

Sugar beets must be processed close to the fields where they are grown. One reason for this is transportation. One acre of land can produce from 15 to 26 tons of beets. Trucks used for hauling beets from the field to the factory can carry 20 to 25 tons or 40 to 45 tons. If one farmer has 200 acres of sugar beets, it will require between 100 to 200 loads to transport all of his beets to the plant. A second reason that beets are processed close to the fields where they are grown is that beets are perishable. Once harvested, sugar beets burn sugar to stay alive. Therefore, sugar beets must be processed on the day they are harvested or frozen until they can be processed.

In regions where it freezes and stays cold for an extended period of time, harvests are stockpiled. Beets are piled in plant yards and stored until they can be processed. There are also some covered deep-freeze storage facilities in Minnesota and North Dakota.

Since the beginning of the beet sugar industry in the United States in 1879, sugar beets have always been grown under a contract. The contract is between the grower and the processor and stipulates how payment is determined, the harvest and delivery dates, the delivery location, the type of seed to be used, and growing practices. These contracts are used to protect both the processor and the grower. The processor must ensure an adequate supply of beets for his factory and the grower needs to ensure a market for his product; his sugar beets will only be useful to a sugar processor. No individual grower negotiates his contract with a processing company. Regional sugar beet grower associations negotiate the contract for their member growers. One grower's contract differs from his neighbor's only with regard to the number of acres and description of the land to be planted.

The beet sugar refining process is essentially the same for all companies. The beets are first washed and then sliced into strips called cossettes. Second, in the diffusion process, the cossettes are immersed in hot water to remove the sugar. The cossettes, free of sugar, are dried and pelletized to make the pulp by-product. The sugar-water solution is called "raw juice." Impurities are removed from the raw juice. A heavy, syrup-like liquid is left. This liquid is boiled until the sugar in it crystallizes. Centrifugal machines are used to separate the sugar crystals from the syrup or the molasses by-product. New technology, molasses desugarization, allows the processor to obtain more sugar from the molasses. In the final production step, the white crystals, now separated from the syrup, are dried. The final product is ready for packaging.

Beet sugar processing factories are large and technically complex. They are very capital intensive. The last processing plant constructed in the United States (built in 1976) cost more than $60 million. Today's costs would be more than $100 million. Several studies suggest that to operate efficiently, a plant must have a daily slicing capacity of 4,000 to 5,000 tons. To supply such a facility (if it operated for 180 days per year), about 55,000 acres of beets would need to be harvested each year. Allowing for a three- to five-year rotation per sugar beet crop, a factory would need at least 200,000 acres of land to support it.

Appendix II

Calculation of Sugar Loss to Molasses

The impurity level and the amount of recoverable sugar are negatively correlated. The main impurities found in beets are sodium (Na), potassium (K), and amino nitrogen (Am-N). The amounts of these elements present in the beet root are measured in parts per million (ppm). These elements combine with other elements to form several kinds of salts. The presence of these salts prevents a certain amount of sugar from crystallizing. The factors for converting the single impurity elements to salts are 3.5 for Na, 2.5 for K, and 9.5 for Am-N.

Carruthers Formula:

(developed by Dr. A. Carruthers of the British Sugar Corporation in the 1960s).

Percent Sugar Loss to Molasses =

$$\left\{ \frac{(ppm\ Na \times 3.5) + (ppm\ K \times 2.5) + (ppm\ Am\!-\!N \times 9.5)}{11,000} \right\} \times 1.5$$

where 1.5 is a standard factor representing 60 percent purity molasses.

Example (using 1993 crop averages for American Crystal Sugar):

$$\left\{ \frac{(469 \times 3.5) + (2,016 \times 2.5) + (450 \times 9.5)}{11,000} \right\} \times 1.5 = \begin{array}{l} 1.495\% \text{ sugar loss} \\ \text{to molasses} \end{array}$$

8 Microeconomics of Agricultural Commodity Grading: Impacts on the Marketing Channel

DAVID A. HENNESSY[1]

Although much work has been done on grading and standards in agricultural marketing, very little has been analytic in nature. The emphasis has been on the determinants and welfare impacts of grading and quality standards (French and Nuckton; Powers). In this paper, microeconomic theory is used to analyze how a grading structure affects resource allocation along the marketing channel. The model emphasizes the role of resources in protecting value and identifies coordination failures between agents along the marketing channel.

Consider the case of the fresh apple industry. While there are many variants on preparing fresh, raw apples for market, a typical sequence of operations is outlined below. After harvest, apples are transported and stored. When the market demands, they are removed from storage and enter the packing line. They are washed, sponged, and air-dried. Waxing is next, followed by a second drying. They are then sorted according to color and size. Culls are removed, and the remaining apples are graded, packed, and shipped. Each operation in this sequence is called a "transformation," and the associated skill a "transformation skill." The words "transformation" and "operation" are used interchangeably. The word "processing" is avoided because it has connotations of a particular subset of transformations. The purpose of this paper is to identify how grade prices affect the level and location of transformation skills along the food marketing chain. The paper will show how resources are allocated to protect the potential value of produce.

There are many perspectives on the motives for grading. Almost all include a quality control aspect, though French, Tamimi, and Nuckton suggested that, with marketing order legislation, "quality controls are really disguised volume controls." French and Nuckton showed how volume controls can be used to ensure orderly marketing in markets with inelastic demand and unpredictable supply. Quality control may play a similar role. In his study of producer surplus maximization, Price explicitly linked the quality and quantity control aspects to determine the producer surplus-maximizing discard grade. Produce below this grade is discarded, and consumers buy average bundles of the remaining produce. Nguyen and Vo generalized on Price's model. Others (e.g., Bockstael 1987) placed the grading system in the context of Rosen's (1974) hedonic pricing model in which the continuum of markets is precluded by the high cost of setting up a market.

The information attribute of grades has motivated another strand of the literature. Grades are used to identify quality for the purpose of transactions in which participants cannot inspect the produce. Further, even without a codified grading system, processors may sort and discard produce that could not be processed further profitably (Armbruster and Jesse). Thus a grading system, even with minimum quality standards, could be the formalization of a language, a public good, whereby all would benefit from the resulting precision and honesty.

At the retail level, if the consumer can identify accurately, or at least as well as graders, the quality of produce, then the only benefit of grading is that it may be more efficient to do so at an aggregate level rather than inconvenience the consumer. In this case, it has been shown (Bockstael 1984) that minimum quality standards cannot increase, and probably will decrease, net social welfare. The role of minimum quality standards may be to increase social welfare whereby quality improvement incurs costs, but consumers cannot identify quality at the point of purchase. This information asymmetry between producers and consumers implies that bad goods drive out the good because there is no reward for quality enhancement, and so the market may be undermined (Akerlof). Reliable grading and minimum quality standards will assure the customer of the market's integrity.

In this paper, a self-protection model (Ehrlich and Becker; Hiebert; Shogren) is constructed that demonstrates how resources in the marketing channel are allocated to protect value. It is also shown that quality enters the food chain multiplicatively. Similar models of multiplicative effects have been analyzed by Rosen (1981) and Kremer while more general models have been specified by Danø (Chapter VIII). This multiplicative aspect of the model may cause coordination failures. Such coordination failures can have far-reaching implications for the structure of processing. They also have interesting implications for sectoral development, and may explain how, in a full information or symmetric information situation, minimum quality standards could improve welfare. This multiplicative attribute can also magnify resource allocation alterations caused by imperfect information. The model's emphasis on coordination failures and imperfect information highlights the potential economic benefits from the provision of extension services to post-harvest agribusiness.

The Model

Production theory has focused almost exclusively on the volume aspects of production at the expense of quality considerations. In the model presented below, the technology of production is partitioned into two distinct sets. First, inputs are transformed into raw produce, i.e., apples. Second, the raw produce is transformed for final consumption. Simplifying, it is assumed that in the first stage, yield is determined, while in the second stage, quality is determined. This paper focuses on second-stage operations. In the fresh apple context, such second-stage operations would include harvesting, storage, transportation, packing, and perhaps some preharvest cosmetic spray or water applications.

These operations are modeled as being performed in a binary manner, good or bad. The probability that the outcome of the transformation is "good" characterizes the skill level associated with the operation in question.[2] The probability of a "good" outcome is determined by the level of resources applied to acquiring the skill. Thus the self-protection model (Ehrlich and Becker) developed here permits agents to have some, but not complete, control over outcomes. For the sake of clarity, in this model only two transformations, the outcomes of which are independent, are considered. These are transformation 1 and transformation 2, each with binary outcomes denoted by $\{g, b\}$ for $\{$good, bad$\}$. Thus the sample space contains four elements, each of which can be described by $\{i, j\}$ where i and j can be either g or b. Each element is mapped onto a retail price as follows: element $\{g, g\}$ maps to P_a; $\{g, b\}$ maps to $P_b < P_a$; $\{b, g\}$ maps to $P_c < P_a$; and $\{b, b\}$ maps to $P_d < \min[P_b, P_c]$. Let the probability that transformation 1 is "good" be q_1, and that transformation 2 is "good" be q_2.

In the initial analysis, it is assumed that the decision maker cannot respond ex post to event 1 by differentiating between the q_2 associated with a "good" outcome 1 and a "bad" outcome 1. This may be because the transformations are simultaneous or because sequential transformations are coupled; in either case, the decision maker has no flexibility. An example of the "sequential, no flexibility" case is one in which fresh apples are transported and stored, but the packer cannot store poorly transported and well-transported apples any differently. The levels of q_1 and q_2 are allowed to be monotonically increasing and concave in inputs X_1 and X_2, respectively. While the probability couple (q_1, q_2) a firm faces depends on many things including effort, innate managerial abilities, local extension, communications infrastructure, and the level of training acquired by the decision maker, for simplicity it is assumed that X_1 and X_2 are the levels of effort applied to the respective tasks. Expected price per unit, P_e, may be written as

$$P_e = P_a q_1 q_2 + P_b q_1 (1 - q_2)$$
$$+ P_c (1 - q_1) q_2 + P_d (1 - q_1)(1 - q_2). \tag{1}$$

Only expected profit-maximizing agents will be considered in this model.[3] Denote the costs of effort as w. Net profit per unit is

$$\pi = P_e - w(X_1 + X_2) - P_0 \tag{2}$$

where P_0 is the unit price of raw produce. If the processing chain is vertically integrated, then one decision maker chooses (X_1, X_2). In this case, (X_1, X_2) is chosen to satisfy

$$\frac{\partial P_e}{\partial q_1} \frac{\partial q_1}{\partial X_1} - w = 0 \tag{3a}$$

$$\frac{\partial P_e}{\partial q_2} \frac{\partial q_2}{\partial X_2} - w = 0 \tag{3b}$$

where

$$\frac{\partial P_e}{\partial q_1} = [P_a - P_c] q_2 + [P_b - P_d](1 - q_2) \tag{4a}$$

$$\frac{\partial P_e}{\partial q_2} = [P_a - P_b]q_1 + [P_c - P_d](1 - q_1). \tag{4b}$$

For the moment, the second-order conditions for maximization are assumed to hold, but this issue will be revisited when stability and equilibrium are considered. If the processing chain is not vertically integrated, then input X_1 (input X_2) will be chosen to satisfy equation (3a) (equation (3b)) for a given level of input X_2 (input X_1). This may give rise to suboptimization as described by Danø (pp. 151–56).

The joint-profit-maximization, or vertically-integrated-industry, problem is analyzed first. The nonintegrated-industry problem will be considered later. Both (4a) and (4b) are positive because $P_a > \max[P_b, P_c] \geq \min[P_b, P_c] > P_d$. We would like to understand what influences the choice of (X_1, X_2), i.e., the choices of effort. In the simplest case, if q_1 and q_2 are identical functions of effort and if $P_b > (=) (<) P_c$, then, by manipulating (3a) and (3b), it is found that $X_1 > (=) < X_2$.

Also, given an increase in X_1, the optimum value of X_2 will increase (decrease) if $\partial^2\pi/\partial X_1\partial X_2 > (<) 0$. Evaluate this expression to get

$$\frac{\partial^2\pi}{\partial X_1\partial X_2} = \Delta^2 \frac{\partial q_1}{\partial X_1} \frac{\partial q_2}{\partial X_2}, \tag{5}$$

where $\Delta^2 = P_a - P_b - P_c + P_d$. Thus X_1 and X_2 are complements if $\Delta^2 > 0$. This means that the price drop due to one defect, $P_a - P_b$ or $P_a - P_c$, exceeds the price drop due to a second defect given the first defect, $P_b - P_d$ or $P_c - P_d$. Alternatively, Δ^2 may be interpreted as $\partial^2 P_e/\partial q_1\partial q_2$, the rate at which the marginal change in expected price as one skill increases changes as the other skill increases. It is analogous to the stochastic complementarity and substitutability conditions found by Hiebert to be important in signing the effects of self-insurance and self-protection.

Because

$$\frac{\partial^2\pi}{\partial X_1^2} = \frac{\partial P_e}{\partial q_1} \frac{\partial^2 q_1}{\partial X_1^2} < 0,$$

condition (3a) holds that an increase in X_1 decreases the value marginal product of X_1 $((\partial P_e/\partial q_1)/(\partial q_1/\partial X_1))$, and denoted by $VMPX_1$). However, $VMPX_1$ increases (decreases) with an increase in X_2 if $\Delta^2 > (<) 0$. Therefore, condition (3a) implies that a sufficient condition for optimum X_1 to increase (decrease), given an exogenous increase in X_2, is that $\Delta^2 > (<) 0$.

If the quality index is additive in the number of defects, and if the fall in quality due to defect i (given defect j) equals the fall in quality due to defect i (given defect j) not occurring, then the condition $\Delta^2 > (<) 0$ means that the retail price is convex (concave) in quality. If $\Delta^2 > 0$, then a mandate to improve a skill (e.g., transportation infrastructure) will either increase the demand for the other skill (e.g., storage infrastructure) or drive the industry out of business. Further, given $\Delta^2 > 0$, if q_1 is influenced positively by extension advice, then not only does the advice increase q_1, but it also induces an increase in q_2.

These examples illustrate how a virtuous circle may evolve in a region. A crop area with high-quality apple packers may attract a good storage infrastructure, quality educational services, good agricultural engineering contractors, etc., thus creating a major, integrated, high value-added growing region. Note further that, in assessing the potential of a region, the weakest link in the chain must be evaluated critically. For example, it is very difficult to alter the microclimate of a region. If a poor local microclimate causes low-quality produce at farm level, then the region will not attract high-quality services. A regional planner must either try to solve the microclimate problem through research and/or extension, or abandon hope of creating a high-value-added production area.

How product transformers in a region will form business alliances may also be deduced from equation (5). If $\Delta^2 > 0$, then high-quality (low-quality) providers of a transformation skill will ally with high-quality (low-quality) providers of the other skill. If $\Delta^2 < 0$, then high-quality (low-quality) providers of a transformation skill will ally with low-quality (high-quality) providers of the other skill. In the case where $\Delta^2 > 0$, high-quality transformers will reject low-quality produce sources because this produce would reduce the marginal productivity of their effort relative to high-quality produce. In this case, providers of low-quality transformations will not buy produce upon which a high-quality transformation has been performed because high-quality providers of the transformation that they perform can outbid them. Thus the region may naturally polarize into a processing chain of high-quality transformations and a chain of low-quality transformations. Kremer found this result in the simple case where $P_b = P_c = P_d = 0$ and likened it to Becker's assortative mating conclusion.

What does this mean for the relationship between raw material and produce as it is presented to the consumer? Quality raw material may receive a lot of attention so that, in probability, it remains high quality when presented to the consumer, while lower quality material is denied attention so that it may be of very low quality indeed when presented to the consumer. Note, if there is very little variability in the quality of raw material, two almost identical units of raw material may be of greatly different quality when retailed, and so their retail prices may differ substantially.

Changing the Grade Prices

Thus far, the relationships between skill (probability) levels, given a fixed set of grade prices, have been studied. In this section, the effects of changes in grade prices on the effort applied to different tasks and the demand for different skill levels are studied. The effect of a change in P_d, where neither transformation has been performed well, on effort when joint profit is being maximized, is analyzed first. Intuitively, one might expect that an increase in P_d would decrease the effort applied to both transformations because the expected return to effort (premium for performing tasks well) is reduced; and effort, through the concavity of q_1 and q_2, is subject to the law of decreasing marginal returns. However, cross effects come into play. Suppose that an increase in P_d decreases the effort X_2. It is possible that the decrease in X_2 increases $VMPX_1$ by such an amount that this indirect effect outweighs the direct X_1-decreasing effect of an increase in P_d. Because the effect of X_2 on the $VMPX_1$ is given by

$$\frac{\partial^2 \pi}{\partial X_1 \partial X_2} = \Delta^2 \frac{\partial q_1}{\partial X_1} \frac{\partial q_2}{\partial X_2}$$

a decrease in X_2 decreases X_1 if $\Delta^2 > 0$. Therefore, $\Delta^2 > 0$ is a sufficient condition for an increase in P_d to decrease both X_1 and X_2, provided that the second-order conditions hold for the maximization of (2). A comparative static analysis of the first-order conditions demonstrates this to be true.[4] Further, an increase in P_a increases both X_1 and X_2 if $\Delta^2 > 0$ because it increases the penalty for performing a transformation poorly. Similarly, for an increase in P_b (P_c), it is found that $\Delta^2 > 0$ is a sufficient condition to ensure that X_1 increases (decreases) and X_2 decreases (increases). The reason is that price P_b (P_c) is paid for a product where transformation 1 (transformation 2) is performed well and transformation 2 (transformation 1) is performed poorly.

Next, the effect of a mean-preserving spread (m.p.s.) in the grading structure on the demand for q_1 is investigated. Here, to simplify, the endogeneity of q_1 and q_2 is suppressed; i.e., q_1 and q_2 are considered to be constants. Using (1), let P_a increase and P_c decrease to compensate,

$$\left.\frac{\partial P_c}{\partial P_a}\right|_{dP_e = 0 = dP_b = dP_d} = -\frac{q_1}{1 - q_1}. \tag{6}$$

Using this relationship, it is found that

$$\left.\frac{\partial^2 \pi}{\partial q_1 \partial P_a}\right|_{dP_e = 0 = dP_b = dP_d} = q_2 + \frac{q_1 q_2}{1 - q_1} = \frac{q_2}{1 - q_1} > 0. \tag{7}$$

The value marginal product for q_1, and so the demand for q_1 given an m.p.s. in (P_a, P_c), increases because the price premium for attribute 1, given a success in event 2, increases. The price premium for successful event 1, given unsuccessful event 2, $P_b - P_d$, does not change. Similarly, from the symmetry of the problem, an m.p.s. in (P_b, P_d), holding P_e and other prices constant, can be shown to increase demand for q_1. Now let P_a rise and P_b fall to compensate. This gives

$$\left.\frac{\partial P_b}{\partial P_a}\right|_{dP_e = 0 = dP_c = dP_d} = -\frac{q_2}{1 - q_2}.$$

Using this relationship, it is found that

$$\left.\frac{\partial^2 \pi}{\partial q_1 \partial P_a}\right|_{dP_e = 0 = dP_c = dP_d} = q_1 - \frac{(1 - q_1) q_2}{1 - q_2} = 0.$$

Directly, given P_e and q_2, the demand for q_1 is unaffected by an increase in P_a at the expense of P_b. This is because P_a and P_b occur under a successful event

1 outcome. Indirectly, a mean-preserving increase in P_a, at the expense of P_b, will increase the demand for q_2, which will induce an increase in the demand for q_1 if $\Delta^2 > 0$. The same logic can be used to get similar results for the effect on q_1 of an increase in P_c at the expense of P_d.

In this section, the concavity of joint profit in (X_1, X_2) was assumed when studying the effects of changes in grade prices. The concavity property is important not only in signing comparative statics, but also because it ensures a unique equilibrium. In the next section, the model's second-order conditions, the implications for equilibrium, and how these may relate to minimum quality standards are considered.

Equilibrium, Stability, and Minimum Quality

Perhaps one of the reasons that minimum quality standard regulations have received slight analytic attention is that this regulation type does not lend itself to comparative static analysis. In this section, it will first be shown that one can expect no simple, global understanding of the economic implications of minimum quality standards. Denote quality by $s(X, \xi)$ where $s(X, \xi) = m(X) + \xi$. Here $m(\cdot)$ is monotonically increasing, X denotes effort, and ξ is an additive stochastic component with a probability density function $f(\xi)$. There is a minimum quality standard, $\bar{m}$, above which produce receives a fixed price, $\bar{P}$, and below which the price is zero. The cost of X is denoted by the increasing, convex function $V(X)$. Thus X is chosen to maximize

$$\bar{P} \int_{\bar{m}-m(X)}^{\infty} f(\xi)d\xi - V(X). \tag{8}$$

The first-order condition is

$$\bar{P} f(\bar{m}-m(X)) \, m' - V' = 0 \tag{9}$$

where a prime denotes a differentiation. There is no guarantee that there is a unique solution to (9). This is because of the presence of an evaluation of the density function. The underlying problem is the nonuniformity of curvature of price as a function of quality.[5] Differentiate (9) with respect to X and $\bar{m}$, to get

$$\frac{\partial X}{\partial \bar{m}} = \frac{\bar{P}f'm'}{\bar{P}(m')^2f' + V'' - \bar{P}m''f} \tag{10}$$

where a double prime denotes a second differentiation. If $m(\cdot)$ is concave, and if the slope of the density function evaluated at $\xi = \bar{m} - m(X)$ is positive, then the minimum standard increases effort and, therefore, mean quality. If $f(\cdot)$ is unimodal and close to being symmetric, then an increase in a low minimum quality standard will probably increase quality while an increase in a high minimum standard may cause the industry to collapse. It will now be demonstrated that the existence of, and an increase in, a low minimum quality standard may increase welfare.

As before, let there occur two transformation operations in the marketing channel. The per-unit profit function is equation (2), as presented previously with first-order conditions (3a) and (3b). Partially differentiate (3a) to get

$$\frac{\partial X_1}{\partial X_2} = \frac{-\Delta^2(\partial q_1/\partial X_1)(\partial q_2/\partial X_2)}{(\partial^2 q_1/\partial X_1^2)(\partial P_e/\partial q_1)}. \tag{11}$$

This is positive (negative) if $\Delta^2 > (<) 0$. Similarly, from condition (3b), X_2 will increase (decrease) with an increase in X_1 if $\Delta^2 > (<) 0$. Because the slopes are of the same sign, there is no guarantee of a unique solution, (X_1^*, X_2^*). There may be multiple equilibria. Cooper and John show that a sufficient condition for multiple equilibria is that the $\partial X_1/\partial X_2$ from condition (3a) and the $\partial X_2/\partial X_1$ from condition (3b), evaluated at a Nash equilibrium, be greater than one.[6,7] If both conditions hold, then it can be shown that concavity is necessarily violated. If $\partial^2\pi/\partial X_1\partial X_2 > 0$, that is, if $\Delta^2 > 0$, then the highest crossing is joint profit maximizing. Therefore, if different transformation operations are run by different agents, an industry may languish in an equilibrium that does not maximize joint profit. This may suggest a motive for vertical integration.

Also, the minimum quality standard may be a mechanism for forcing an industry to a higher equilibrium. If all agents realize that an industry is operating at a low equilibrium, all may consent to minimum standards provided that either the profits associated with each operation increase or side payments are made. In a vertically integrated industry, the task of coordination will be easier. Consumers may benefit from a minimum quality standard, relative to a suboptimum status quo, because the increase in sector productivity may outweigh the possible waste of some substandard produce.

Until now it has been assumed that, while the outcomes of transformations 1 and 2 are random, the probability of their occurrence, q_1 and q_2, are fixed, given the level of resources applied to these transformations. However, the determinants of q_1 and q_2, (i.e., effort, education, and innate ability) may not be measurable. The associated uncertainty concerning the actual levels of q_1 and q_2 will affect the willingness of transformers to invest in upgrading skills and in applying their full effort. In the next section, the effects of this uncertainty on the quality of product transformations will be analyzed.

Uncertainty of Effort

There are many ways in which uncertainty of effort can be introduced into the model. One way is that agent 1 may employ agent 2 at a fixed wage to complete transformation 2, but he may not be sure about how hard his employee works. In this case, agent 2 is indifferent to the effort decision of agent 1. Another way is that agents 1 and 2 control transformations 1 and 2, respectively, that the incentive structure is conducive to maximizing expected joint profit, and that there is uncertainty about the effectiveness of agent 2's effort. Each of these two cases will be investigated in turn. The general model is a variant of Shogren's stochastic self-protection model.

Let the uncertainty about the effectiveness of X_2 be summarized by adding a zero mean, white-noise, random variable, ω, to X_2. If effort is measured in terms of productive hours worked, then ω can be interpreted as uncertainty concerning productive hours worked. Agent 1, a maximizer of expected profit, seeks to maximize over X_1 the value of

$$\mathcal{L} = P_a q_1(X_1)E\{q_2(X_2+\omega)\} + P_b q_1(X_1)[1 - E\{q_2(X_2+\omega)\}]$$

$$+ P_c[1 - q_1(X_1)]E\{q_2(X_2+\omega)\}$$

$$+ P_d[1 - q_1(X_1)][1 - E\{q_2(X_2+\omega)\}]$$

$$- w(X_1 + X_2) - P_0$$

(12)

where $E\{\cdot\}$ denotes the expectation over ω, and where w is the unit opportunity cost of effort. For the employer-employee case, the following result holds:

PROPOSITION 1: *If both q_1 and q_2 are concave in effort, then an m.p.s. in the riskiness of agent 2 (the employee) effort will decrease (increase) agent 1 (the employer) effort when $\Delta^2 > (<)\, 0$.*

Proof. Denote the cumulative density function for ω by $F(\omega;\gamma)$, where γ is an index of mean-preserving riskiness. The first-order condition is

$$\{\, [P_a - P_b - P_c + P_d] \int_{-\infty}^{\infty} q_2(X_2 + \omega)\, dF(\omega;\gamma)$$

$$+ [P_b - P_d]\,\}\, \frac{\partial q_1}{\partial X_1}\, -\, w\, =\, 0.$$

(13)

Denote the term in braces by H. It can be shown to be positive by factoring out $P_b - P_d$ and noting that $P_b - P_d > 0$ and $P_a - P_c > 0$. Differentiate (13) partially with respect to X_1 and γ, to get

$$\frac{\partial X_1}{\partial \gamma}\, =\, \frac{-\, \Delta^2\, (\partial q_1/\partial X_1)\, \partial \left[\int_{-\infty}^{\infty} q_2(X_2 + \omega)\, dF(\omega;\gamma) \right] / \partial \gamma}{(\partial^2 q_1/\partial X_1^2)\, H}.$$

(14)

The denominator is negative because of the concavity of $q_1(\cdot)$. For a concave function, the expression

$$\partial \left[\int_{-\infty}^{\infty} q_2(X_2 + \omega)\, dF(\omega;\gamma) \right] / \partial \gamma$$

is negative (Rothschild and Stiglitz). The results follow from evaluating (14) when $\Delta^2 > (<)\, 0$.

Note that a second-degree stochastically dominated change in the distribution of ω can be decomposed into a reduction (or no change) in the mean of ω added to mean-preserving spreads. Further, a reduction in the mean of ω is equivalent to a reduction in X_2. Therefore, from this decomposition of a second-degree stochastically dominated shift (SSD) in the riskiness of effort, from proposition 1 and from equation (11), it can be concluded that if both q_1 and q_2 are concave in effort, then an SSD in the riskiness of employee effort will decrease (increase) employer effort according as $\Delta^2 > (<) 0$.

Having considered the employer-employee case, the effect of uncertainty when the two transformations are conducted by independent operators will now be addressed.

PROPOSITION 2: *If the incentive structure is conducive to expected joint profit maximization, the second-order conditions for concavity of joint profit in (X_1, X_2) hold and the third derivative of q_2 is negative, then X_2 decreases with an m.p.s. of ω, while X_1 increases (decreases) with an m.p.s. of ω if $\Delta^2 < (>) 0$.*[8]

The motive of agent 2 is easiest to understand. If the third derivative of q_2 is negative, then the first-order condition facing agent 2 is concave in ω, i.e., the derivative of (12) with respect to X_2 is concave in ω. An m.p.s. will decrease the first-order condition away from equilibrium, and a decrease in X_2 is the only action available to agent 2 to restore equilibrium (Diamond and Stiglitz, p. 340). The forces at play here have been identified by Shogren (Proposition 2). This reduction affects agent 1 through the effect of X_2 on $VMPX_1$; i.e., through Δ^2 as previously discussed.

Vertical integration and extension services may be interpreted as methods of improving information flows between different transformation operations. The two propositions show that, while vertical integration and extension services will increase expected profit, the effects on X_1 and X_2 are not at all clear. It is worth noting that the sign of Δ^2 is generally a necessary and sufficient condition to sign effects in this paper. This is in contrast to the self-protection model of Hiebert where, due to utility function considerations, stochastic complementarity (substitutability) turns out to be either necessary or sufficient, but not both.

Until now, this paper has modeled only operations that either occur simultaneously, or in sequence, but in which agents cannot react to prior outcomes. In the next section, agents are permitted the flexibility of reacting to prior outcomes. The section will identify how a company allocates its resources along the product transformation chain. In the case of fresh apples, flexibility would permit allocating resources of different skill levels to shipping extra fancy versus fancy apples.

Quality in a Flexible, Sequential Model

Consider a two-operation scenario with $P_a > \max[P_b, P_c] \geq \min[P_b, P_c] > P_d$. The schematics are laid out in Figure 8.1. The unit price of the raw material remains P_0 as before. Operation 1 succeeds with probability q. The price of the intermediate good, given that operation 1 is a success, is P_h. Given a successful operation 1, the probability of a successful operation 2 is q_h. This probability is determined by the quality of resources applied to operation 2 for produce where operation 1 is a success. Two successful operations render a retail price of P_a whereas an initial success followed by a failure renders a retail price of P_b. The price of the intermediate good, given a failed operation 1, is P_{low}. Given a failed operation 1, the probability of a successful operation 2 is q_{low}. An initial failure followed by a success renders a retail price of P_c, while two failures render a retail price of P_d.

To simplify the analysis, the probabilities of successful outcomes, (q, q_{low}, q_h), are made exogenous; i.e., effort is not modeled.[9] The question to be addressed is where to place high-quality resources, i.e., resources with low failure rates. In the second operation, should quality resources be applied to

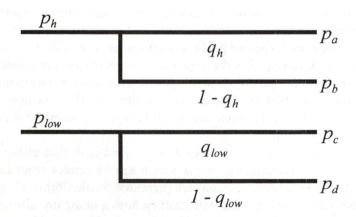

Figure 8.1 Two-operation scenario

high- or to low-quality intermediate produce? Should high-quality resources be applied to the first or second operation? The technique used is the revealed preference argument employed by Kremer.

Industry revenue is calculated under one allocation and then under another. Because identical resource levels are used, the allocation giving the higher industry revenue must be the competitive allocation if resource markets function well. Industry revenue from the allocation schematized in the diagram above is

$$\pi_{q,q_h,q_{low}} = P_a q_h q + P_b (1 - q_h) q + P_c q_{low} (1 - q)$$

$$+ P_d (1 - q_{low})(1 - q) - P_0. \tag{15}$$

Interchange q_h and q_{low} and take the difference to get

$$\pi_{q,q_h,q_{low}} - \pi_{q,q_{low},q_h} = (q_h - q_{low})[(P_a - P_b)q$$

$$- (P_c - P_d)(1 - q)]. \tag{16}$$

If the diagrammed allocation is optimal, then this expression is positive, and $q_h > (<) q_{low}$ when $(P_a - P_b)q > (<) (P_c - P_d)(1 - q)$. Thus the better-quality resources are allocated to transform the higher (lower) quality intermediate produce if the ratio of the price premium for success in operation 2 (given success in operation 1) to the price premium for success in operation 2 (given failure in operation 1), $(P_a - P_b)/(P_c - P_d)$, exceeds (is less than) the odds of failure in operation 1, $(1 - q)/q$. Because the odds ratio can be any positive number, knowledge of $(P_a - P_b)/(P_c - P_d)$ is insufficient to determine where resources are allocated within the second operation.

Now consider the issue of whether to employ high-quality resources in the first or second operation. The sum of profits from operation 1 and operation 2 performed on high-quality intermediate produce is

$$\pi_{q,q_h} = P_a q_h + P_b (1 - q_h) - P_h + P_h q + P_{low} (1 - q) - P_0. \tag{17}$$

Interchange q and q_h and take the difference to get

$$\pi_{q,q_h} - \pi_{q_h,q} = (q_h - q)(P_a - P_b - P_h + P_{low}). \tag{18}$$

This is positive for an optimal allocation. Thus the better-quality resources are allocated to transform the better-quality intermediate produce rather than the raw produce if the premium for success in the second operation, given success in the first operation, $P_a - P_b$, exceeds the premium for success in the first operation, $P_h - P_{low}$. Note that, unlike the problem of allocating within operation 2, the result does not depend on any probability values, i.e., resource quality values. Repeating the revealed preference technique for whether to allocate high-quality resources to operation 1 or to low-quality intermediate produce, we find that the better-quality resources are allocated to transform the low-quality intermediate produce, rather than the raw produce, if $P_c - P_d > P_h - P_{low}$. It can be concluded, therefore, that if $\min[P_a - P_b, P_c - P_d] > P_h - P_{low}$, then only low-quality resources are allocated to operation 1.

Conclusions

This paper highlights two main issues. First, grade structure and grade pricing are important in determining how a processing industry is organized. Resources are used to protect price premiums, so grading determines the level and sequencing of resources along the processing chain. Second, the quality of information flow along the processing chain may provide an incentive to vertically integrate and may fundamentally influence the intensity of value-added to the raw produce. Some product transformation operations are integrated while some are not. It may not be feasible for a firm that retails agricultural produce to extend its control over harvesting, storing, and transporting the raw crop. In this case, there is a role for the extension agent to facilitate information flows between the nonintegrated portions of the transformation chain. Extension agents currently do this through advising producers, writing information bulletins, and organizing industry conferences. The role of the extension agent does not stop at reducing uncertainty. Different agents along the food processing chain act contingent upon actions of other agents along the chain. It may be that all agents are perfectly informed and seek to maximize profit, yet industry profits are not maximized due to a coordination failure. Extension personnel, conversant with all aspects of the industry, may be in a position to communicate the situation to all parts of the chain.

The implications of grading and structure of the marketing channel for on-farm production decisions, and of production decisions for grading and marketing channel operations, are many faceted. The trade-off between quality and output of raw produce depends on the price-quality schedules facing producers. This, in turn, depends on how price-quality schedules facing the marketers of retail produce filter back through the marketing system. These interactions warrant further study.

Notes

This paper was previously published as "Microeconomics of Agricultural Grading: Impacts on the Marketing Channel" in the *American Journal of Agricultural Economics*, 77(1995):980–89, and is used here by permission of the American Agricultural Economics Association.

1   This paper was written while the author was on the faculty of Washington State University. He is very grateful to two anonymous referees, to Tom Schotzko, and to several other faculty members at Washington State University for very helpful comments.
2   A transformation may be considered to be an experiment in the statistical sense.
3   With high-volume throughput along a transformation chain, the central limit theorem ensures that, at any point in time, the percentages of transformed output receiving each of the prices P_a, P_b, P_c, and P_d are almost constant. Thus risk aversion does not matter when there is high-volume throughput along the marketing channel.
4   The proof is available from the author upon request.
5   The price function is not continuous, and so violates both global convexity and global concavity.
6   A more general condition is that both $\partial X_1/\partial X_2$ from condition (3a) and $\partial X_2/\partial X_1$ from condition (3b) are positive at a Nash equilibrium, and that their product at this equilibrium exceeds one.
7   The conditions outlined in the text hold if

$$\Delta^2 > -\frac{(\partial P_e/\partial q_1)(\partial^2 q_1/\partial X_1^2)}{(\partial q_1/\partial X_1)(\partial q_2/\partial X_2)}$$

for condition (3a) at a Nash equilibrium, and if

$$\Delta^2 > -\frac{(\partial P_e/\partial q_2)(\partial^2 q_2/\partial X_2^2)}{(\partial q_1/\partial X_1)(\partial q_2/\partial X_2)}$$

for (3b) at a Nash equilibrium.
8   The proof is available from the author upon request.
9   Because the two intermediate goods are different, it could be that the nature of the intermediate good affects the probability of a successful subsequent transformation. This possibility is ignored, and it is assumed that the sole determinant of the probability of a successful subsequent transformation is the quality of resources applied in the transformation procedure, i.e., the probability of subsequent success is disembodied from prior outcomes.

202 *The Industrialization of Agriculture*

References

Akerlof, G. A. 1970. "The Market for 'Lemons': Quality Uncertainty and the Market Mechanism." *Quarterly Journal of Economics* 84:488–500.
Armbruster, W. J., and E. V. Jesse. 1983. "Fruit and Vegetable Marketing Orders." *Federal Marketing Programs in Agriculture: Issues and Options*, ed. W. J. Armbruster, D. R. Henderson, and R. D. Knudson, pp. 121–58. Oak Brook, Ill,: Farm Foundation.
Becker, G. 1973. "A Theory of Marriage: Part I." *Journal of Political Economy* 81:813–46.
Bockstael, N. E. 1984. "The Welfare Implications of Minimum Quality Standards." *American Journal of Agricultural Economics* 66:466–71.
———. 1987. "Economic Efficiency Issues of Grading and Minimum Quality Standards." *Economic Efficiency in Agricultural and Food Marketing*, ed. R. E. Kilmer and W. J. Armbruster, pp. 231–50. Ames, Iowa: Iowa State University Press.
Cooper, R., and A. John. 1988. "Coordinating Coordination Failures in Keynesian Models." *Quarterly Journal of Economics* 53:441–64.
Danø, S. 1966. *Industrial Production Models.* Vienna, Austria: Springer-Verlag.
Diamond, P., and J. E. Stiglitz. 1974. "Increases in Risk and Risk Aversion." *Journal of Economic Theory* 8:337–60.
Ehrlich, I., and G. S. Becker. 1972. "Market Insurance, Self-Insurance, and Self-Protection." *Journal of Political Economy* 80:623–48.
French, B. C., and C. F. Nuckton. 1991. "An Empirical Analysis of Economic Performance Under the Marketing Order for Raisins." *American Journal Agricultural Economics* 73:581–93.
French, B. C., N. Tamimi, and C. F. Nuckton. 1978. *Marketing Order Program Alternatives: Use and Importance in California, 1949–1975.* Giannini Foundation Information Series 78-2, Bulletin 1890, University of California–Berkeley, May.
Hiebert, L. D. 1983. "Self Insurance, Self Protection, and the Theory of the Competitive Firm." *Southern Economic Journal* 50:160–68.
Kremer, M. 1993. "The O-Ring Theory of Economic Development." *Quarterly Journal of Economics* 58:551–75.
Nguyen, D., and T. T. Vo. 1985. "On Discarding Low Quality Produce." *American Journal Agricultural Economics* 67:614–18.
Powers, N. J. 1990. *Federal Marketing Orders for Fruits, Nuts, and Specialty Crops.* Washington, D.C.: U.S. Department of Agriculture, Economic Research Service, Agricultural Economic Report 629, March.
Price, D. W. 1967. "Discarding Low Quality Produce with an Elastic Demand." *Journal of Farm Economics* 49:622–32.
Rosen, S. 1974. "Hedonic Prices and Implicit Markets: Product Differentiation in Pure Competition." *Journal of Political Economy* 82:34–54.
———. 1981. "The Economics of Superstars." *American Economic Review* 71:845–58.
Rothschild, M., and J. E. Stiglitz. 1970. "Increasing Risk I: A Definition." *Journal of Economic Theory* 2:225–43.
Shogren, J. 1991. "Endogenous Risk and Protection Premiums." *Theory and Decision* 31:241–56.

PART III
INDUSTRIALIZATION IN THE PORK SECTOR

9 The Changing U.S. Pork Industry: An Overview

KELLY ZERING

Rapid change in technology, structure, and methods of coordination have made the U.S. pork industry the center of much discussion. The purpose of this paper is to provide an overview of the current U.S. pork industry and the changes that are occurring. The following sections describe the swine production sector, the packing and processing sector, and provide a glimpse of pork retailing. The description focuses on profit as a motive for change; productivity and efficiency; technology; and implications for methods of coordination.

Swine Production is Undergoing Rapid Change

Since 1920, the number of farms in the United States and the percentage of all U.S. farms that keep pigs have been falling (Figure 9.1). Since 1900, the total inventory of pigs in the United States has varied little so that the average inventory per farm has risen steadily. The marketing of pigs in the United States has risen steadily over the period, reflecting increased productivity and decreased farm slaughter (Figure 9.2).

The number of farms keeping swine has continued falling since 1981, and most of those ceasing to keep swine had fewer than 100 head in inventory (Figure 9.3). Total inventory on farms with at least 2,000 head in inventory is growing rapidly (from 16.6 million head on December 1, 1992, to 28.6 million head on December 1, 1996). The 4,880 U.S. farms with at least 2,000 pigs in inventory accounted for 51 percent of total U.S. swine inventory on December 1, 1996 (Figure 9.4). They represented 3.1 percent of all farms in the country that had at least one pig.

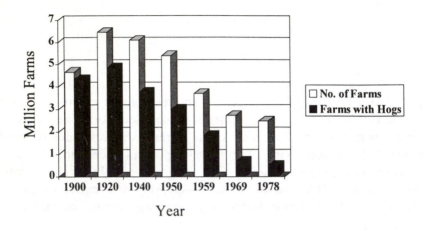

Figure 9.1 U.S. farms and U.S. hog farms

Source: U.S. Department of Commerce.

A geographic shift in swine production has accompanied the shift in size of operations. North Carolina accounted for 37 percent of the increase in national inventory on farms with at least 2,000 pigs between 1992 and 1996. Since 1989, North Carolina rose from seventh to second among states in swine inventory. Missouri added 700,000 hogs and pigs, and Minnesota added 150,000 head to its inventory. Rapid growth in swine production is also occurring in Oklahoma, Kansas, Mississippi, Arkansas, Texas, Colorado, Utah, Wyoming, Arizona, and other places not known for swine production. Traditional hog producing states experienced sharp declines in inventory between 1992 and 1996, including Iowa (-2.7 million head), Illinois (-1.5 million head), Nebraska (-1.0 million head), Indiana (-0.8 million head), and South Dakota (-0.63 million head). Even more striking is the decline in swine kept for breeding in Iowa (-450,000 or -26 percent), Illinois (-180,000 or -26 percent), Nebraska (-130,000 or -22 percent), Indiana (-90,000 or -16 percent),

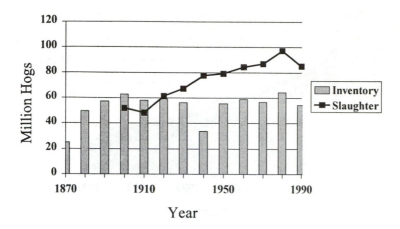

Figure 9.2 U.S. swine inventory and slaughter, 1870–1990

Source: U.S. Department of Commerce.

and South Dakota (-80,000 or -34 percent). The data reflect a shift from farrow-to-finish farms to "finishing only" farms in these states.

Costs of hog production vary widely across farms, creating incentives for the expansion of profitable farms and liquidation of unprofitable farms. The U.S. Department of Agriculture (USDA) benchmark North Central farrow-to-finish cost of producing market hogs served as a reasonably accurate predictor of supply response: hog prices above this benchmark preceded expansion while prices below this cost were followed by contraction of national hog supply. The North Central farrow-to-finish cost was near or above market hog prices between 1992 and 1996.

Many of the rapidly growing swine production firms claim long-run total costs of $38 to $40 per cwt. of live hog while the North Central benchmark ranged from $43 to $48 in recent years. Hurt (p. 185) estimated that specialized 1,200-sow farms have total costs of production that are $6.29 to $13.63 per cwt. (15 to 28 percent) lower than those of 150-sow farrow-to-

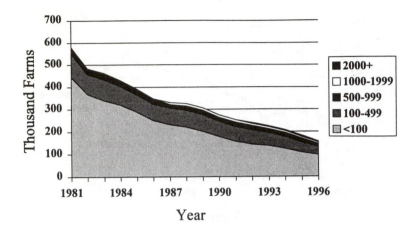

Figure 9.3 Number of U.S. hog farms by inventory size

Source: U.S. Department of Agriculture.

finish farms. The importance of economies of size and scale cannot be overstated in explaining the structural change now occurring.

A large supply of hogs and inadequate packing capacity pushed hog prices below $30 per cwt. in the fourth quarter of 1994. Hog prices remained low through the first half of 1995. Severely reduced national corn yields in 1995 raised feed prices and forced the North Central benchmark cost above $60 per cwt. in 1996. The combination of low hog prices in 1994–1995 and high feed costs in 1996 created financial stress for all hog producers. Many older farms and some newer, highly leveraged farms liquidated their operations in 1995 and 1996.

Modern swine production is highly specialized, highly coordinated, and very efficient. For example, farms with at least 2,000 pigs in inventory averaged 8.8 pigs saved per litter while farms with fewer than 100 pigs saved 7.3 pigs per litter (U.S. Department of Agriculture). Similar differences can be noted in litters per breeding animal per year. USDA does not routinely

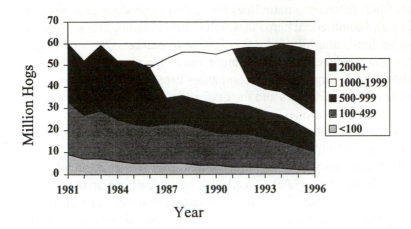

Figure 9.4 Number of hogs in the United States by farm inventory size

Source: U.S. Department of Agriculture.

report feed conversion. The rapidly growing firms report feed conversion of 3.0 pounds of feed per pound of live hog produced while the North Central benchmark uses more than 4.0 pounds of feed and many records systems report averages above 3.5.

Efficiency is achieved with a wide range of technology and organization. Genetic stock defines a limit to productivity. The breeding stock sector produces genetic stock for hog producers. A pronounced shift from on-farm breeding stock replacement programs to purchased hybrid breeding stock has accompanied the shift in farm size and organization. Purebred breeders tend to be small and produce purebred breeding stock primarily for local or regional markets. The modern commercial breeding stock companies (in many cases, international firms) tend to be much larger than purebred breeders and sell hybrid breeding stock.

The traditional breeding system based on purebred breeding stock usually mates purchased purebred boars with females selected from the commercial herd (the commercial herd is defined as the herd producing hogs for slaughter). The breeding system based on hybrid breeding stock suppliers includes nucleus herds (herds that are the source of basic genetic stock supplied to crossing herds), crossing herds or multiplier herds (herds in which sows and boars from different genetic lines are mated to produce crossbred or hybrid stock), and commercial herds in which hybrid breeding stock is acquired from crossing herds and all production is sent to market. Johnson suggests that larger hog producers are much more likely than small producers to obtain seedstock from large genetics companies because they can provide the large number of gilts and boars and the uniformity that large producers require. A number of international swine genetics companies initiated or expanded operations in the United States when U.S. packers began paying premiums for leaner hogs in 1992.

A recent innovation in swine breeding is the widespread adoption of artificial insemination (AI). An AI boar can inseminate up to twenty sows for each sow inseminated by a boar by natural mating. The emerging swine breeding stock sector is capable of selecting highly productive pigs with traits that consumers value and broadly distributing those genes to commercial hog producers in a short period of time.

The hog production sector has been substantially restructured over the past decade. Prior to 1993, most pigs were raised on farms with fewer than 1,000 hogs and pigs in inventory. Farrow-to-finish operations with 50 to 100 sows typically have a total inventory of 500 to 1,000 head. Traditional farrow-to-finish operations have a breeding herd and raise pigs from birth to market. Many farrow-to-finish operations are located on farms that also grow corn and soybeans. Farms of this type process their own feed by grinding and mixing their corn with purchased soybean meal, vitamins, and minerals. Prior to 1993, separate feeder pig and finishing operations were also common. Feeder pig operations include a breeding herd, but pigs are typically sold as feeder pigs when they reach 45 to 55 pounds. The feeder pigs are sold to finishing operations that raise the pigs to market weight—about 250 pounds. The volume of feeder pigs moving through public auctions has declined dramatically since 1985 because of large-scale finishers' demand for large lots of genetically uniform pigs of the same age. Concerns about commingled feeder pig auctions include high transactions costs, transportation costs for small lots, lack of information about health and genetics, variable supply, and performance loss due to commingling small lots. Finishers find cost savings in all-in/all-out production scheduling. However, they receive severe discounts (called sort loss) from packers if their pigs vary too much in weight.

Therefore, they desire pigs of a uniform age with very similar growth characteristics. Truckloads of up to 1,000 feeder pigs can economically be moved long distances.

Modern, highly specialized, large-scale commercial hog production may be separated into three distinct phases. Weanling pigs are produced in farrowing facilities, feeder pigs are produced in nursery facilities, and market hogs are produced in finishing facilities. Weanling pigs from farrowing operations (often 1,200 sows or more in inventory) are transferred to nurseries at a weight of 12 to 16 pounds. Feeder pigs are then transferred from nurseries to finishing operations at about 45 to 55 pounds. The finisher grows the hogs to market weight and then sells them to packers. Many hogs are now raised at three sites (farrowing, nursery, and finishing) while being owned by one hog producer. The hog producer may own the facilities at each site or the facilities may be owned by another producer raising the pigs under a production contract with the pigs' owner. Some pigs are sold at the weanling stage and some are sold at the feeder pig stage. Technologies and organizational innovations of modern hog farms include segregated early weaning, all-in/all-out pig placements, split sex feeding, phase feeding, network buying and selling, and high throughput facility scheduling. Hurt (p. 188) provides an estimate of the marginal profit associated with these innovations.

Many of the large, specialized farms do not process feed on the farm. Instead a large, centralized feed mill manufactures complete feeds, which are then trucked to farms. The mill may be owned by a large hog producer or by a producer cooperative, or it may have a term contract to manufacture feed for the farm. The larger feed mills are able to operate nearly twenty-four hours per day and employ technology such as pelleting lines not feasible for smaller mills. The larger feed mills may also be able to achieve higher precision and uniformity in nutrient levels, buy ingredients in large volumes at lower cost, and switch ingredients more frequently in response to changing relative prices. These advantages are weighed against the additional cost of transporting corn to market and transporting complete feeds back to the farm.

Labor is highly specialized on many modern hog farms. Labor in farrowing operations is skilled, full-time, and specialized in farrowing or breeding and gestation. Nursery labor may be full-time at the same site or part-time at a separate site. Finishing labor may be part-time or full-time, usually at a separate site.

Producers are seeking economies of scale to buy ingredients at lower prices, market hogs at lower cost and at higher prices, coordinate specialized production across farms, and obtain access to the highest quality genetic stock at lower prices. The definition of independence is being rewritten as hog producers band together to capture the efficiencies of scale, specialization, and coordination that contract production has brought to others. Aspects of the evolving relationship between "independent" hog farmers are variously referred to as networking, cooperation, marketing associations, or limited corporations (Martinez, Smith, and Zering).

Production contracts are widely used in regions with rapidly expanding new hog production operations. The common production contract makes the grower responsible for providing facilities, labor, utilities, waste disposal, land, and water. The contractor provides feed, livestock, veterinary care and medicine, and managerial support, and markets the hogs. The contractor bears all market risk and keeps any residual profits or losses. Lenders have found contracts with reputable contractors to provide steady cash flow with little or no record of default. The contracts are generally written for one to five years with automatic renewal and include emergency out clauses for both parties (i.e., the contracts as such offer no security). Contractors anxious to grow and in need of lender support are careful to screen growers and work with existing growers to avoid failure. The contracts are generally calibrated to pay growers their total cost of production plus a slim profit margin for average productivity. Incentive clauses provide larger profits for superior productivity and breakeven for below average productivity. Many growers have achieved exceptional rates of return on equity by borrowing 70 percent or more of their initial investment. Loan guarantee programs from the Farmers Home Administration, Small Business Administration, and a smaller state agency have helped limited resource farmers enter production. In addition to the risk sharing and specialization benefits of contract production, contracts have allowed utilization of underemployed or unemployed labor on the farm. Many of those owning contract nurseries or finishing floors work off the farm or in other activities on the farm. Contract farrowing operations exist but employ full-time labor. Approximately 21 percent of the U.S. swine inventory was being raised by contractees on December 1, 1996 (U.S. Department of Agriculture).

In summary, economies of size and scale in hog production stem from several features. Large, specialized facilities minimize capital investment per hog produced and employ people full-time in high-skill jobs. Multi-site production with segregated early weaning allows improved disease control, use of smaller tracts of land, and use of part-time labor for some nursery and finishing operations. Close coordination between farrowing, nursery, and finishing facilities organized in production pyramids allows high throughput and minimum cost. Large groups of market hogs allow sorting to minimize size discounts and full utilization of large trucks to minimize trucking costs. Pecuniary economies accrue to hog producers when they are able to buy inputs and market pigs in large volume. Large-scale producers gain other economies such as the ability to employ full-time veterinarians, nutritionists, field supervisors, accountants, and engineers. They may also conduct research with multiple replications in "the field." Profits are increased when producers can try alternative diets, genetic stock, facility designs, health programs, etc., and replicate the best. The trend to large, specialized facilities is profit driven.

The Packing and Processing Sector is Also Changing

Economies of size are also driving changes in the packing and processing sector. In 1982, 40 percent of U.S. hog slaughter capacity was in plants that slaughtered fewer than one million hogs annually (Hayenga et al.). By February, 1996, only 6.2 percent of U.S. hog slaughter capacity remained in these smaller plants (Meyer). Competitive pressures are causing many packers to reevaluate their "commodity"-based hog pricing and procurement practices and move toward coordinated marketing. Cassell and West found that packing costs decrease with plant size, but that procurement and transportation costs rise. Improved coordination is used to offset the otherwise larger procurement costs. While traditional packers employ hundreds of buyers to procure hogs, others employ a dozen or so to schedule deliveries of hogs procured through long-term written agreements with large producers. Uncertain supplies day to day and season to season also impose costs on packers when facilities are not used to capacity and when labor is underutilized. The sharp reduction in hog production in Iowa and surrounding states caused at least three packing plants to close their second shifts and another large plant to be closed entirely in 1997.

Close coordination between packers and producers has enabled growth of hog production and construction of new large packing plants in areas that previously had few hogs. Smithfield Foods built the largest plant in the country at Tar Heel, North Carolina, when hogs were already at a deficit in the region. Agreements with several large producers to simultaneously expand their production allowed rapid growth in both packing and production. A similar sequence of events occurred in Guymon, Oklahoma, where an old beef packing plant was refurbished and is now the center of a large pork production region. Both of these plants run constantly near capacity with little supply uncertainty from day to day and season to season.

Carcass merit pricing systems have been adopted by most U.S. packers since 1992. Technology to accurately measure carcass backfat and weight at low cost has enabled packers to reward producers of hogs with large, lean carcasses. Producers are not rewarded for backfat or gut-fill. Small carcasses are heavily discounted (up to 30 percent or more) since packer cost per carcass varies little with size but income varies directly. Small cuts may be worth less per pound than standard cuts. Clear price signals have resulted in a steady increase in carcass weight and yield and a steady decrease in backfat depth. Recent increased attention to meat quality characteristics that are difficult to measure is creating greater incentives for direct communication between packers, producers, and genetics suppliers.

An important element of coordination is the transmission of information up and down the marketing channel. Some export customers demand assurance that the pig has been produced in a certain manner. Such assurance is difficult to provide without close coordination between packer and producer. Direct communication is more feasible with a few large producers than with many small producers. Some networks of smaller producers create lines of communication similar to those in larger firms.

Retail Markets are Evolving

Closer coordination is allowing purveyors of fresh pork to consider their product in something other than generic terms. A National Pork Producers Council taste test (National Pork Producers Council) found that consumers were willing to pay more for pork with specific levels of various quality traits including intra-muscular fat (marbling), acidity (pH), tenderness, color, and drip-loss. A number of pork packers have introduced "store-ready" and branded fresh pork products in recent years. Some distinguish their products as being leaner while others promote their products as juicier and better tasting. Others identify their products as being from a specific breed of pig or as being raised on family farms.

Restaurant and institutional markets are major outlets for food producers in the United States. Meals eaten away from home now account for more than half of U.S. consumer spending on food. Large quantities of chicken and beef are sold through restaurants and institutions while pork is missing from the menus of many large restaurant chains. The addition of ham to the menu of

Boston Market restaurants and the addition of bacon (via the Arch Deluxe sandwich) to McDonald's lunch and dinner menus created new markets for millions of pounds of pork in the past few years.

Volume, regular delivery, and uniform, consistent quality are important product attributes when the customer is a large regional or national chain. Traditional hog and pork marketing systems may have difficulty providing such a product. A reliable supply of consistent quality hogs may be critical to supplying such markets.

The United States became a net exporter of pork for the first time in several decades in 1995. Much of the growth in pork exports has been in the form of high-valued cuts being sold to Japan. Smithfield Foods formed a partnership with Sumitomo Corporation to sell pork in Japan under its own retail labels. The ability to know where and how the pigs were raised and the ability to inspect the production and packing process were critical to establishing the brands. A recent outbreak of hoof and mouth disease in Taiwan and that country's loss of its export market in Japan has underscored the importance of food safety and quality control in maintaining export markets. U.S. exports are expected to continue growing.

Closer coordination and large-scale production and processing are likely to characterize the U.S. pork industry for the next few years. Retailers are recognizing that different segments of the population have different preferences for attributes in pork: lean versus marbled, fresh versus flavored or marinated, pink versus darker pink, and ready-to-eat versus ready-to-cook. The availability and variety of pork products is expected to increase steadily over the next few years.

Conclusion

Economies of size and scale, economies of improved coordination, and the desire to capitalize on consumers' demand for quality, convenience, and variety are drivers of the dramatic restructuring of the U.S. pork sector. Rapid adjustments in the size, organization, and location of swine farms are occurring. A substantial amount of social conflict has arisen around the rapid change. Environmental advocacy groups have sought strict regulations to control siting and waste management on new large hog farms. Public health officials and neighbors have sought to block or control development of new large hog farms to avoid potential exposure to odor, pathogens, or water pollution. Advocacy groups for small "family" farms have attempted to impede the growth of large "industrialized" or "corporate" swine farms. Environmental officials and researchers have scrambled to learn more about the effects of large hog farms on the environment and to develop new regulations to prevent air and water pollution. A considerable amount of research is underway to improve nutrient management and odor control on hog farms. The U.S. pork sector is in the midst of dynamic adjustment and seeking a new, sustainable, prosperous equilibrium.

References

Cassell, G. R., and D. A. West. 1967. *Assembly and Slaughter Costs for Hogs in North Carolina*. Research Report 3, Department of Economics, North Carolina State University.

Hayenga, M., V. J. Rhodes, J. A. Brandt, and R. E. Deiter. 1985. *The U.S. Pork Sector: Changing Structure and Organization*. Ames, Iowa: Iowa State University Press.

Hurt, C. 1995. "Summary and Conclusions." *Positioning Your Pork Operation for the 21st Century*. ID-210, Cooperative Extension Service, Purdue University, July.

Johnson, N. 1995. "The Diffusion of Livestock Breeding Technology in the U.S.: Observations on the Relationship Between Technical Change and Industry Structure." Staff Paper P95-11, Department of Applied Economics, University of Minnesota, October.

Martinez, S. W., K. Smith, and K. Zering. 1997. *Vertical Coordination and Consumer Welfare: The Case of the Pork Industry*. Washington, D.C.: U.S. Department of Agriculture, Economic Research Service, Agricultural Economic Report 753, August.

Meyer, Steve. 1996. "U.S. Hog Slaughtering Capacity, February, 1996." *1996 Pork Industry Economic Review*. Clive, Iowa: National Pork Producers Council, March.

National Pork Producers Council. 1995. *Pork and the U.S. Consumer Conference*. Clive, Iowa, March.

U.S. Department of Agriculture. Various, 1984–1996. *Hogs and Pigs*. Washington, D.C.: National Agricultural Statistics Service.

U.S. Department of Commerce. Various, 1910–1990. *Statistical Abstract of the United States*. Washington, D.C.: Bureau of the Census.

10   The Industrialization of Hog Production

V. JAMES RHODES[1]

Industrialization was once considered a polar opposite of agriculture. What is industrialized hog production? In this paper, it is treated as production in specialized facilities, tended typically by specialized labor using routine methods. The sizes of hog producers once depended on the acres of associated corn land; now they vary with the size and number of facilities.

Most are familiar with the transition of pioneer, self-sufficient farming into today's specialized and commercialized enterprises. Hog production has changed tremendously from seventy-five years ago when nearly every farm raised some hogs. The period from the Great Depression until 1970 brought the commercialization of hog production; butchering hogs for home consumption largely ended, and the number of farms with hogs declined from 3,768,000 in 1940 to 604,000 in the 1969 Census of Agriculture (U.S. Department of Commerce). The current industrialization began in the 1970s with rapid transition of hog production into partial or total confinement. The census reported only 374 farms with hog sales exceeding 5,000 head and a trivial share of national output in 1974. Since then, a continuing series of advancements in technology and management have made a science of hog production in large factory-like units staffed with specialized labor.

Changes in Hog Marketings of Units and Firms

There have been large, compensating changes in the number and size of the basic production units referred to as farms in the agricultural censuses. Changes in numbers of hog production units have been strongly related to size (Table 10.1). What may be surprising is the small sizes of the units that were

217

Table 10.1 Number and changes in number of U.S. farms selling hogs and pigs by size groups, 1959–1992

Census year	Total farms	Size group of number head sold per farm (thousand farms)					
		1–99	100–199	200–499	500–999	1,000+
1959	1,273	1,018	161	81	10.0	1.5
1969	604	361	109	101	25.0	6.6
1978	470	281	69	74	30.0	15.8
1982	315	162	44	56	30.0	21.6
1987	239	110	33	45	27.5	23.9
1992	188	77	23	35	25.0	27.8

Changes in numbers of farms between censuses as percentage of earlier census

1959–1969	-52	-64	-32	+25	+150	+340
1969–1978	-22	-22	-36	-27	+20	+139
1978–1982	-33	-42	-36	-24	0	+36
1982–1987	-24	-32	-25	-20	-8	+11
1987–1992	-21	-30	-30	-22	-9	+16

Source: U.S. Department of Commerce.

viable enough to grow in numbers as late as the 1960s. Production units in the 200 to 499 head of annual sales did not begin declining until the 1970s, and those in the 500 to 999 group first began declining in the 1980s. In the 1980s, attention shifted to the pattern of change in producers having greater than 1,000 head sales. In 1978, the census showed one-third of output produced by units marketing 1,000 head or more per year, but only 7 percent by those large units marketing 5,000 head or more. Nine years later 58 percent was marketed by the 1,000 head group and 17 percent by the 5,000 head group. Those percentages rose to 69 percent and 28 percent in the 1992 census.

Changes in Firms

The most interesting changes in the structure of hog production in the past ten to fifteen years have not been measured by either the census or the U.S. Department of Agriculture (USDA) because (1) their top size categories are outmoded and (2) they focus on the production unit rather than the ownership (firm) unit. More and more operations (firms) produce hogs at multiple sites; these sites number into the hundreds for some of the largest producers. Since the size of the operation is no longer limited to the feasible number of hogs at a site, the production of hogs has become attractive to new groups: large corporations and wealthy investors.

Growth in Marketings by Firm Size

Rhodes and others have made numerous surveys estimating change in firm sales at the upper end of the distribution. Rhodes, Finley, and Grimes stated their purpose in the introduction to their first publication in 1974. "Hogs are often cited as the major farm commodity which may be next to shift along a route similar to cattle feeding. Although it is widely known that there are some large-scale hog units around the country, systematic information about them has not been available" (p. 3). In those days, "large" meant inventories of 3,000 head or annual marketings of 5,000 head. In their second survey in 1975, the few producers they found marketing more than 50,000 head annually were ignored as an anomaly; their ensuing research focused on measuring the growth of the 1,000 and the 5,000 head groups (Rhodes and Grimes 1975). Finally in their 1989 survey, they tried to identify all the largest producers and counted 33 producers marketing 50,000 head or more in 1988 with a total output of 5.7 million market hogs, or 6.5 percent of the national slaughter (Rhodes 1990b). Further surveys (see Table 10.2) showed 41 producers in the

Table 10.2 University of Missouri estimates of the growth in market hog marketings of very large producers, 1988–1994

Year	Producers marketing over 50,000 head		Producers marketing over 500,000 head	
	Number of producers	Number of market hogs (million)	Number of producers	Number of market hogs (million)
1988	33	5.7	*	*
1991	41	8.1	6	4.4
1992	45	9.5	6	5.4
1993	57	12.4	7	6.7
1994	66	16.1	9	9.3

* Not available.

Source: Grimes and Rhodes, various.

50,000 or more group in 1991, 57 producers in 1993, and 66 in 1994 (Rhodes and Grimes 1992a; Grimes and Rhodes 1994). Those figures document what industry leaders recognize as an amazingly swift evolution in hog production. Nine of those 66 firms in 1994 each marketed more than 500,000 hogs (designated as megaproducers) and averaged marketings of slightly more than one million.

An extreme example of the rapid growth of these new big operations is shown by Premium Standard Farms (PSF). PSF began construction of its first hog facilities in 1989, reached a production rate of 1.6 million head of market hogs per year by early 1995 in Missouri, and purchased a unit in Texas with 17,000 sows in 1994 (Marbery 1994b). PSF illustrates the multi-unit production that is typical of large producers. In Missouri, PSF farrows in dozens of complexes of 1,000 sows and finishes in buildings holding 1,100 head; production is distributed over three northern Missouri counties.

PSF was an unusual megaproducer in other ways: it was largely financed by Wall Street money with a high proportion of debt; it did virtually no production contracting so it had high capital requirements; it built and operated a packing house; and it is now in Chapter 11 bankruptcy reorganization in which it appears that its junk bond holders will become the major holders of equity (Stroud; McMahon 1996).

Contract Production and Contractors' Marketings

Many large producers use contract production to increase the number of units producing their hogs. Contract production is an effective method of obtaining a larger output while economizing on the contractor's capital and hired labor. Contract production of hogs involves the following relationships and activities. An owner of feeder pigs engages a producer/grower to take custody of pigs and finish them in the latter's facilities to slaughter weight with feed and health items furnished by the pigs' owner (the contractor). This producer/grower (hereafter called a grower) usually receives from the contractor a set fee per pig received and/or per hog marketed, and often some performance incentives for providing superior custodial care. The pigs' owner (contractor) bears all market risks and most of the production risks. Alternatively, the owner of breeding stock may engage a grower to produce feeder pigs or to produce farrow-to-finish under the same type of contractual arrangement. In composition, Midwestern growers typically have been experienced hog producers before their contract growing while growers outside the area typically have been new to hog production.

Since the early 1970s, the techniques of efficient, large-scale production have gradually been developed. Many producers have utilized production contracts to rapidly expand their output. Rhodes, Flottman, and Procter estimated there were about 1,000 contractors in 1986, ranging in size from annual sales of about 1,000 head to more than 500,000. Of the very big contracting operations, some were begun by large firms (e.g., Cargill and Tyson) while others began as small producers.

One of the best known big contractors that had a humble beginning is Murphy Family Farms. Wendell Murphy, fresh out of college in the early 1960s, bought a small feed mill in North Carolina and bought some feeder pigs to better utilize the mill. Good profits led Murphy into contract finishing by growers, and then into farrowing and finishing in rapidly expanding facilities of his own as well as contracting with more grower units.

The marketings of contractors are estimated to have grown from 9.5 million head of market hogs in 1988 to 13.2 million in 1991, and 22.8 million in 1994. The marketings of the very large contractors (50,000 head or more) have grown more swiftly from 4.1 million in 1988 to 14.4 million in 1994. The marketings of the small contractors grew from 5.4 million head in 1988 to 8.4 million in 1994 (Rhodes 1990b; Rhodes and Grimes 1992a; Grimes and Rhodes 1995a).

In measuring the size and significance of contracting, it is important to distinguish between two sources of contractors' marketings: growers' or contractors' facilities. Contractors, with a few exceptions such as Cargill, farrow and finish in their own units as well as in those of growers. Hence, the volume of hogs produced under contract by growers is considerably less than the total marketings of contractors. In 1994, an estimated 10.4 million of the 14.4 million hogs marketed by very large contractors were finished by their growers, while 5.4 million of the 8.4 million head marketed by small contractors were finished by their growers (Grimes and Rhodes 1995b). The larger contractors depended more on contract finishing than the smaller contractors. Generally, contractors have relied less on growers for farrowing than finishing. It has not been unusual for popular press reports of our research findings to overstate the significance of contract production by using the contractors' total marketings rather than the much smaller output of their growers.

Changing Location

Large-scale operations are proportionately more important outside the two North Central regions. For example, according to the 1992 Census of

Agriculture, total hog/pig marketings by units marketing 5,000 head or more were 82 percent of total marketings in North Carolina and 73 percent in Arkansas, compared to 21 percent in Illinois and 14 percent in Iowa. Approximately one-third of the superproducers (50,000 head or more) are located—or headquartered—in North Carolina. Because these very large operations are attracted to thinly populated areas with cheap land and lower priced labor, their growth is less likely in the Iowa-Illinois-Indiana corridor than elsewhere. Contract production of hogs has been easier to introduce in areas in which farmers have had experience with poultry contracting. Such areas are mainly to the south and east of the Corn Belt. Considerable numbers of pigs continue to be farrowed outside the Corn Belt but finished inside (U.S. Department of Agriculture).

Forces Driving Structural Change

Innovational Profits

As economists, we can explain this growth in size of operation as an integral part of the general substitution of capital for labor characterizing a developing economy and seen, in varying degrees, in all parts of U.S. agriculture. A farm management specialist would probably emphasize the efficiency gains experienced by specialization in the various crop and livestock enterprises that have replaced the general farms of earlier periods. An animal scientist could explain the development of techniques, procedures, equipment, medicines, and feeds that have made feasible the handling of far more animals in one location than was feasible a quarter century ago (e.g., 3,500 sows in a single complex). The scientist could also cite the advances in genetics and in management practices that have significantly increased the pigs farrowed per sow per year and reduced the pounds of feed required per pound of lean pork. Some of these practices include artificial insemination, early weaning, separation of farrowing and finishing, sex-separated finishing, and feeding formulas varying with the age and type of animal.

Economies of Size

Together, these advances in technology, organization, and management have extended the size of the efficient production unit to many times that which existed in the 1960s. In 1970, relatively few producers could manage a farrowing unit large enough to produce 3,500 pigs; today, a farrowing unit of 3,500 sows (producing 70,000 pigs) is a standard size for some firms. Hurt at Purdue recently estimated a cost advantage of nearly $2 per cwt. of live hogs for a unit with 3,400 sows, compared to one of 650 (Vansickle 1995). These advances have also multiplied greatly the feasible size of the production firm via ownership and/or management of hundreds of production units. Such a multi-unit organization was unthinkable as long as production was an art in which success depended upon widely differing sets of fixed resources and management on each and every farm. Completely comparable costs are not publicly available to distinguish between a declining or flat average cost curve in the long run, but what is clear is that diseconomies of size are not limiting the growth of firms with 95,000 sows.[2] In sharp contrast, the studies of size in the 1970s were divided on whether economies extended to as much as 1,000 sows (see a review by Hayenga et al., pp. 19–20).

Thus the driving force of structural change in hog production has not been unusual. It has been the prospect of significant profits or rather a stream of profits obtainable by those who seize the new technologies and practices and continue to develop more of their own. Numerous state farm records show a range of about $10 in average costs per cwt. between the best one-third and the poorest one-third of producers. The bulk of the rapidly expanding large operations were understood to be operating at costs that are $3 to $5 per cwt. below the bulk of more traditional producers (Iowa State University Swine Task Force). That kind of cost advantage will eventually be competed away, but large innovational profits have been available for a decade or more and probably will continue to be available for much of another decade.

Other Forces

Various other events contributed to the recent rapid changes in structure. Profitable hog prices during most of the period from 1965 to 1979, combined with investment tax credits for building new facilities, encouraged a general substitution of capital for labor—on a per hog basis—through the building of specialized hog facilities and encouraged the general surge toward larger units documented in the census data (Rhodes and Grimes 1980). Then the farm crisis of the early 1980s squeezed out numerous farmers—including some hog producers—and expedited entry and/or expansion into that gap by those with continuing access to capital. During the later 1980s, profits were available to all but the most inefficient producers so that entry and expansion of efficient large operations were facilitated by larger than normal competitive profits.

Late 1994 was the first period in which expansion of production led to prices so low that virtually every producer temporarily experienced losses.[3]

Organizations Conducive to Continual Growth

Larger producers are winning larger market shares because they are, on average, more efficient than a majority of the smaller ones and because their large corporate organization is more conducive to continual expansion. Successful, efficient producers must (1) have access to, and quickly adopt, new technology, (2) have access to, and use, market information, (3) have increased specialization so the first two points are feasible, (4) have equal or superior access to all inputs including capital, and (5) produce the volume and quality of hogs that attract packer premiums rather than discounts. These success factors are less available to smaller producers; good managers of larger organizations are more likely to obtain them. While a consistently efficient operation provides the profit incentives for expansion and generates the equity capital base, efficiency does not necessarily provide sufficient conditions for growth. Surveys show that many family operations limit their growth, not wanting to take larger risks or supervise nonfamily labor, or because further expansion seems irrational given the operator's age or poor health and lack of a family successor (Rhodes and Grimes 1992a).

Has Changing Demand Been a Driving Force?

Some have argued that the main push for structural change has come from the demand side rather than from the capture of a stream of innovational profits in production. For example, Barkema and Cook recently argued: "Primarily responsible for the changes underway in the U.S. pork industry are today's discriminating consumers" (p. 49). In their view, these consumers are reached more effectively by new market channels of communication such as production contracts and vertical integration. Others have picked up the theme that a push for quality in pork (leanness with palatability) has been the driving force behind this huge structural change in hog production. These views give a central role to packers who convey the rising consumer demand for better pork to producers via production contracts and even direct production. The rise of contract production, documented above, is cited by Barkema and Cook to support their demand-pull interpretation.

The demand for hogs of more uniform, and higher, quality is becoming more important. To service those segmented markets, packers may bypass the open market by use of production contracts or direct production. But that demand clearly has not been an important driving force over the past quarter century. First, since 1970, packer-controlled production has been, and still is, tiny—about 3 percent of the national slaughter in 1994. Before 1987, only one packer controlled any sizeable volume of hog production and it was less than 0.5 percent of the national slaughter. In contrast, the massive shift in the structure of production has directly affected a majority of the national slaughter. Second, much, if not most, of so-called packer-controlled hog production has been motivated more by high returns in hog production than by returns to vertical integration. For example, Cargill began hog production in 1973 and steadily expanded what it found to be an enterprise with a high return on investment; however, it did not enter pork packing until 1987. Many of its produced hogs are not slaughtered in Cargill plants, and most of the Cargill slaughter does not come from Cargill production. That is hardly a picture of hog production driven by changing consumer demands, and yet it is one of the few examples of packer/producers. However, there is increasing recognition of the quality opportunities in pork. PSF and Smithfield now emphasize the role of quality in their vertical integration. Whether the most efficient road to continuous quality improvement involves vertical integration, contract production, or other devices is an important research question. Meanwhile, analysis should not confuse what may be with what has been.

Are Broilers a Model for Hogs?

A related idea is that hogs will follow broilers; it is an old analogy that can both inform and mislead because there are significant differences as well as similarities between hogs and broilers. As soon as the sweeping change in broilers became evident in the mid-1950s, agricultural economists and others were suggesting vertical integration in broilers as a model for hogs. Commercial feed companies and packers soon attempted it.

In the Corn Belt, their efforts to contract hog production largely subsided within a few years. The better producers were seldom interested in a quasi employee status that did not provide access to the profits of the good years of the hog cycle. Grower recruitment was greater in the South in areas already accustomed to broiler contracts, but success was fairly limited. As a result, many of the large packers and feed companies lost their enthusiasm for vertical integration in hogs in any form.

Contract hog production as vertical integration by commercial feed companies or meat packers has been the most vivid image of structural change.

For traditional hog producers, it has been the most feared image; for those agricultural economists expecting hogs to follow broilers it has been the anticipated change. But here hogs have deviated from the broiler model.

The popular term for big operations is "integrators" and many people—following the broiler metaphor—assume that contract production is undertaken by packers or commercial feed companies. As illustrated by Murphy Family Farms, most contractors are simply hog producers and not commercial feed companies or packers. Among the 66 very large producers providing 1994 data, only 38 percent of the 16.1 million market hogs were produced by vertically integrated producers (such firms as Carroll-Smithfield, Cargill, Farmland, and Goldkist) (Grimes and Rhodes 1995b). As of 1994, a big majority of contract production was horizontal—between producer and grower—rather than vertical. On the basis of their 1995 national survey, Grimes and Rhodes estimated that 8 percent of the national slaughter of hogs was vertically integrated into packing or commercial feed companies in any way (ownership, joint ventures, or production contracts) in 1994.

Vertical Integration and Transaction Costs

Williamson's approach to explaining vertical integration in terms of lesser transaction costs than market exchange has become the conventional wisdom. If we define transaction costs to include the most effective control of quality, the above arguments about driving forces can be put in that framework. Evidence suggests that vertical integration and/or production contracts can reduce transaction costs in certain situations. Cargill slaughters most of the hogs it contract produces near its Iowa plants, but it does not haul its North Carolina hogs to Iowa. PSF built a plant sized to slaughter its own daily hog production in its nearby Missouri sites. Efficiencies can be expected from such close coordination of packing and production. Tyson, almost a decade after becoming a megaproducer (500,000 head or more marketed), purchased a packing plant in Missouri adjoining its production sites centered in Arkansas. Cargill, Tyson, and PSF were each major producers before they acquired packing plants. Their motives appear consistent with minimization of transaction costs. Note, however, that these are not cases of packers moving to control hog production—the popular bugaboo of family farmers—but conversely producers grown big that acquired packing plants.

Tyson's sale of its packing plant after less than two years of operation suggests vertical integration was not profitable. As already noted, the vertical integration of PSF into pork packing appears to have been costly rather than profitable. Operating a pork packing plant requires very different skills than producing hogs.

Minimization of transaction costs is also consistent with feed milling being tied to major feed consumers such as hog operations. These ties exist but most of the feed mills do not belong to commercial feed companies. Most big producers, including the above three packer/producers, produce most of their own feed in big mills central to their production sites. In 1991, about half of the small contractors and two-thirds of the large ones milled their own hog feed—just as do many independents, large and small. At the same time, 81 percent of small contractors and 77 percent of the large ones did not sell any commercial feed and only 13 percent of each group rated commercial feed sales as of great importance in the overall business (Rhodes and Grimes 1992b). Thus the vertical integration of commercial feed companies into hog production is minor. While corn and hog production were once "vertically integrated" on nearly all hog operations, that type of integration has steadily declined while feed milling for hog production is now typical.

The model for explaining horizontal contracting cannot be vertical transaction costs. The approximate model may be the fast food franchise in which a franchisor such as McDonald's saves on capital while obtaining highly motivated local managers and greatly increasing its sales by contracting with individual franchisees. Likewise, the hog contractor can employ all, or most, of his capital on hogs and feed, rather than on land and facilities while the grower avoids certain market risks and obtains a key role in a hog operation that he could not capitalize on his own.

In summary, the profits achieved by being a leader in reducing production costs has been the main incentive for structural change; reducing transaction costs by vertical relationships has been a minor one. The volume of hogs produced in vertical integration is not yet important; furthermore, much of it has been attracted more by high returns on equity in hog production than by the small savings achievable in transaction costs (Rhodes 1993b).

Vertical Coordination and Spot Markets for Slaughter Hogs

The traditional method of selling slaughter hogs on the spot market is gradually being replaced. I define spot market as taking hogs to market (public market, buying point, or packer dock) and taking the going price for that specific weight and quality range. The spot market is gradually being replaced by a set of prior agreements that are short of vertical integration but are usually categorized as forms of vertical coordination.

Grimes and Rhodes (1995a) obtained information on marketing methods in their 1995 survey of medium and very large producers of hogs. They found that marketing methods were highly related to size of producers; the larger the operations, the less reliance on spot markets. The medium-size producers (those marketing 1,000 to 49,999 head annually) sold 71 percent of their hogs on spot markets, 17 percent on formula prices (prices based upon a formula previously agreed upon), 3 percent on a fixed price set previous to delivery (a cash contract), 2 percent on a risk-sharing deal with the packer, and 7 percent other (a catchall of miscellaneous answers and nonanswers). In contrast, the very large producers (those larger than medium) sold only 10 percent of their hogs on the spot market, 78 percent by formula pricing, 1 percent on fixed price contracts, 2 percent on risk-sharing deals with packers, and 9 percent other ("other" for the very large producers referred mainly to internal transfer pricing of vertically integrated packers). Grimes and Rhodes summarized: "The low usage of spot markets by the superproducers and zero usage by the mega producers [those marketing more than one-half million head annually] raises a red flag for price discovery as the industry trends toward a larger size. If most everyone in the next century tries to free ride on the prices discovered by those using spot markets, those spot markets will lack the volume necessary to provide reliable price discovery" (Grimes and Rhodes 1995a, p. 4).

Implications of Structural Change

Consumers are obvious winners as these large gains in production efficiencies and the smaller gains sometimes available in vertical relationships are passed up to consumers in terms of lower prices and better products. Innovative producers are winners. Losers include those producers that hang on to obsolete ways. Probably 80 percent of current producers will exit the industry within the next twenty years. To exit is not necessarily to lose in economic terms; however, some exiting producers will experience economic loss and some will suffer emotional loss. Hog production once provided an entry into farming for young people with a high ratio of time and energy to capital; that entry route is rapidly closing except for the possibility of becoming a grower. The limited independence of growers is repugnant to many farmers —especially in the major production areas of the Corn Belt—and the opportunity to be a grower is sharply limited geographically (Rhodes and Grimes 1992a).

As hog production becomes more concentrated in units and firms, it also becomes more concentrated geographically. As some communities gain thousands of sows, more communities will lose hog farmers and hogs, with contrasting economic impacts. North Carolina has gained a major industry as it has moved in fifteen years from being a minor player to second only to Iowa. Some state economic development agencies view megaproducers as they would any major employer and are welcoming them.

However, some people in growth areas—including potential ones—are not pleased. Modern hog production has the reputation in many quarters of being a "dirty" industry (in the same class as smokestack industries). Those not getting employment or direct economic benefits from new hog production may be most conscious of certain social costs. A major group of losers may be the rural neighbors. The odors allegedly associated with freshly applied effluent and overloaded lagoons induce increasingly the most common and vociferous complaints. Occasionally, overflowing lagoons have polluted streams. Communities often sharply divide in their opinions about the importance of such effects (Stroud; Hendricks; Marbery 1994g). The reality is that courts have awarded nuisance damages and have ordered operations to clean up or close down offending units (Marbery 1994d; Bell). A recent article in *Choices* cites research findings that the sales prices of North Carolina rural homes have been adversely affected by the building of nearby hog facilities (Vukina, Roka, and Palmquist), so markets are recognizing the odor problem as real. Several states have recently tightened regulations relating to lagoons and their operation.

Large, specialized hog operations must develop financial reserves in the high-price phase of the hog cycle to survive the low-price phase because they lack income from other sources to carry them when hogs are losing money. Specialized broiler operations have often struggled with that problem. However, even diversified public corporations such as Ralston Purina eventually exited broiler production with the comment that their stockholders did not appreciate the cyclical earnings associated with broilers. Perhaps risk will encourage more vertical integration of packing and hog production since their earning cycles tend to partially offset one another. If so, the more closely held companies may do better, as has been true in broilers. Most of the big producers of hogs, including the few packer producers, are closely held operations that have less need to calm panicky stockholders when hog prices dive. Some producers, stung by the low prices of late 1994, are currently showing interest in risk-sharing marketing contracts with packers (King). In any case, rising risk and ways to handle it are implications of the current structural change.

One of the major concerns of smaller producers associated with these structural changes is market access. Will packers favor those producers that can regularly supply 1,000 hogs per week or even per day and give lower prices to small producers—or even refuse to buy from them when supplies are abundant? The South Dakota Pork Council board of directors recently considered a proposal to study the feasibility of producer-owned packing plants (Marbery 1994i). While one may think these fears overblown, even the megaproducers on the East Coast are much concerned about "shackle space" among their few packer-buyers. If the Midwest markets were to become as concentrated, market access could become a serious problem there.

It appears commercial feed companies are currently in the process of losing most of their market for hog feeds—complete rations, especially—although some high-tech operations may preserve a specialized role and a few firms such as Cargill and Continental are engaged in major hog production. Many Corn Belt feed dealers, including local cooperatives, are losing, or expecting to lose, much of their hog feed sales. Some have turned to production contracts to try to maintain their volume. Farmland, a large regional cooperative in the Midwest, has struggled to save feed business and maintain supplies for its packing plants while minimizing the resentment of some members who feel that their cooperative is competing against them (Bodus and Knudsen; Marbery 1994a). Most cooperatives probably lack the organizational attributes that will enable them to keep up in this race toward bigness (Rhodes 1993a).

In an interrelated economy, other firms and agencies will have to adjust. Those in extension and experiment station research must adjust if they are to remain relevant to large producers that have (1) direct relationships with equipment and drug manufacturers, (2) highly educated specialists on the payroll or as consultants, and (3) the capacity to test new ideas with thousands of animals. There are only three specialized hog magazines left, and magazine ads may not be the most effective way for major drug companies and equipment suppliers to reach the few hundred decision makers controlling the bulk of hog production in the twenty-first century.

State producer associations face considerable adjustment as their numbers shift. In the Midwest, some associations have had a difficult path to tread as some members resist the entry of major producers from outside while others do not.

There is some action resulting in—and a great deal more discussion about—producers cooperating together and—sometimes—forming networks with allied industries such as packers and veterinarians. Some producers are achieving economies through joint purchasing of inputs, joint marketing, sharing data, etc. Growth in participation has been rapid, and Grimes and Rhodes (1995a) estimated that networking producers marketed about one-fifth of the national slaughter in 1994.

Marketing agencies serving smaller producers, such as the terminal livestock markets, dealers, and independent buying stations, will suffer further loss of volume. Veterinarians with general practices will lose hog business in many cases. (See Hurt for a complementary discussion of implications of the industrialization of hog production.)

Policy Alternatives

Although federal macro policies involving taxes or interest rates have impacted structural change, it is highly unlikely that any national policies will be formulated specifically to either directly hamper or accelerate changes in the structure of hog production. The most significant effect of national policies may be on whether merger policy is enforced to prevent any move toward high concentration of packers in the Corn Belt. Thus the policy struggles of large producers and their opponents will remain mostly at the state or local level.

State Protection of Family Farms

Several Corn Belt states have laws designed to protect the more traditional-size farm operated by a family (Hamilton and Andrews). State policy makers face a basic economic quandary. If family farmers in states A and B obtain, or keep, anticorporate legislation that effectively bars big firm hog production, and then that production goes to welcoming states C and D, the economic benefits of a new employer have been lost. Moreover, the family farmers in states A and B have not been saved, because in a national market for pork, the impact of the new production in states C and D on hog prices is the same as if it were in states A and B. Realization of that economic limitation to state regulation has led to considerable pressures for change in the several Midwestern states with restrictive regulations (Bodus and Penner; Marbery

1994c). For example, Kansas and Oklahoma have recently lowered barriers. Kansas has gone to a county option on corporate farms (Perkins; Marbery 1994b, 1994e, 1994h). However, a new group of citizens has become concerned about the development of new hog operations.

Zoning and Nuisance Complaints

"Not in my backyard" (NIMBY) opposition has become very real for large, and even for smaller, producers seeking to locate or expand in the Corn Belt. There seems to be an increasing willingness of neighbors to take their complaints to court—sometimes against long-existing units and even against fairly small ones (Bell; Hendricks; Marbery 1994d, 1994f, and 1994e; *National Hog Farmer*). Organized community opposition is slowing the issuance of the necessary regulatory permits and sometimes scaring away potential developers. The protagonists of family farms and those fighting to keep out a "dirty" industry are natural allies in the fight against big hog units (Marbery 1994f). In my state, dozens of angry neighbors watch closely for any infractions of state water quality regulations by the large corporate producers (Stroud).

These attitudes are causing large producers to think more about locating in arid, sparsely populated areas with abundant supplies of cheap land although water rights can be a problem (Marbery 1995; McMahon 1994). The Circle Four group of producers starting up in a rural Utah valley have agreed to locate new production units more than three miles from any residence (Marbery 1994g). There are probably only a trivial number of hog production units in this nation today that could meet that site distance criterion. While such a site distance policy would probably greatly minimize the valid complaints about odors, it would be a very costly policy to implement in areas of expensive land and typically dense rural populations in the Corn Belt. In fact, to maintain the current distribution of hogs among 200,000 farm operations would be virtually impossible under such a siting policy. Thus the NIMBY-generated policies may cut against the smaller producers as much as the larger ones. There are difficult policy trade-offs between clean air and economic development being made rather hastily on a state and/or local level.

County, or even township, zoning is being tried as a way to serve the NIMBY interests (Hamilton and Andrews; Hendricks; Vansickle 1994; Marbery 1994g, 1994h). Farmers and other rural people have often tended to oppose the rules and regulations inherent in zoning, but some entities are voting it in. If an operation has already sunk considerable capital into a locality, it will not yield readily to local opposition. However, given that many areas have welcomed new hog operations, a larger operator searching for sites may pass by those areas that organize opposition. Thus the main effect of NIMBY policies is more likely to be micro than macro. Such policies are likely to affect more the where than the how of hog production. While it is too soon to know how much effect NIMBY forces will have, it is conceivable that sizeable production will move west to more sparsely populated and cheaper rangeland where an economic boost can be obtained with little affront to the nostrils of its residents.

Movement west might rely mainly on vertical integration. While considerable development has occurred in northeast Colorado by nonintegrated producers that sell their hogs in Nebraska and Iowa, the movement to more distant areas such as Utah may be typified by Circle Four that includes Smithfield Packing among its members. Any producer venturing far from established packers must consider market access. On the other hand, big lots for cattle feeding developed far from packers on the High Plains in the 1960s and eventually drew packers to them via open-market mechanisms (Marbery 1994c). Is the cattle feeding or the broiler model to be our guide in this case?

Research Suggestions

The following are a few suggestions rather than an attempt to propose a full research agenda. What are the feasible roles for producer organizations in increasing competitiveness and handling risk? Such organizations may include, but not be limited to, producer networks and alliances, existing and new cooperatives, and other legal entities.

How efficiently can packers obtain the production of the optimum quality mix of pork using open-market mechanisms compared to more closely coordinating institutions such as marketing or vertical production contracts or joint ventures?

What are the minimum sizes of units and firms that allow 98 percent of the maximum obtainable economies of size and specialization?

What is the variance in income arising solely from variations in productivity over a five-year period in well-managed operations? Even factory-produced hogs cannot be stamped out like widgets; disease organisms are remarkably resilient, and they can devastate productivity at times. Variance in income becomes an important influence on the entry and exit of firms with large sunk costs and complete commodity specialization.

What institutions can redistribute risks to those most willing and able to bear them? Who will be the main risk takers? Are there societal concerns about the locus of risks?

What legal protections for growers make sense in terms of efficiency considerations, market and political realities, and mainstream ethics? Agricultural economists cannot provide the complete answer, but they can play a larger role in an area now dominated by attorneys and sociologists.

What are the long-term prospects for the competitive viability of horizontal production contracts under a variety of plausible scenarios?

What are the trade-offs for various current and potential production areas in terms of input costs, production efficiencies, markets, and social costs? Can we develop some institutional rules that could greatly reduce social costs?

Summary

U.S. hog production has mostly been industrialized in the past twenty-five years. Much further concentration of ownership and control is in process. About 10 percent of the nation's hog producers marketed almost 83 percent of all commercial slaughter in 1994. Each of the largest producers generally controls many production units through ownership of some facilities and contract production in others. Production through multiple units allows a firm to attain great size; almost 17 percent of the national slaughter in 1994 came from only 66 producers. Diseconomies of size do not appear to exist for several firms that have each surpassed a volume of 90,000 sows in production. The volume of hogs finished by contract growers has been rising and reached almost 17 percent of the national slaughter in 1994. However, contrary to public perception, only a minority of the contractual volume is vertical—between growers and packers and/or growers and feed companies—while a majority is horizontal—between contractor-producers and growers. Both horizontal and vertical contracts have extended the capital of entrepreneurial contractors and speeded growth of large units. However, contract production is neither a necessary nor a sufficient condition for the large operations.

The driving force of structural change has been the dynamic exploitation of profit opportunities associated with new technologies and managerial techniques. It is argued that changes in consumer demand have not been a primary force in the past. The primary route for such expression would have been through production directly controlled by packers, but that output has been a trivial part of the national slaughter. However, it is now a growing part because a few packers are increasing their controlled hog production and two large producers, Cargill and PSF, have recently become pork packers. Packers' control of hog production, and hence their ability to directly reflect changes in consumer demand into production specifications, could conceivably become quite important in the next few years.

Consequences are being felt by displaced hog producers, packers, commercial feed companies, trade associations, hog industry magazines, extension, neighbors, and communities. As extremely widespread production is being concentrated into fewer production units and areas, communities and states debate whether they shall compete for, or try to bar, these allegedly dirty industries. While trying to save family farms by anticorporate legislation at the state level has not worked, a new force for regulation is the NIMBY reaction of rural neighbors. Continuation of the currently growing trend of neighbors and neighborhoods legislating and litigating against odor nuisances may drive more hog operations toward the wide open spaces of the arid West. Such removal could accelerate a more rapid concentration in ownership and vertical integration.

Notes

This paper is a reprint, with updating, of a paper of the same title published in the *Review of Agricultural Economics* 17(1995):107–118 and is republished by permission of that journal, which holds the copyright.

1 It is a pleasure to acknowledge the long-time collaboration of my extension colleague, Glenn Grimes. Thanks to the thousands of hog producers who have filled out question-naires in the past twenty-one years. Thanks, without any accompanying liability, are extended to Glenn, Marvin Hayenga, and Michael Monson for their comments on this paper.

2 Four operations with 95,000 or more sows in full production were reported in October 1994 (Tyson, 95,000; PSF, 97,000; Carroll Foods, 110,000; and Murphy, 180,000) (Freese).

3 USDA Acting Chief Economist Keith Collins was quoted in the December 12, 1994, *Feedstuffs* as saying at the November 29, 1994, House Agricultural Subcommittee hearing on pork margins: "With pork supplies expected to remain near record levels for several years, prices will remain under pressure, and low cost, typically larger operations will continue at a distinct advantage" (Carlson, p. 7).

References

Barkema, A., and M. L. Cook. 1993. "The Changing U.S. Pork Industry: A Dilemma for Public Policy." *Economic Review* 78, Second Quarter, pp. 49–65. Kansas City, Mo.: Federal Reserve Bank of Kansas City.

Bell, A. 1994. "Size Is No Protection in Nuisance Suits." *Pork '94*, November, pp. 44–45.

Bodus, T., and K. Knudsen. 1989. "Farmland Looks at a Changing Future." *Pork '89*, May, pp. 52 and 54.

Bodus, T., and K. Penner. 1988. "The Corporate Giant: Friend or Foe?" *Pork '88*, April, pp. 22–24.

Carlson, Gordon S. 1994. "Hearing on Pork Price Spreads Yields Little Good News." *Feedstuffs*, December 12, p. 7.

Freese, B. 1995. "Pork Powerhouses." *Successful Farming*, October, pp. 20–22.

Grimes, G., and V. J. Rhodes. 1994. *Marketings of the Nation's Very Large Producers of Hogs*. Agricultural Economics Report 1994-3, University of Missouri–Columbia.

———. 1995a. *1994 Hog Production and Marketing Activities of Medium and Very Large U.S. Hog Producers*. Agricultural Economics Report 1995-5, University of Missouri–Columbia.

———. 1995b. *1994 Marketings of the Nation's Medium and Very Large Producers of Hogs*. Agricultural Economics Report 1995-7, University of Missouri–Columbia.

Hamilton, N., and G. Andrews. 1992. *State Regulation of Contract Feeding and Packer Integration in the Swine Industry*. White Paper 92-4, Iowa Agricultural Law Center, Drake University.

Hayenga, M., V. J. Rhodes, J. A. Brandt, and R. E. Deiter. 1985. *The U.S. Pork Sector: Changing Structure and Organization*. Ames, Iowa: Iowa State University Press.

Hendricks, M. 1994. "Farms Causing a Stink." *Kansas City Star*, November 29, section A, pp. 1 and 10.

Hurt, C. 1994. "Industrialization in the Pork Industry." *Choices*, Fourth Quarter, pp. 9–13.

Iowa State University Swine Task Force. 1988. *The Iowa Pork Industry: Competitive Situation and Prospects*, pp. 59–63. Iowa State University STF1, December.

King, M. 1995. "Producer/Packer Contracts Take Center Stage." *Pork '95*, March, pp. 34–37.

McMahon, K. 1994. "Westward Bound!" *National Hog Farmer*, May 15, pp. 34–36.

———. 1996. "'Newco' Picks Up the Pieces." *National Hog Farmer*, August 15, pp. 10, 14, and 19.

Marbery, S. 1994a. "Hog Industry Insider." *Feedstuffs*, February 7, pp. 22–23.

———. 1994b. "Hog Industry Insider." *Feedstuffs*, April 18, pp. 18–19.

———. 1994c. "Hog Industry Insider." *Feedstuffs*, May 2, pp. 58–59.

———. 1994d. "Hog Industry Insider." *Feedstuffs*, June 20, pp. 22–23.

———. 1994e. "Hog Industry Insider." *Feedstuffs*, August 1, pp. 22–23.

———. 1994f. "Hog Industry Insider." *Feedstuffs*, September 5, pp. 22 and 27.

———. 1994g. "Hog Industry Insider." *Feedstuffs*, November 7, pp. 40–41.

———. 1994h. "Hog Industry Insider." *Feedstuffs*, November 21, pp. 20–21.

———. 1994i. "Hog Industry Insider." *Feedstuffs*, December 19, pp. 22–23.

———. 1994j. "Minnesota Reformers Push Corporate Farming Debate." *Feedstuffs*, May 2, pp. 1 and 44.

———. 1994k. "PSF Sues Township Over Zoning That's Keeping Hogs Out." *Feedstuffs*, August 22, p. 5.

———. 1994l. "PSF to Acquire National Farms of Texas." *Feedstuffs*, April 18, p. 1.

————. 1995. "Hog Industry Insider." *Feedstuffs*, February 27, p. 21.

Miller, M. 1995. "Group Marketing: More Than Pooling Hogs." *Pork '95*, March, pp. 38, 43, and 44.

National Hog Farmer. 1994. "Corporate Farming Debate Heats Up." November 15, pp. 22–24, 28, 30, and 32.

Perkins, J. 1994. "Hog Boom: Making It Happen." *Des Moines Register*, May 22, section J, pp. 1–2.

Rhodes, V. J. 1990a. *Structural Trends in U.S. Hog Production.* Agricultural Economics Report 1990-5, University of Missouri–Columbia.

————. 1990b. *U.S. Contract Production of Hogs.* Agricultural Economics Report 1990-1, University of Missouri–Columbia.

————. 1993a. *Cooperatives' Role in Hog Contract Production.* Washington, D.C.: U.S. Department of Agriculture, Agricultural Cooperative Service, Research Report 116.

————. 1993b. "Industrialization of Agriculture: Discussion." *American Journal of Agricultural Economics* 75:1137–39.

Rhodes, V. J., R. Finley, and G. Grimes. 1974. *A 1974 Survey of Large-Scale Hog Production in the U.S.* Extension Special Report 165, University of Missouri–Columbia.

Rhodes, V. J., D. Flottman, and M. H. Procter. 1987. "Basic Data on U.S. Medium/Large Size Hog Operations, 1986–87." Agricultural Economics Working Paper 1987-17, University of Missouri–Columbia.

Rhodes, V. J., and G. Grimes. 1975. *Large Volume Hog Production in the U.S.: A 1975 Survey.* Agricultural Experiment Station Report SR114, University of Missouri–Columbia.

————. 1980. "The Changing Structure of the Hog Industry." *Farm Structure.* Washington, D.C.: U.S. Senate Committee on Agriculture Print, April.

————. 1992a. *Structure of U.S. Hog Production: A 1992 Survey.* Agricultural Economics Report 1992-3, University of Missouri–Columbia.

————. 1992b *U.S. Contract Production of Hogs: A 1992 Survey.* Agricultural Economics Report 1992-2, University of Missouri–Columbia.

————. 1994. *Marketings of the Nation's Very Large Producers of Hogs.* Agricultural Economics Report 1994-3, University of Missouri–Columbia.

Stroud, J. 1996. "Farm's Fallout: Busted Banks and a 'Hog Fog.'" *St. Louis Post-Dispatch*, August 18, section E, pp. 1 and 8.

U.S. Department of Agriculture. 1992. *Meat Animals Production, Disposition and Income, 1991 Summary.* Washington, D.C.: National Agricultural Statistics Service, April.

U.S. Department of Commerce. *1959–1992 Census of Agriculture.* Washington, D.C.: Bureau of the Census.

Vansickle, J. 1994. "Expansion Dream Survives Roadblocks." *National Hog Farmer*, June 15, pp. 12, 14–15, and 18.

————. 1995. "The Midwest Can Compete." *National Hog Farmer*, March 15, pp. 28 and 30.

Vukina, T., F. Roka, and R. Palmquist. 1996. "Swine Odor Nuisance." *Choices*, First Quarter, pp. 26–29.

Williamson, O. E. 1989. "Transaction Cost Economics." *Handbook of Industrial Organization*, ed. R. Schmalensee and R. D. Willig, vol. 1, pp. 135–182. Amsterdam, The Netherlands: North- Holland.

11 Vertical Relationships and Producer Independence

DENNIS R. HENDERSON

My purpose herein is to present a case for why we should interpret evidence of increasing industrialization in the food and agricultural sector, including the pork subsector, as indicative of reduced farm-operator independence. Specifically, I argue that industrialization is synonymous with interdependence; interdependence being an antonym to independence. My argument is conceptual; I present it without empirical elaboration. Yet it is based on a perception of structural change in the sector that seems hardly debatable—a trend toward fewer and larger agro-industrial complexes that orchestrate the food chain, if not from "conception to consumption," then at least from "the farm gate to the dinner plate."

I hold a few truths to be self-evident: (1) farm production enterprises are becoming fewer and larger, (2) a relatively small and declining share of farm production is sold through a transaction in which all terms of exchange are set "on the spot" once production is complete, and (3) both (1) and (2) result from the competitive drive among firms in the sector to supply customers with an array of appealing products at sales-enhancing prices. In short, I believe observed trends associated with industrialization are logical outcomes of efforts by firms in the sector to increase profits by expanding sales, reducing costs, and gaining market share, i.e., these trends are economically rational. Within the livestock/meat complex, I lift up the relative commercial success of poultry meat as casual but persuasive evidence.

Industrialization can be defined in many ways. As put forward many years ago by my mentor Jim Shaffer, the concept I find most compelling is a process in which the production or supply of a product is broken down into specialized steps. An automobile manufacturing assembly line comes readily to mind. Certainly, today's food chain is better characterized as a system composed of specialists (e.g., breeders, nutritionists, veterinarians, feeders, environmental managers, sorters, deboners, formulators, fabricators, packagers, advertising copywriters, media buyers, retail electronic check-out technicians) than an amalgamation of family farms and general stores.

The "flip side" of specialization is, of course, interdependence. Interdependencies arise from the need for close coordination among specialists making up the chain of supply in order for that chain to function effectively and efficiently. A group of interdependent specialists may be clustered into a common firm, but more likely they are less formally amalgamated through coalitions, contracts, alliances, standard operating practices, and other forms of mutual agreement. Relevant to this discussion is the question, to what extent do farmers (or others in the chain, for that matter) give up independence of decision making as a result of the industrialization (i.e., specialization) process?

I submit that the answer can be found, at least in part, in the nature of the exchange arrangements used within the chain. Because exchange typically occurs between upstream and/or downstream enterprises, this is inherently a vertical phenomenon. Even in instances in which a group of producers pool or coordinate acquisitions and/or sales through horizontal agreements (e.g., farmer cooperatives), I maintain that the nature of the vertical exchange carries important intelligence regarding who is directly influencing the behavior of whom. Given considerable evidence of grower-to-grower contracting in the pork subsector, understanding the nature of the vertical arrangements of the contractor-growers would seem to be particularly germane to understanding producer interdependence.

I also submit that a spot transaction is the most purely independent form of exchange. By spot transaction, I mean that *all* terms of exchange are determined on the spot of the exchange, including, inter alia, price, quantity exchanged, assessment of quality, time of delivery, and form of payment. Independence prevails because neither party has an obligation to alter her/his business behavior in response to the desire or need of the other. Essentially, with a spot transaction there is no agreement, or *understanding*, between the parties with regard to *any* manner of doing business prior to, or subsequent to, the time of exchange.[1]

To extend this argument, the existence of any method of exchange other than a spot transaction can be taken to be a sign that some degree of interdependence is at least tacitly recognized by the parties to the exchange. Something as simple, for example, as an agreement on delivery time indicates it is in the interest of one party for the other to behave in a specific manner regarding the giving or taking of physical control over the good being exchanged. Obviously, the number of terms that may be subject to such an agreement can vastly exceed time of delivery; location, quantity, quality, time, and/or method of payment, bonus for superior performance, and penalty for shirking come immediately to mind.

To clarify, this view contrasts with the often-cited conclusion that the demise of spot markets has led to an industrial structure in agriculture (see Barry, for example). Rather, it is based upon the perception that it is the process of industrialization, i.e., specialization and its corollary, interdependence, that have given rise to exchange arrangements other than spot markets—specifically, arrangements that recognize or codify interdependency.

One feature of spot transactions is the linear nature of the compensation scheme. That is, total payment (y) typically equals price (p) times quantity (q), price being uniform across the relevant range of quantities. Given this linear payment scheme, it is relatively straightforward for each party to the transaction to determine profit-optimizing behavior. However, interdependence disrupts that calculus. In the interdependent case, one party's ability to optimize depends upon another party's performing in a specific manner. In a simple example, the ability of a meat packing firm to set a profit-maximizing price on its output rests on its ability to acquire livestock at marginal cost. If a livestock producer has some degree of market power, let us say, because he or she is producing a differentiated good that has been genetically tailored to meet the packer's idiosyncratic processing requirements, marginal cost pricing is quantity dependent; price is nonlinear.

What, then, is the calculus of optimization? There is a fairly sizeable literature dealing with this problem. Some of this follows the form of principal-agent. I find this to be particularly helpful in thinking about exchange agreements other than spot transactions, that is, transactions with nonlinear prices or compensation schemes. It can help advance our understanding of what motivates the terms of such agreements and the implications of such schemes for how one party influences the behavior of another.

In the standard principal-agent problem (see Stiglitz), one party (the principal) seeks a contract that will maximize his or her expected profits provided the second party (the agent) undertakes a set of complementary actions. The contract specifies a compensation scheme that creates incentives for the agent to undertake those actions. That is, the compensation scheme is one that, when the agent behaves in a way that maximizes his or her returns, ensures that the principal's profits also will be maximized. In other words, the agent is compensated for putting forth effort, such as growing out lean, meaty-type hogs, that benefits the ability of the principal to pursue an optimal marketing strategy, such as the sale of lean, low-fat meat.

While these compensation schemes may take many forms, they can be generalized into the relatively simple case of a two-part tariff: $y = pq + s$ where y, p, and q are as before and s represents some variety of an incentive payment (or penalty). Examples of the latter could be a bonus to a grower for hogs that exceed a specified lean-to-fat ratio or penalties for late delivery or light weights. The key feature is that total compensation is set by a combination of ad valorem and lumpy, or lump-sum, components, the purpose of the latter being an incentive for the agent to conduct her/his business in a way that directly benefits the principal. If the principal could maximize profits simply by dealing with the agent on an arm's length (spot) basis, there would be no reason for other than an ad valorem payment.

Katz, among others, has demonstrated the efficiency-enhancing (or profit-maximizing) outcomes of two-part tariff schemes in markets for intermediate goods that exhibit the following characteristics:[2]

1. Large transactions by sophisticated buyers.
2. Products with complex bundles of attributes.
3. Interdependent demands by buyers.
4. A buyer's downstream game is affected by its upstream behavior.
5. Buyers can credibly threaten backward integration.

These appear to be conditions that are prevalent in the food chain; they may be norms in the pork subsector.

The appeal of the nonlinear compensation scheme is, even though one party directly influences the behavior of the other in order to deal with the condition of interdependency, both parties act rationally. Thus, while the size of the incentive payment may reflect the relative bargaining power of the two parties, neither party exercises power in the sense of forcing suboptimal behavior by the other. To me, this seems to be a remarkable accomplishment when viewed in the light of the numerous competitive imperfections in the sector that would lead neoclassical microtheorists to predict less-than-optimal market outcomes. Indeed, a careful reading of the principal-agent literature seems to reveal how commonly cited rationale for vertical contracts (e.g., assure market, reduce risk) generalize into the case of a nonlinear payment scheme.

One of the undone tasks is getting about the business of properly identifying the nonlinear payment schemes embodied in the marketing arrangements, agreements, and contracts that are actually used throughout the sector. This means more than identifying the existence of written contracts; it means identifying and classifying *all* forms of exchange arrangements, delving into the terms of those agreements, and perfecting measurement and analytical techniques that are both tractable and robust in terms of assessing market performance. We should look wherever there are transactions that resemble something other than a spot exchange—even where those transactions appear on the surface to be among horizontal counterparts. The existence of such schemes, I allege, is prima facie evidence of subsector interdependencies.

While I offer no empirical evidence, I believe that it is reasonable to interpret the general trend toward industrialization in the pork subsector as indicative of real vertical interdependencies. These interdependencies reach from far upstream, through all stages of swine production, downstream to the point of retail sale. These interdependencies mean that many—perhaps most—growers among others in the subsector are not independent operators but function in concert with those at other stages. Evidence of these interdependencies can be found in a careful examination of compensation schemes. Compensation schemes with the general form of a per-unit price plus an incentive payment signal interdependency. Such contracts, I submit, do not impose suboptimal behavior on growers, but do put them in the status of agents responding to principals elsewhere in the sector.

Notes

1   Exception would be rules of trade that have been accepted as standard within a specific exchange or market (e.g., delivery dates and locations associated with organized trading in commodity futures contracts).
2   A more detailed discussion of how nonlinear compensation schemes resolve problems, such as moral hazard and opportunism that are common to exchange under these structural conditions, can be found in Henderson and Frank.

References

Barry, P. J. 1995. "Industrialization of U.S. Agriculture: Policy, Research, and Education Needs." *Agricultural and Resource Economics Review* 24:128–35.
Henderson, D. R., and S. D. Frank. "Quantifying Vertical Coordination: Refinement of the Frank-Henderson Vertical Coordination Index." In this volume, pp. 99–112.

Katz, M. L. 1989. "Vertical Contractual Relations." *Handbook of Industrial Organization*, ed. R. Schmalensee and R. Willig, vol. 1, pp. 655–721. Amsterdam, The Netherlands: North-Holland.

Stiglitz, J. J. 1987. "Principal and Agent." *The New Palgrave—A Dictionary of Economics*, ed. J. Eatwell, M. Milgate, and P. Newman, pp. 966–72. London, England: Macmillan.

12 Alternative Models for the Future of Pork Production

ROGER G. GINDER

Pork production in the United States has typically taken place on diversified "family" farming operations in which the operator independently makes virtually all critical production and marketing decisions. The decisions include breeding stock genetics, feeding programs, health programs, the facilities used, farrowing cycles, and all other key production decisions. Marketing decisions such as time of sale, weight at sale, and the choice of packer have also been made independently by individual operators. In nearly all cases, these producer-level decisions were made in response to open-market prices on both the input and output sides of the market.

The demand in the input markets and the supply in the output markets have been largely determined as an aggregated result of uncoordinated decisions by individual producers acting independently. Suppliers have responded to the input demand, packers have slaughtered and processed the supply farmers placed on the market, and consumers have purchased the available quantity supplied. Open-market prices have served as the coordinator for the system through a set of broadly defined commodity grades (see Figure 12.1).

Several conditions have served as a foundation for the producer-centered commodity pork production system:

1. Farmer position as low-cost producer.
2. Independent farmer capability to finance production.
3. Access to production technology and genetics by farmers.
4. Access to competitive open markets by independent farmers.
5. Little or no coordination in the system by large firms.
6. Consumer acceptance of product as produced.

247

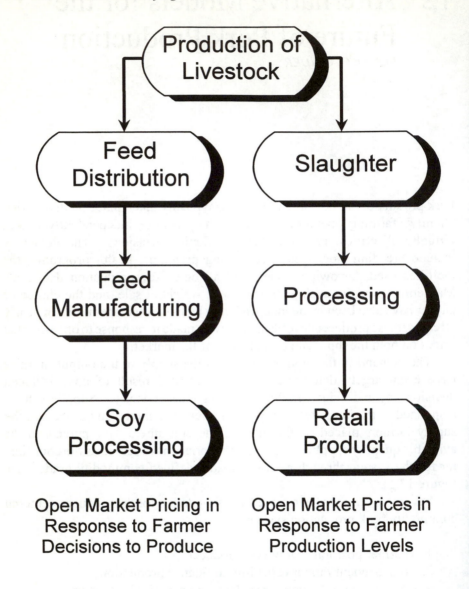

Open Market Pricing in
Response to Farmer
Decisions to Produce

Open Market Prices in
Response to Farmer
Production Levels

12.1 Traditional independent producer-centered market channel for livestock

These conditions taken together have made the decentralized independent producer system the dominant means of production in the United States through most of its history.

First, this system has been the low-cost means of production. No competing system has been willing or able to match the cost performance of the system. Second, the independent producer system has had the capability to finance the production of all the pork demanded by consumers. Third, most independent producers have had open access to production technology and genetics on a competitive basis. Beyond that, independent producers have had open access to slaughter markets and, until recently, no significant attempts had been made by large firms to coordinate the production and marketing of hogs. Finally, consumers have been willing to purchase the product the system produced with prices adjusting to move the volume produced. But these conditions may not be assured in the future.

Virtually every one of these critical underpinnings has been challenged in one way or another over the past decade. Low-cost coordinated systems have developed outside the Midwest and are moving into the core hog production areas of the Corn Belt. New technology and production practices, including uniform genetics, three-site production, phased feeding, split-sex feeding, and all-in/all-out occupancy, have raised the fixed cost commitment for farrow-to-finish operations. Entry of at least one large poultry integrator and large industrialized producers has also resulted in unequal access to production technologies and genetics. Research and development activities are increasingly lodged in the private sector rather than the U.S. Department of Agriculture and land-grant universities where public access is assured. Research findings and even operating efficiency measures are increasingly treated as proprietary information and are largely unavailable to the independent producer sector.

While markets remain open and the majority of the volume still originates from independent producers, the number of hogs sold by large contractors has steadily increased over the past decade and continues to accelerate. Large industrialized producers and contract integrators such as Premium Standard Farms, Seaboard, Tyson, ConAgra (Monfort), Cargill, and Smithfield have entered the market. Integrated and industrialized operations are in a position to operate increasingly outside the commodity hog markets and rely on internally controlled production. Large production contractors are in a position to bring large volumes of hogs into open markets and command price premiums.

Finally, the consumer sector is demanding low-cost, high-quality, consistent retail pork cuts and products. Increasing per capita consumption of chicken and turkey products implies that pork must meet similar cost, quality, and nutritional standards if it is to maintain or increase its per capita consumption levels.

The Bifurcated Production and Marketing Channel

The hog production and marketing channel has been irrevocably changed as a result of the entry of the industrialized producers and the integrated processors. The producer-centered monolithic channel of the past is being supplanted, and new relationships are being forged among levels. A bifurcated channel (Figure 12.2) is developing with a specialty hog side dominated by the industrialized producers with packing and processing facilities and a commodity hog side dominated by independent producers and a few large production contractors without packing and processing facilities. At this time, the commodity hog channel still has the vast majority of the volume and most of that volume is sold through the spot-market transactions between independent producers and packers just prior to slaughter. Only a very modest amount of cash-forward contracting occurs in which the producer retains title to the product but contracts for delivery (at some point during the production period) to a packer. The open spot market remains dominant with the majority of commodity channel volume priced in the market at the time the hogs are delivered for slaughter.

The specialized side of the channel is different in that a significant amount of volume is owned or controlled by a corporation throughout the production and marketing process. This internally owned volume varies from all (or nearly all) of the hogs produced and slaughtered by a firm to cases in which fewer than half the hogs slaughtered are internally owned. In most cases, however, the objective of firms operating on the specialized side of the channel leans toward direct ownership or contractual control of a very high percentage of the production and marketing activities. The span of control extends from the acquisition of the breeding animals to the marketing of final meat product in systems such as Smithfield. Tyson, Seaboard, or Premium Standard would also fall into this general category.

On both sides of the bifurcated channel, trends exist toward cost reduction and increased efficiency as well as providing a higher quality of product for consumers. The two sides of the channel are attempting to generate two

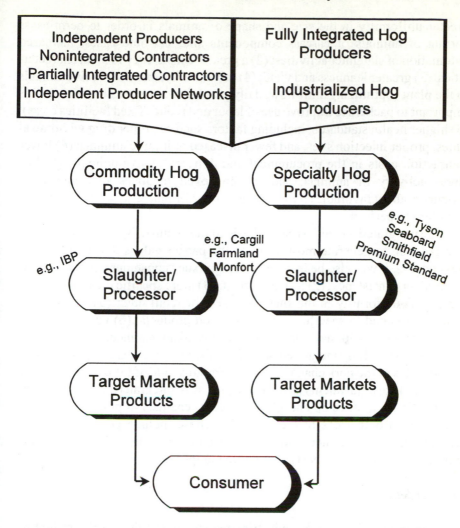

Figure 12.2 The bifurcated pork channel

distinct kinds of values, however. As they seek to create value, both sides of the channel will continue to create significant changes at the production level. Neither side will leave the production system of the past unaffected.

The commodity side of the channel is more likely to pursue "packer values" that translate into lower cost and better-quality commodity meat output for sale at the wholesale level. These "packer values" include (1) greater uniformity in the size and shape of animals in order to permit less sorting of animals or carcass components and, in some cases, increased automation of slaughter activities; (2) a greater consistency in meat characteristics; (3) greater leanness and yield; (4) more predictable flow of live animals to the plant (optimizing shift flow, daily plant flow, or even seasonal flow is important to packers to improve use of labor and reduce fixed facilities costs); (5) higher health standards; including factors such as proper drug withdrawal times, proper injection sites, and fewer diseased or injured animals; (6) lower transaction costs in the procurement and delivery of live animals; (7) low stress delivery of animals; and (8) improved feedback mechanisms to producers about favorable characteristics or performance, as well as problems or failure to perform.

The integrated and industrialized side of the channel, by its nature, will be in a position to generate most or all of the packer values discussed above. Beyond that, it will also be in a position to pursue "consumer values" such as (1) product consistency; (2) leaner product; (3) more specific meat texture and flavor; (4) uniformity in the shape and size of retail cuts; (5) meat that is adapted or suited to specific markets for food products; (6) wholesomeness and safety; (7) nutritional content; and (8) visual appearance.

The entry of fully integrated or industrialized systems is creating changes in both sides of the pork channel. The commodity side of the channel is being forced to make adjustments as the emerging fully integrated or industrialized side continues to develop and grow. Several changes in practices are now occurring on both sides of the channel. These include genetics, channel relationships, procurement practices, pricing and payments, production emphasis, slaughter emphasis, and market emphasis.

Channel Relationships

The commodity side and the industrialized side of the dual pork production and marketing channel are exhibiting very different channel relationships than have existed in the traditional channel of the past. The industrialized side of the channel, by definition, involves very tight coordination and direct control throughout the channel. Coordination and control on this side of the channel are enforced through either contract specification or outright ownership. Virtually all inputs production, activities, and slaughter are brought under one management system.

The commodity side of the channel preserves more of the traditional channel relationships among input suppliers, producers, slaughterers, and processors than the industrialized side. Despite this fact, even the commodity side of the new bifurcated channel is becoming more coordinated than in the past. Nonintegrated contractors prescribe uniform production practices among their contract producers and employ common genetics. Some contractors have integrated backward and own feed mills that they operate as a cost center. At this point, the coordination is aimed more toward generating packer values than final consumer values. Coordination is enforced using less formal means such as price premiums and discounts offered to producers from individual packers. While there are some common factors that are rewarded or discouraged, coordination between producer and packer is usually not tight. Furthermore, there is a great deal of variation among packers in the factors they choose to reward and the level of price premiums or discounts they place on any given factor.

The commodity side continues to produce commodity-end products, but the range of acceptable variation in both live animals and the end products is being noticeably narrowed. The movement of animals to market is becoming more standardized, a larger number of production and health practices are being influenced, and, finally, transaction costs are being more accurately apportioned to producers. Control mechanisms on the commodity side (price premiums and discounts and selective rejection) are less formal than those on the integrated industrialized side, but they are, nonetheless, creating changes in production practices. This represents a fundamental change in the traditional channel relationships between packers and producers.

Procurement Sources

Procurement of livestock on the industrialized side of the channel is accomplished primarily through production contracts for company-owned pigs or through production in facilities that are internally owned and operated by employees. In a few cases, production using company genetics and pigs may be done by either a nonintegrated production contractor or a partially integrated contractor using the contractor's network of producers. Networks of independent producers could also be used. However, in such cases, the input specification and production processes are rigidly defined by the integrated or industrialized firm.

The primary procurement source on the commodity side is still the independent producer. However, a growing fraction of the volume is now being supplied by nonintegrated production contractors who purchase (or contract for) inputs in the open market and do not own packing facilities.

Partially integrated contractors (who own feed mills as well as livestock) are also a growing source of hogs on the commodity side. Producer networks that coordinate marketing genetics and health practices also serve as a source of animals for the commodity hog side of the market. These networks are usually coordinated around some entity such as a veterinarian or feed supplier.

Genetics

The industrialized integrated side of the channel is adopting very specialized genetics. Genetics are selected not only for meat quality, but also for their suitability to specific production practices and facilities and their ability to deliver low, per-unit production costs. It is conceivable that, in the future, genetics may be selected for specific meat characteristics such as flavor, texture, or suitability for processing into highly differentiated food products. But, at the present time, genetics selected by the industrialized side appear to be aimed primarily toward uniformity and production efficiency.

In contrast, the commodity side of the channel continues to handle animals with more varied genetics. Nevertheless, there has been a measurable move toward discouraging some types of genetics by some packers. There is anecdotal evidence of some lots being rejected upon delivery or the producer being told to deliver future loads elsewhere.

Perhaps more significant is the move toward a pricing system that more effectively rewards lean, high-yielding carcasses with minimal backfat and punishes poor carcass quality. The market news price report shown in Table 12.1 provides an example of how commodity packers have responded to the need for improved genetics and quality. A base packer-style carcass of 170 to 191 pounds is priced (with head off) and departures from the base packer carcass are priced based on the lean percentage and carcass weight.

Pricing from the Packer

Packer pricing on the fully integrated or industrialized side of the channel is done mostly through fixed-payment production contracts with contract growers. There may be a few long-term agreements with partially integrated or nonintegrated production contractors with strict performance criteria attached. In a few cases, there may be similar agreements with producer networks.

Pricing on the commodity side of the channel remains open-market with some cash-forward contracting. Once again, while open-market pricing prevails, the use of pricing as an informal means of coordination has resulted in a wider range of premiums and discounts related to the seller's ability to provide the desired packer values.

Production-level Emphasis

Emphasis at the production level on the industrialized/integrated side of the channel is currently focused on production efficiency and per-unit cost of production. There is also a second emphasis on quality and consistency in the meat products produced. The potential exists for emphasis on special meat characteristics as well, but it is not a major factor at this time.

The production-level emphasis on the commodity side of the channel is currently focused on gaining production efficiency. A secondary emphasis is placed on improving management and producing "high-quality" commodity animals that will receive price premiums or at least not be discounted. Commodity-side producers are also concerned about gaining sufficient volume to obtain price premiums from packers. The partially integrated contract producers are attempting to reduce production costs by internalizing feed production as a cost center in some cases. Finally, both the integrated and nonintegrated contractors are adopting the large-scale, three-site production technologies used by the fully integrated or industrialized systems.

Slaughter and Processing Level Emphasis

The primary slaughter emphasis on the fully integrated/industrialized side of the channel is now processing efficiency. However, the potential exists for shifting the efficiency emphasis toward generating brand margins from specialized products in the future. Direct control over genetics, feeding programs, health programs, and other production factors could be used to develop identifiable differentiated consumer-level products. These potentials remain unrealized, however. Although there are currently some product development efforts on the full integrated/industrialized side of the channel, these are not a major emphasis at this time.

On the commodity side of the channel, slaughter-level emphasis is heavily focused on processing efficiency and cost control. Obtaining the volume of animals required to operate plants at (or near) the minimum average cost point remains an important goal for most commodity packers. High-yield, reasonably uniform animals are important in reaching the goal of marketing a high-quality commodity pork competitively.

Table 12.1 Sample market news price report

GS LS232
SPRINGFIELD, IL.
THIS IS A NEW REPORT WHICH WILL BE CODED GX LS232 AS OF JAN. 11, 1993

JANUARY 6, 1993

FEDERAL-STATE

Eastern Cornbelt Direct Hog Trade
Hot Carcass Value Information
Based on Individual Packers Plant Delivered Prices
Lean Value Buying Programs & Weight Differentials

Estimated Deliveries ---> 12,100
Hog Carcass Value STEADY TO MOSTLY 1.00 LOWER

					Percent Lean					
	41-42	43-44	45-46	47-48	49-50	51-52	53-54	55-56	57-58	59-60
Weights	-5.00	-5.00	-3.00	0.84	0.00	1.40	2.50	3.50	3.92	3.92
	-3.25	-1.63	-0.58	0.00	1.25	2.44	3.86	4.88	6.00	7.00
Carcass Wt 140-154	34.50	34.50	35.50	37.50	39.20	40.60	41.72	42.84	43.12	43.12
-17.00 / -8.00	43.39	43.75	45.30	46.00	47.25	48.25	49.25	50.50	51.75	53.00
Carcass Wt 155-162	46.10	47.73	48.78	49.36	50.50	51.75	52.75	53.00	53.50	54.00
-4.88 / -2.00	48.50	49.75	51.30	52.00	53.25	54.25	55.25	56.50	57.75	59.00
Carcass Wt 163-169	49.90	51.50	52.50	53.16	54.00	55.25	55.93	56.50	57.00	57.50
-1.08 / 0.00	51.50	52.36	53.48	54.60	55.44	56.84	57.96	59.08	59.75	61.00

Lean Value***

Carcass Wt 170-191									
49.50	50.50	52.00	54.00	54.50	56.25	57.02	58.50	59.12	59.12
51.80	52.92	54.04	55.16	56.00	57.50	59.50	59.64	60.50	61.50

Lean Value***

Carcass Wt 192-199									
49.25	51.25	53.25	54.00	55.03	56.25	56.61	58.50	58.52	58.52
51.80	52.92	54.25	57.25	57.25	59.25	61.25	61.25	61.25	61.25

Carcass Wt 200-207									
48.50	50.50	52.80	53.38	54.58	55.82	56.15	58.26	58.26	58.26
51.80	52.92	54.04	56.50	56.50	58.50	60.50	60.50	60.50	61.00

Carcass Wt 208-222									
48.00	49.56	50.68	51.53	52.64	53.97	54.31	56.28	56.41	56.41
49.75	52.00	56.00	58.00	58.00	60.00	60.00	60.00	60.00	60.20

Backfat at 10th Rib									
More Than 1.4"	Less Than 1.4"	Less Than 1.25"	Less Than 1.15"	Less Than 1.0"	Less Than .9"	Less Than .75"	Less Than .6"		
Inches								----------->	
Millimeters 36mm	36mm	32mm	30mm	26mm	23mm	20mm	15mm		

Backfat in Tenths at									
<----	1.35	1.20-1.35	1.10-1.25	.95-1.15	.80-1.00	.60-.85	.70	----------->	

Continued on next page

Table 12.1 *Continued*

SUMMARY

DELIVERIES WEDNESDAY　Estimate:　12,100

TREND: STEADY TO MOSTLY 1.00 LOWER

CARCASS WEIGHT	EVALUATION (BACKFAT AT 10TH RIB)	PRICE RANGE
170-191	45-46% Lean/Backfat less than 1.25"	52.00 - 54.04
170-191	47-48% Lean/Backfat less than 1.15"	54.00 - 55.16
170-191	49-50% Lean/Backfat less than 1.00"	54.50 - 56.00
170-191	51-52% Lean/Backfat less than .90"	56.25 - 57.50
170-191	53-54% Lean/Backfat less than .75"	57.02 - 59.50

Actual Paying Prices may not always fall within price ranges. Primary basis for value is lean, determined on individual packer fat measurements may be adjusted for superior or inferior muscling.

This report a service of the USDA and Illinois Department of Agriculture Livestock and Grain Market News (217)782-4925.

Market Emphasis

The market-level emphasis on the industrialized side of the channel is currently focused on selling both commodity and differentiated meats. Some firms are selling differentiated branded products such as hams, bacon, and cold convenience meats. Some have (or are now in the process of developing) branded nonfrozen shelf products and hot processed products such as TV dinners. Most are capable of providing consistent, high-quality meat products to specialty contract buyers with very stringent and narrow quality specifications.

The potential for providing differentiated branded products is not fully developed at the present time. However, as the fully integrated or industrialized firms get slaughter and processing facilities properly designed and operating efficiently, their ability to expand branded product activities is more likely to be exercised. The major impediment at that point will be consumer demand and willingness to pay for specialized products.

The market emphasis on the commodity side of the channel is currently aimed toward providing quality wholesale meat products. This side of the channel now provides the majority of wholesale meat volume to independent processors, institutional buyers, and commodity-oriented contract buyers. It is the principal source of undifferentiated fresh meat case products at the retail food distribution level. These markets tend to be more price conscious and have less rigid quality specifications. They account for a large fraction of total meat sales and are likely to be important markets for at least the next decade.

Future Production Models

The dual channel is by no means static. As stated above, the fully industrialized, integrated side is now attempting to consolidate a low-cost position at the production, slaughter, and, in some cases, processing level. Marketing opportunities for specialized end products are, as yet, largely unrealized, but they remain a potential source of further competitive advantage for firms on the fully industrialized, integrated side of the channel. The efforts in the commodity channel to increase packer efficiency and quality of commodity meat are creating greater (but less formal) coordination between the input level, the production level, and the slaughter level. A variety of producers now coexist in the commodity channel, including small independent producers, large independent producers, nonintegrated production contractors (i.e., production contractors who have partially integrated backward), and networks of independent producers.

There is a great deal of concern about the future viability of the various types of producers in the commodity channel—especially the independent producers. The cost data and study results are somewhat confusing and seem to carry a conflicting message about the relationships between size and the per-unit cost of production. Much of the confusion arises from differences in accounting practices, inventory measurements, and the type of data used. Nevertheless, widely varying results are leading researchers to disagree on the industry direction (i.e., Good et al., using a budgeting approach to compare the costs of a 3,500-sow operation in the Midwest to units with 650 sows and 250 sows). Budgeted costs for the 3,500-sow unit were estimated to be $35.94 per cwt., compared to $37.80 per cwt. for a 650-sow operation and $40.22 per cwt. for a 250-sow operation. This would imply that the 650-sow operation might be cost-competitive with a 3,500-sow operation operated by a partially integrated or nonintegrated production contractor. Presumably smaller operations would be somewhat less cost-competitive with a disadvantage of $4–$5 per cwt., or more than $10 per head produced.

In contrast, Duffy has shown, using actual farm records from two independent sources (Swine Enterprise records and Iowa Farm Business Management Association records), that average costs do not fall significantly beyond about 150 sows. Citing Swine Enterprise records from 1992, 1993, and 1994, he shows the average production cost for the top one-third of the responding producers to be approximately $36 per cwt. in all years and the average size of the top one-third operations to be approximately 120 sows.

To further confuse the issue, Bruns et al., in a six-year study using the Swine Enterprise records, showed that there was remarkable variation in performance by individuals reporting into the system from year to year. Of forty producers tracked over a six-year period, 73 percent were among the lowest one-third in total production cost per cwt. in at least one of the six years. However, only 25 percent of the producers were in the lowest one-third in total production cost for four years or more. Hardly any of the producers (only 3 percent) were in the low-cost one-third for all six years. Similar patterns were found for most other efficiency measures studied. This brings into question the presumption that one segment of the independent producer sector consistently outperforms the rest and attains unit cost levels competitive with the production contractors delivering to the commodity side of the channel.

It is generally agreed that the issue of production cost will play a significant role in the future of the commodity hog side of pork industry. But the different studies lead to quite different conclusions. If the Duffy interpretation of existing cross-sectional data is accurate, small- to modest-size independent producers can continue to produce competitively for the commodity hog side of the channel. In that event, it will be possible for independent farmers to coexist side by side with nonintegrated contract producers on sound economic footing. Although the partially integrated producer (operating feed manufacturing as a cost center) may gain some cost advantage, there would be little need for radical change by the independent producer.

If the budgeted cost data from Good et al. is accurate, a much different picture emerges. Smaller independent producers with fewer than 650 sows will be at a significant cost disadvantage. Independent producers will be forced to make heavier investments in production facilities in order to be cost-competitive with the nonintegrated and partially integrated production contractors. Alternatively, they will be forced into "networks" with other producers in order to match the per-unit costs of the production contractors operating on the commodity side of the channel.

The Duffy findings indicate that a significant portion of independent producers are now cost-competitive at an average size of 120 sows. This implies that these producers are capable of competing with their current complement of fixed assets and labor. It is reasonable to expect they would be viable for five to seven years. These producers appear to be able to compete at least in the short run. But there is evidence that at least some of these producers may encounter difficulty reinvesting when their present facilities are no longer suitable for use. Work by Shaffer shows that investment per breeding female is very low and quite variable among those contributing to swine enterprise records. This may reduce their current average cost below the cost levels that would exist after facilities are renovated and/or replaced. Higher depreciation costs after replacement could place them at a cost disadvantage.

Because cost studies are inconsistent, the current cost of production may not be the best indicator of the future structure of the industry. In the final analysis, investment in facilities may actually provide a better indication of how commodity-side production will occur in the future than either cross-sectional or budgeted cost estimates. The part of the industry investing most heavily in production assets is likely to have the largest share of future production. The vast majority of the new investment in production facilities over the past four years has been made by nonintegrated and partially integrated production contractors. The unwillingness or inability of the independent producer sector to reinvest in production assets will (over time) reduce their position in the industry. This may be more a reflection of the absence of technologies within the financial reach of individual producers than a lack of interest or competence in hog production. But the net result will be to steadily shift a larger and larger percentage of production away from the small- and medium-size independent producers to production contractors and larger independent producers.

The heavy capital investment requirements for the larger operations place the independent producer (particularly the beginning producer) in a difficult situation. Greater amounts of capital, which is usually in short supply, are being substituted for operator and family labor, which is more abundant. Lower capital requirement approaches to production in the commodity side of the channel would be desirable. The establishment of producer networks using "segregated early wean" (SEW) and three-site production holds some promise. This approach would permit more labor-intensive farrowing to take place in existing facilities on individual farms. The pigs (SEW) farrowed would be moved to a common nursery at two weeks of age then on to finishers at a third site after seven weeks in the nursery.

While this approach may use less capital, it requires that producers organize networks and work together. In the process, some decision making sovereignty must be given up by individual producers. This is likely to make the establishment of producer networks difficult and slow, but not impossible.

Summary and Conclusions

The production and marketing channel is now bifurcated. There is an industrialized, fully integrated side capable of producing very specialized pork products for specific end uses. There is also a commodity side with traditional producers and production contractors providing hogs. Most production now moves through the commodity side of the channel. There is increased coordination on the commodity side although it is of the more informal kind.

At present, independent producers are supplying the majority of the volume through the commodity side of the channel, and this is not expected to change precipitously. However, nonintegrated and partially integrated production contractors have been steadily increasing their share of the total marketing. A serious question exists about whether independent producers can coexist alongside production contractors in the future. Cost data from different sources provide a conflicting message. The revealed investment behavior of independent producers indicates that the production contractors are making larger investments in new production facilities. They will account for an increasing percentage of commodity production in the future if these trends continue and the slower rate of investment in the independent sector persists. Networks of individual producers can be formed to better utilize the existing assets and labor of independent producers to help overcome any production cost disadvantages to the traditional production technology and size of operation. Under those circumstances, this kind of model may be the only viable alternative for producers with limited access to capital and limited ability to accept risk. The process of forming networks will be somewhat difficult and will require conscious effort on the part of producers, but it shows a great deal of promise.

References

Bennink, D. 1994. "In Hogs, Bigger Is Not Necessarily Better." *Iowa Farm Business Association Newsletter*. Ames, Iowa.

Bruns, M., J. Kliebenstein, J. Lawrence, and E. Stevermer. 1992. *Iowa Swine Enterprise Return and Production Variability*. Swine Research Report ASL-R971, Cooperative Extension Service, Iowa State University, December.

Duffy, M. 1995. "Profitability in Farming: Today and Tomorrow." Paper presented at 5th annual conference, Leopold Center for Sustainable Agriculture, Iowa State University, Ames, Iowa, March 3.

Ginder, R. G. 1991. "Changing Structure of the Pork Industry." Staff Paper, Department of Economics, Iowa State University.

Good, K., C. Hurt, K. Koster, J. Kadlec, and K. Zering, 1995. "Comparative Costs of Hog Production in the Midwest and North Carolina." Paper presented at Pork Global Competitiveness Seminar, St. Louis, Mo., January 9.

Iowa State University Extension Service. 1992. *Iowa Livestock Enterprise Summaries*. Cooperative Extension EJS-206, ASB.

———. 1993. *Iowa Livestock Enterprise Summaries*. Cooperative Extension EJS-206, ASB.

———. 1994. *Iowa Livestock Enterprise Summaries*. Cooperative Extension EJS-206, ASB.

Shaffer, J. 1995. "Critical Success Factors for Iowa Swine Producers." Staff Paper, Department of Economics, Iowa State University.

13 Sustainable Agriculture: An Alternative Model for Future Pork Producers

JOHN E. IKERD

The expansion of large corporate hog operations has fundamentally transformed the basic nature of the hog/pork sector of the U.S. agricultural economy during the decade of the 1990s. Large-scale, industrial hog operations have gained a position of dominant market power that eventually will make it impossible for independent hog farmers to compete using conventional methods of production and marketing. It is not simply a matter of independent hog farmers staying competitive in terms of costs of production. Profit margins will be squeezed to the point that it may take thousands of sows just to generate an acceptable level of living for a family—at average, or even below-average, costs of production. Even those independent producers who survive the first few rounds of expansion will eventually lose access to markets as the industry completes the process of vertical integration.

Industrial corporations are driven to continually increase returns to "their" capital investments. Historically, this has meant lower returns to labor and hands-on management and higher levels of output per worker employed. Economists have called this trend increasing "labor efficiency." It might be more accurately called increasing "worker displacement." Those who have capital to invest, benefit. Those who have mostly themselves to invest, their ability to work, and to think, lose. There is no reason to believe that the outcome of industrializing the hog/pork sector will yield results that are different. It would take far fewer "hog production workers" to produce the nation's supply of pork than there are "hog farmers" today. Unless hog farmers are offered a viable alternative to the industrial model of production, there will be few if any of them left after another decade.

Hog farmers who fail to recognize this fundamental change, who just try to ride out the cycle as they have in the past, will soon face serious financial stress and a high probability of financial failure. Many undoubtedly will choose to produce on contracts with the large corporate integrators and will become "hog production workers." Hog farmers, who choose to remain independent farmers, rather than someone else's worker, must find a fundamentally different way to farm. Independent hog farmers of the future will be those who develop systems that capitalize on their individual ingenuity and creativity to produce more value with less capital. They will produce in a new economic arena in which the large, vertically integrated hog operations cannot compete. The emerging concept of sustainable agriculture represents independent hog farmers' best hope for finding this viable alternative to survive and even prosper until the industrialization of agriculture becomes a thing of the past.

Sustainable Agriculture: A New Paradigm for Farming

A new agricultural paradigm is emerging under the conceptual umbrella of sustainable agriculture. Sustainable agriculture has been given a variety of different definitions. However, there seems to be a growing consensus that the central theme of sustainability is one of permanence. A sustainable agriculture must be capable of maintaining its productivity and value to human society indefinitely, must meet the needs of current generations without compromising the ability of future generations to meet their needs as well, and must be capable of sustaining human life on earth forever.

Most agree long-run sustainability is a logical, reasonable goal for any agricultural system. Disagreements, for the most part, arise over alternative means of pursuing this goal. The proposed means range from perennial polycultures and organic farming, on the one hand, to genetic engineering and prescription farming on the other. Differences in opinion concerning means will not likely be resolved, at least not in the foreseeable future. However, agreement is not a prerequisite for progress. Simultaneous pursuit of alternative means quite likely improves the odds of success.

Some of the most challenging questions of sustainability are linked directly to either the consequences or failures of the industrial model—environmental degradation, reliance on nonrenewable resources, and growing social inequities, just to name a few. Champions of industrialization are searching desperately to find industrial solutions to problems caused by industrialization. The current search for solutions to problems of waste disposal and odors in large-scale confinement hog operations is a prime example.

Others see efforts to solve problems created by a paradigm by using the same paradigm as inherently futile. They are searching for something fundamentally different, a new paradigm capable not only of solving the problems created by industrialization, but of realizing a whole new set of opportunities for human progress in a post-industrial era. The sustainable agriculture issue is characterized by this fundamental conflict between those who are trying to "fix" the industrial model of farming and those who are seeking a new paradigm for farming in the post-industrial era.

The Industrialization of U.S. Agriculture

Paradigms, such as industrialization, become dominant because they are found to be capable of exploiting new opportunities or solving problems that previous paradigms could not solve (Barker). The industrial era was fostered by a host of interrelated and complex developments, but among the most important was discovery of, and accessibility to, large supplies of fossil fuels. The industrialization of the U.S. economy was made possible, in large part, by the various means of exploiting vast supplies of fossil energy.

U.S. agriculture was industrialized in support of industrialization of the U.S. economy as a whole. At the turn of the century, America was an agrarian society. Most of our total resources were spent on the necessary tasks of feeding and clothing ourselves. People had to be freed from producing food and fiber to provide workers for the factories and offices of a growing industrial society. The costs of food and fiber had to decline if consumers were to have discretionary income to buy the things the factories and offices would produce.

U.S. agriculture was mechanized, specialized, routinized, and otherwise industrialized to make it possible for fewer people to feed more people better for less money. Industrialization began in earnest when tractors replaced horses as sources of power on U.S. farms. The agricultural sector has been among the last to become fully industrialized, but the driving force of change has long been to make farms perform as factories without roofs, with fields and feed lots operating as much as possible like factory assembly lines.

Industrial strategies of the past century were highly successful in reducing the claim of food and fiber production on the nation's human resources. For example, the *1895 Yearbook of Agriculture* indicated that 42 percent of people in the United States were employed on farms in 1890 (U.S. Department of Agriculture 1895). This compares to less than 2 percent of the total U.S.

population living on farms a century later. In addition, those living on farms today earn more than half of their income from nonfarm sources (U.S. Department of Agriculture 1990). U.S. consumers now spend slightly more than 11 percent of their income on food, and farmers receive only about 22 cents out of each dollar spent for food (Dunham). About half the farmer's share goes to pay for purchased inputs, leaving the farmer little more than a dime out of each dollar spent for food to cover costs of value added on farms.

The industrial paradigm succeeded in exploiting the opportunities of cheap fossil energy and a multitude of related industrial technologies. The U.S. food system is now the envy of the rest of the world. Farmers and others have been freed from the subsistence living that characterized earlier times. However, known stocks of fossil energy are being depleted rapidly as potential societal gains from still further increases in agricultural efficiency are dwindling. In addition, the industrialization of agriculture has generated a whole new set of growing economic, environmental, and social concerns that may soon outweigh its declining benefits.

Industrialized Crop Production

First, concerns are growing regarding the continuing effectiveness of inputs and technologies necessary to support large-scale, specialized cropping systems. Increased concentration of a single crop within a geographic region increases pest pressures on that crop. In addition, insects are becoming resistant to pesticides, weeds to herbicides, and both require higher rates of application or new, more costly chemicals for control. Previously fertile soils in some areas have lost organic matter and natural fertility through monocropping, conventional tillage, and removal of crop aftermath year after year. Lower organic matter has meant less microbial activity, less ability to hold water, and less availability of nutrients in root zones, meaning lower yields from a given level of water and fertilization or higher fertilizer and irrigation costs to maintain yields.

Water tables in some of the major irrigated areas are declining as rates of irrigation surpass rates of natural regeneration of aquifers. Irrigation supports some of the largest of the large farming operations. Salinization of soils has also become a major concern in some irrigated farming regions. Soil conservation rose to the top of the political agenda in 1985 primarily because of rising soil erosion rates. Soil losses went up as farmers abandoned forage grass and legume-based crop rotations in the 1960s and rose still further as farmers intensified row crop production for growing export markets during the

1970s. Farmers have made significant progress in conserving soil through conservation tillage and other conservation measures; however, soil erosion remains a major public issue.

Other costs of industrialized crop production are beginning to show up in the environment of farm families, farm workers, and rural residents. Health risks in handling pesticides, for example, have become a major issue in farm safety. Risks of chemical contamination of drinking water and risks of pesticide residues in food are important public perceptions, regardless of the facts concerning actual risk levels. Nitrate leaching into groundwater may be attributed to organic sources, such as livestock waste and crop residues, as well as the use of commercial fertilizer. However, this issue, as much as any other, has increased awareness in rural areas of the potential environmental hazards of chemically dependent farming.

Industrialized Livestock Production

Questions are also being raised concerning industrial systems of livestock production. Water pollution associated with livestock feedlot wastes may prove more challenging than controlling nutrient leaching and runoff from commercial fertilizers used on crops. The energy required to produce meats, compared with direct human consumption of grain, is an oft-stated resource concern. Drug and hormone residues in meats may be at least as common as pesticide residues in fruits and vegetables. And animal welfare is a public issue of increasing social concern that could have major impacts on livestock production in the future.

Large-scale, commercial cattle feeding, poultry, and dairy operations have been the primary focus of past concerns. However, the rapid growth in large-scale hog operations has shifted the public spotlight to pork production. Water and air pollution from livestock wastes; residues of antibiotics and growth additives in meats and milk; welfare of animals raised in confinement; and impacts of large, corporate operations on opportunities of smaller livestock producers are all issues raised by those concerned about the sustainability of livestock production industrial systems.

The practice of feeding grain to livestock and poultry raises questions regarding the sustainability of meat production. Grain-fed beef yields only a fraction of the energy embodied in the feedstuffs consumed by cattle in the production process. Consumption of poultry and pork is more energy-efficient than beef consumption, but all are far less efficient than direct human consumption of grains. In addition, concentration of livestock and poultry feeding outside of major grain-producing regions makes it impractical to recycle nutrients contained in animal waste back to the fields from which they were removed by grain production.

Most environmental questions for livestock producers also relate to confinement feeding operations. Nutrient runoff from feed lots is an obvious potential source of water pollution. But mismanagement of manure removed from cattle feed lots or confinement hog and poultry facilities can be just as important. Farmers may apply manure at such times or by methods that result in most of the nutrients being volatilized, eroded, or leached rather than used by growing plants. Air pollution has proven to be one of the most persistent problems of large hog operations. Odors drifting from hog waste treatment lagoons to neighboring residences has probably triggered more lawsuits than any other single environmental problem associated with confinement livestock production.

Confinement livestock and poultry operations are also the primary users of subtherapeutic levels of antibiotics. Such practices may result in pathogenic resistance, thus reducing the effectiveness of these antibiotics for therapeutic uses in humans. Growth hormones have also been used extensively in feed lots. The association of DES with cancer has resulted in heightened public concern regarding the use of growth hormones in general. The concern about the use of growth hormones is combined with public distrust of biotechnology in recent public controversy concerning use of genetically engineered growth hormones, BST in milk and PST in pork.

Social questions regarding animal welfare are also most frequently associated with large-scale, confinement livestock operations. To date, producers of veal and caged layer chickens have received most of the animal welfare publicity. However, the basic issues are the same for all animals produced in confinement. To what extent can the activity of animals be restricted for purposes of production or economic efficiency without violating our social values concerning humane treatment of animals?

Industrialization Impacts on Farming Communities

The industrialization of agriculture has changed rural landscapes. Farmers planted "fence row to fence row" during the 1970s and many tore down the fences and plowed out the fence rows. Farming areas were no longer patchworks of fields, meadows, grassy hills, and valleys separated by rows of trees. Rural landscapes became field after field of corn, soybeans, wheat, and cotton across the hills and valleys. Timber was cleared to make room for cow herds. Cattle feeding, poultry production, and now pork production are being moved from aesthetically diverse family farms to large factory-like animal production units.

Larger, more specialized farming operations have meant fewer farming families. Fewer people are needed on farms with industrial farming technologies. Not only have purchased inputs been substituted for land and climate, but machines have been substituted for labor, and technology has been substituted for management. The unneeded human resources have been squeezed out of agriculture as a natural economic consequence of the substitution of technology-based inputs for both natural and human resources.

Industrial technologies reduced costs of production and provided incentives for expanded production which, in turn, reduced market prices and ultimately reduced farm incomes. Attempts to mitigate the effects of surplus production through export expansion have instead created a system that is even more dependent on cost-reducing technologies to remain competitive in global markets. Only those farmers who were among the first to adopt emerging technologies have realized profits. Those who lagged behind were forced to adopt the technologies in order to survive. Those who could not adopt or adapt quickly enough were forced to sell out to their more "progressive" neighbors.

The continual repetition of this process over time has ensured that economic returns to those remaining in agriculture were kept well below those of growing sectors of the economy. This process was an economic necessity for moving unwilling people and resources out of agriculture and into other uses. But there were costs associated with this migration out of agriculture. These costs have included "social disorganization, shrinking rural economic bases, declining rural communities and institutions, and the specter of a permanent underclass in the cities" (Glover).

In earlier times, a greater social good was likely achieved by moving farmers off the land and out of rural communities. Today, however, few people are left on farms to be moved to the cities, even if the cities had productive jobs for them to fill. Today, there is little left for society to gain from continuing to squeeze the farmer's penny from the dime the average consumer spends for food. Food prices would average only about ten percent lower if farmers got nothing for their efforts. Consumers spend more for packaging and advertising than they pay the farmer for producing the food.

The Business of Paradigms

A growing number of people are looking to a fundamentally different paradigm for farming as they search for answers to the economic, ecologic, and social questions arising from industrial methods of farming.

Joel Barker, in his book *Paradigms*, defines a paradigm as a set of rules that does two things: (1) establishes or defines boundaries and (2) sets standards for success and behavior within the boundaries. He uses the game of tennis as an analogy to illustrate these concepts. Tennis courts are standard in size and out-of-bounds is clearly marked. The ball must hit within these bounds to "stay in play." The ball must be struck with a tennis racket, not a baseball bat or anything else, and the ball is allowed to bounce only once before it is returned over the net.

Paradigms may be simple, as in the case of games, or extremely complex, as in the case of a model for economic development. However, the industrial model has some clearly defined boundaries. The natural environment and natural resource base are considered to be "external," or out of bounds, by industrial managers. Society, likewise, is considered to be an "external" factor that constrains or sets bounds on what industrial firms can do. Success for an industrial firm is measured in terms of profits and growth. Within the limits allowed by nature and society, industrial firms may take a wide range of actions to maximize short-run profits and long-run growth. Almost anything that is possible and legal is encouraged if it leads to profits and growth.

The industrial model or paradigm for farming may or may not be sustainable over time. No one can possibly know the future with certainty. It may be possible to fine tune, refine, or redesign the industrial model, resulting in a new model that will meet the ecological and social standards required to sustain long-run productivity without changing the fundamental approach to farming. On the other hand, an approach or philosophy of farming that is fundamentally different from the industrial model may be required. This alternative paradigm may represent the independent hog farmer's best hope for remaining competitive with large-scale corporate hog producers in the future.

The new paradigm emerging from sustainable agriculture may not be fully understood for some time to come. However, this post-industrial approach to farming is fundamentally different from the industrial paradigm in several ways. The new paradigm for agriculture clearly considers ecologic and social impacts to be "within" rather than "outside" its boundaries. Ecological soundness and social responsibility are seen as positive goals rather than negative constraints. The new constraints or boundaries are the laws of nature, including human nature.

The new paradigm considers economic, ecologic, and social dimensions of sustainability to be inseparable. Fields, farms, and communities are considered to be wholes that are made up of smaller wholes and make up still larger wholes. Thus the approach to farm decision making and management must be "holistic." The challenge is to comprehend the complexities of wholes rather than attempt to reduce wholes to simpler and more easily understood elements. Success in the new paradigm is measured against the goal of sustainable economic, ecologic, and social progress rather than profits and growth.

The new sustainable model implies greater reliance on human resources, in terms of the quality and quantity of labor and management, and relatively less reliance on land and capital. Each complex whole is unique and requires a unique management strategy. The human mind may be the only mechanism capable of coping with the multitude of complexities implied by this new paradigm for farming. Success of the new paradigm for farm decision making may well depend on success in empowering more people with information and knowledge needed to manage holistically. Table 13.1 outlines some points of comparison between the industrial and sustainable paradigms for farming. These differences cannot be defined as two specific sets of production practices or methods, for hogs or for any other enterprise, but must be defined in terms of differences in approaches or philosophies of farming.

Farming with the new sustainable paradigm would require more farm operators, more farm laborers, and more farm families than would an industrial system of farming. In addition, operators of these new-paradigm farms would be motivated by a new mix of objectives. Social considerations are balanced with environmental and economic goals. Social goals may cause such farmers to show a preference for local markets and local input supply sources, so long as this preference does not threaten their economic survival.

A fundamental shift in the balance of returns to people versus land and capital must be brought about, by one means or another, if the new paradigm is to be successful and more families are to be able to farm successfully. Smaller, diversified farms will remain commercially competitive with larger, specialized farms only if human resources can be substituted economically for other resources and commercial inputs. By implication, farmers who succeed with the new paradigm must be more productive as "people." They cannot expect to earn a larger return for their management and labor, thereby reducing

Table 13.1 Alternative paradigms for decision making

Industrial	Sustainable
Reductionist (seeks to simplify)	Holistic (seeks to comprehend)
Complex systems (interconnected parts)	Complex wholes (wholes within wholes)
Inductive reasoning (parts → wholes)	Deductive reasoning (wholes → "parts")
Separable goals (multiple goals)	Inseparable goals (multidimensional)
Focus on productivity and profits	Focus on sustainable progress
Ecologic and social constraints	Ecological and social objectives
Economic, ecologic, social—separable	Ecologic, economic, social—inseparable
Constrained profit maximization	Economic, ecologic, social balance
Strategy: linear/sequential	Strategy: spiral/simultaneous
Values conformity/specialization	Values uniqueness/diversification
Driven by problem solving	Driven by problem prevention
Technology based (applies knowledge)	Knowledge based (applies technology)

Stresses knowledge of facts	Stresses human ingenuity
Management extensive (manage more)	Management intensive (more managers)
Management by objectives	Management by principles
Promotes sound management practices	Promotes disciplined use of judgment
Tests decisions against objectives	Tests decisions against goal
Monitors objective-based results	Monitors impacts on whole system
Balances independence/dependence	Balances independence/interdependence
Quality of life is a result of success	Quality of life is the process of success
Motivates people	Empowers people

their reliance on land and capital, unless they possess unique management skills and working abilities.

Knowledge: The Key to Systems Management

The trend toward industrialization in agriculture seems likely to continue. Thus those who voice the possibility of a positive future for family farms and rural communities may be disregarded as unrealistic idealists. But the world is continually changing. A growing number of people who make their living forecasting the future, the futurists, see a new, post-industrial era in which there is room for more than one model for economic and human progress.

Alvin Toffler, in his book *Power Shift*, points out that many forecasters simply present unrelated trends, as if they would continue indefinitely, without providing any insight regarding how the trends are interconnected or the forces likely to reverse them. He contends the forces of industrialization have almost run their course and already show signs of reversing. He labels the industrial models of economic progress as becoming increasingly obsolete. Old notions of efficiency and productivity are no longer valid. Mass production is no longer a symbol of "modern" business operation. The new "modern" model is to produce customized goods and services aimed at niche markets, to constantly innovate, to focus on value-added products and tailored production.

He goes on to state "the most important economic development of our lifetime has been the rise of a new system of creating wealth, based no longer on muscle but on the mind" (Toffler, p. 9). He contends that "the conventional factors of production—land, labor, raw materials and capital—become less important as knowledge is substituted for them" (p. 238). "Because it reduces the need for raw material, labor, time, space and capital, knowledge becomes the central resource of the advanced economy" (p. 91).

Toffler also provides some insights into the nature of knowledge-based production. He states that separate and sequential systems of production are being replaced with synthesis and simultaneous systems of production. Synergism is replacing specialization as a source of production efficiency. Tailoring products to the desires of specific customers is replacing low prices as the source of value. Simultaneity, synthesis, synergism, tailored production; this is the "mind work" of the future.

The new knowledge-based paradigm for development requires a holistic, systems approach to decision making. Development systems embody enormous complexity in simultaneous and dynamic linkages among a multitude of interrelated factors. Cognitive scientists have shown that humans can deal consciously with only a very small number of separate variables simultaneously. Yet humans can perform enormously complex tasks such as driving a car in heavy traffic, playing a tennis match, or carrying on a conversation, activities that baffle the most sophisticated computers. People are capable of performing such tasks routinely by using their well-developed, subconscious minds.

The subconscious human mind appears to be virtually unlimited in its capacity to cope with complexity. As organizational theorist Charles Keifer puts it, "When the switch is thrown subconsciously, you become a systems thinker thereafter. Reality is automatically seen systemically as well as linearly. Alternatives that are impossible to see linearly are surfaced by the subconscious as proposed solutions. Solutions that were outside of our 'feasible set' become part of our feasible set. 'Systemic' becomes a way of thinking and not just a problem solving methodology" (as quoted in Senge, p. 366). The subconscious mind is capable of assimilating hundreds of feedback relationships simultaneously as it integrates detail and dynamic complexities together (Senge, p. 367). The human mind may be the only mechanism capable of dealing effectively with the systems complexities embodied in a knowledge-based development paradigm.

Peter Drucker, a noted business consultant, talks of the "Post Business Society," in his book, *The New Realities*. He states, "the biggest shift—bigger by far than the changes in politics, government or economics—is the shift to the knowledge society. The social center of gravity has shifted to the knowledge worker. All developed countries are becoming post-business, knowledge societies. Looked at one way, this is the logical result of a long evolution in which we moved from working by the sweat of our brow and by muscle to industrial work and finally to knowledge work" (Drucker, p. 173).

Drucker contends there is an important, fundamental difference between knowledge work and industrial work. Industrial work is fundamentally a mechanical process whereas the basic principle of knowledge work is biological. He relates this difference to determining the "right size" of organization required to perform a given task. "Greater performance in a mechanical system is obtained by scaling up. Greater power means greater output: bigger is better. But this does not hold for biological systems. Their size follows function. It would surely be counterproductive for a cockroach to be big, and equally counterproductive for the elephant to be small. As biologists are fond of saying, "The rat knows everything it needs to know to be a successful rat." Whether the rat is more intelligent than the human being is a stupid question; in what it takes to be a successful rat, the rat is way ahead of any other animal, including human beings" (Drucker, p. 259).

Differences in organizing principles may be critically important in determining the future size and ownership structure of economic enterprises, including farms. Other things being equal, the smallest effective size is best for enterprises based on information and knowledge work. "'Bigger' will be 'better' only if the task cannot be done otherwise" (Drucker, p. 260).

As American business has struggled to maintain its competitiveness in global markets, management strategies have begun to reflect these new economic realities. The old model of large-scale, centralized production characterized by high-volume production, standardized units, and little flexibility has fallen out of favor. The largest corporations are downsizing; most of the new nonfarm jobs are being created by small business.

The most successful large companies have begun to rely on small business management strategies, with more employee involvement and attention to improving quality through quality circles, zero-defect quality standards, and just-in-time inventory management. Many large, industrial organizations such as Sears, IBM, GM, and AT&T are facing stiff competition from much smaller competitors. IBM is in the process of breaking up into a series of smaller independent businesses that will be more flexible and quicker to respond to changing economic conditions (Stein). GM created a new, much smaller automobile company to produce the Saturn. Wal-Mart's success may be due, in no small part, to its ability to motivate local Wal-Mart employees to work as if they owned their local store.

Large corporations are clearly decentralizing to smaller, more flexible problem-solving units. However, the primary advantage of being big arises from an ability to specialize, mechanize, routinize, and realize the economies of scale of "mass" production methods. As large corporations decentralize, become more flexible, and target niche markets, they become more like small firms and thus more vulnerable to small-firm competition. As amassing capital and controlling the means of mass production become less critical to success, smaller firms will find it easier to compete.

In *The Atlantic Monthly*, Robert Reich writes, "Worldwide competition continues to compress profits on anything that is uniform, routine, and standard—that is, on anything that can be made, reproduced, or extracted in volume almost anywhere on the globe." What better description of basic agricultural commodities such as corn, soybeans, cotton, beef, and pork? Even if industrial systems dominate future production of basic agricultural commodities, such systems are likely to employ far fewer people and generate far less profit than have farming systems of the past. Reich contends that higher earnings in the future will be concentrated in businesses that are knowledge-intensive, solve problems for customers, and meet social needs.

"Modern" agriculture tends to be characterized by an industrial model that is considered obsolete by many leaders in the general economy. At first, it might appear illogical that what is "modern" in agriculture is "obsolete" elsewhere. However, according to Barker, new paradigms typically appear while the "old" paradigm is still doing well in many areas of application. In fact, he contends that new paradigms are routinely rejected by practitioners of "old" paradigms as being neither needed nor wanted (Barker pp. 47–48).

Paradigms are applied first in areas in which they are best-suited and are likely to be most effective. After the most promising opportunities have been exploited, they are applied to problems for which they are less well-suited, and thus likely to produce smaller gains. Thus old paradigms continue to solve problems and realize opportunities in some areas of application even after they have become obsolete in others.

New paradigms emerge as it becomes apparent old paradigms cannot solve all problems equally well and cannot solve some problems at all. In addition, paradigms may "create new problems" in the process of solving old ones. It may be quite logical to continue to use the old paradigm to solve the problems it is capable of solving while a new paradigm is emerging to solve the problems it cannot solve and the problems it has created. Industrial farming methods may be needed to ensure continuing production of low-cost, basic commodities until an equally "productive," sustainable system can be developed and implemented. According to Barker, competing paradigms typically coexist over extended periods of time. As old paradigms solve fewer and fewer problems and create more, the new paradigms solve more and more problems while the problems new paradigms may create are yet to emerge.

Rural community development strategies are also undergoing a significant change consistent with the new paradigm of economic development. The old strategies of industrial recruitment through building industrial parks by offering tax breaks has given way to growth-from-within policies. The new strategy, in line with the business theories of Reich and others, invests in entrepreneurs within the community to build small businesses and strengthen the local economy. Local buyer-supplier projects plug the loss in dollars leaving the community by replacing imports with locally produced goods and services.

As large companies and branch plants move overseas for cheap labor, efforts to attract these low-quality, low-paying jobs are increasingly regarded as an expensive and ineffective strategy for economic development. Large companies, although they may provide a large number of jobs, often pay poorly and may be unstable since there is no local commitment; they are expensive to attract and maintain; and they are slow to respond to new economic conditions. Economic development professionals are beginning to concentrate on improving the quality of jobs rather than quantity as the number of working poor—workers with full-time jobs who live below the poverty line—continues to increase.

The sustainable agriculture paradigm supports a growth-from-within approach to rural economic development. It is an asset-based rather than deficiency-based strategy wherein human capital is more highly valued than financial capital. Intellectual capital, as it is employed, is enhanced in value rather than depleted as are other resources. It is the "virtuous cycle" of education, increased innovation, increased investment, increased value, and higher wages. Sustainable development offers an alternative to the vicious cycle of industrial recruitment, low wages, declining emphasis on education, declining communities, and resulting downward spiral (Reich).

Sustainable agriculture relies on a knowledge of the land and the ecology that supports the production of food and fiber. The strength of this approach lies in the human intellectual capacity to work with nature and maintain productivity. It focuses on empowering the farmer and the local community through its dependence upon people rather than money and strengthens the local society and economy.

Implications for Pork Production

The past may provide a graphic picture of the future of Midwest family farms and rural communities as hogs and pork now take the lead in agricultural industrialization. Hogs and pork constitute an important sector of the Midwest agricultural economy. But, more importantly, hogs are the economic "backbone" of many diversified family farms.

Hogs have provided a value-added market for crops, stabilized farm income, recycled nutrients, and scavenged wastes. Hogs and other livestock provide year-round employment for members of the farming family who are underemployed in specialized cropping systems. Hogs on farms provide a classic example of synergistic productivity. Hogs on family farms are capable of adding far more to such farming systems than is apparent from even the most critical examination of the hog enterprise in insolation. If Midwest farms lose their ability to produce hogs competitively, thousands of farming families and scores of rural communities may feel the negative impacts for decades to come.

An Example

A 1992 University of Missouri report began with the following statement: "The State of Missouri is poised at a crossroads with respect to pork production. Developments within the state in the next five years will likely determine the future of pork production in Missouri well into the twenty-first century" (DiPietre). However, the report might lead one to believe the major problem confronting Missouri's hog producers and rural communities is a drop in total pork production, and the solution to this problem is to bring in large, multi-state corporate hog producers. The report states that "because of direct and indirect economic linkages of the swine production sector to ag and non-ag business throughout the state and region, the economic impact of reversing [the] significant decline [in Missouri's pork production] could very well prove pivotal to the economic survival of many towns and regions of the state." Much of the report focused specifically on the potential positive economic impacts of increasing large-scale, contract swine production in Missouri.

The primary purpose here is not to challenge assessments of direct employment or net direct employee compensation associated with contracting or any other system of large-scale hog production. The question is whether increasing contract swine production, or any system of large-scale hog production, is a logical rural economic development strategy for Missouri or any other state.

The fundamental challenge to the future of Missouri's farms and rural communities would seem to be the declining availability of quality employment opportunities for farmers and others who choose to live and work in rural areas. More hogs may or may not result in more quality employment opportunities. Thus increased hog production may or may not contribute to economic development of rural communities.

Large-scale confinement hog operations tend to reduce total costs by using production methods that allow fewer people to produce more hogs. The substitution of capital and mass-production technologies for labor and management is the primary advantage that large, specialized hog production units have over smaller, diversified operations. Thus the displacement of family farms by large-scale hog production systems might be expected to reduce rather than increase total employment pork production.

The production environment in large-scale operations is controlled through utilization of buildings and equipment that require large capital investments but greatly reduce labor requirements. Production technologies associated with large-scale, contract production also change the basic nature of the management function. Mass-production technologies (which standardize genetic selection, breeding, feeding, herd health, and marketing functions) transfer most of the management function from on-site hog producers to corporate production supervisors who travel among production units and, to an even greater extent, to production managers back in corporate headquarters who design and refine production strategies. Large-scale, specialized hog production replaces people with capital-intensive, mass-production technologies and centralized management.

A simple comparison of results from the Missouri contract production report to reports from actual Missouri hog operations serves to illustrate the basic principle of input and resource substitution. Figures in the first three columns in Table 13.2 were taken from the University of Missouri study. The first column shows the relevant numbers, taken from the contract production report, for a basic 600-sow farrowing unit, producing 12,000 pigs a year. A $550,000 investment would be expected to result in 2.5 on-site jobs with a total direct employee compensation of $57,000 per year or $22,800 per job. The assumed 2.22 impact multiplier results in a total of 5.55 jobs, including on-site and off-site employment.

The second column in Table 13.2 shows the similar implications associated with 3.5 finishing units, a number sufficient to feed out 11,900 hogs per year, a number generally comparable to the number of pigs produced by one basic contract farrowing unit. Note, in this case, the investment, number of jobs, and total direct employee compensation have been multiplied by 3.5. The total employment associated with the 3.5 finishing units is 1.75 jobs on-site and 3.89 jobs in total.

The third column represents a composite of one farrowing unit and 3.5 finishing units capable of producing approximately 12,000 slaughter hogs per year. Note that the total investment is approximately $1 million, which includes buildings and equipment costs but no land cost. Total dollar sales are based on 11,900 hogs sold at 250 lbs. for $46 per cwt. The number of hogs and price were the same as those assumed in the original study. A market weight of 250 lbs. was the average reported in 1992 Management Information Records (MIR) production data for hog finishers (Plain). The composite operation results in an estimated 4.25 on-site jobs; total direct employee compensation of $93,750, or $22,059 per job; and 9.44 on-site and off-site jobs in total.

The fourth column in Table 13.2 is based on actual production data reported in the *Missouri Farm Business Summary, 1992* (Ehlmann and Hein). A total of twenty-five farms participating in the MIR program in 1992 were classified as hog farms. Sales of livestock accounted for about 90 percent of total sales on these farms, and livestock accounted for all of the net returns. In fact, crop returns, except for crops fed, showed a net average $12,000 loss to operators of MIR hog farms in 1992. Average sales per MIR hog farm in 1992 were about $265,000 per farm. Slaughter hog prices in 1992 averaged about $42 per cwt., $4 per cwt. less than the average used in the contract units in Table 13.2. Total dollar sales for 4.5 MIR hog farms are estimated at $1.3 million, by adjusting 1992 sales upward to reflect the $4 per cwt. price difference. This brings total sales for MIR hog farms in column four roughly in line with sales for the composite contract farrow-to-finish unit in column three.

Note that total investment in buildings and equipment is about the same for the composite contract and MIR hog operations. Additional investment in land and other assets nearly double the "total" investment in MIR operations in comparison to the composite contract unit. Contract operations presumably would require a significant investment in land for manure disposal. However, total assets for contract units in Table 13.2 reflect only the building and equipment investment.

A key difference between contract and individually owned hog production is found in management and labor requirements. The composite farrow-finish contract operation employs only 4.25 people in the process of generating $1.3 million in sales of hogs. On the other hand, independently operated hog farms in Table 13.2 employ 12.60 people in the process of producing a slightly smaller dollar value of hog sales. Large-scale, specialized operations produce more hogs per person employed and, consequently, create fewer jobs per hog produced.

Indirect and induced impacts on related economic sectors of the economy are estimated to create 2.22 jobs in total for each person employed in hog production. Thus the total number of people needed to produce 12,000 hogs is estimated at 9.44 persons for corporate contract production and 27.79 persons for independent hog farms. If corporate, contract production replaced independent hog farmers, approximately three independent hog farmers will be displaced for each new job created.

Table 13.2 Comparisons: Contract and individually owned hog production

	Contract farrowing	Contract finishing	Contract system	1992 MIR hog farms
Production units	1.0	3.5	1.0	4.5
Pigs/year	12,000	11,900	11,900	<11,900
Investment in buildings and equipment (dollars)	550,000	455,000	1,005,000	1,192,500
Sales (dollars)			1,368,500	1,306,071
Sales (cwt.)			28,510	27,210
Farmers employed	—	—	—	6.17
Production workers employed	2.50	1.75	4.25	6.44
Total production employment	2.50	1.75	4.25	12.60
Total investment (dollars)	550,000	455,000	1,005,000	2,452,500
Investment per person employed (dollars)	220,000	260,000	236,471	194,643

Returns to investment, labor, and management (dollars)	57,000	36,750	93,750	349,307
Returns per person employed (dollars)	22,800	21,000	22,059	27,723
Employment multiplier	2.22	2.22	2.22	2.22
Total employment	5.55	3.89	9.44	27.97
Employee displacement			18.54	
Displacement ratio			2.96	

Regardless of the specific numbers, contract production allows the production of more hogs with fewer people. Consequently, large-scale, contract production employs far fewer people than would be employed to produce the same number of hogs in typical owner-operated hog farms.

Some of the difference in employment is accounted for by the fact that many hog farmers produce a significant portion of their own feed whereas contract operators typically purchase their feed from outside suppliers. Management functions performed by independent hog farmers are performed by off-farm supervisors and corporate managers in contract operations. However, when feed is produced on the farms where it is fed and returns to management accrue to local farmers, there is little doubt about whether the economic impacts will be felt in the local community. In addition, other enterprises on the farm may be critically interdependent with, and thus fundamentally inseparable from, the hog operation on many owner-operated hog farms. Therefore, "total" employment on many hog farms may well be dependent on the economic viability of the hog enterprise.

Note also that total assets per person employed in contract production are considerably higher than for MIR hog farms even though land needed for the contract unit is not included. Total investments on MIR farms include all land, machinery, and equipment associated with all enterprises, including on-farm feed production. However, the contract production asset figures are based on new investment costs whereas facilities on MIR hog farms were likely of varying ages in 1992 and were reported at depreciated values. Thus asset comparisons in Table 13.2 reflect the reality of 1992 rather than an average over some future time period.

The Missouri report includes only direct employee compensation, or returns to labor, in reported estimates of economic performance for contract units. Direct employee compensation for contract production is net of interest and principal payments on buildings and equipment. If the useful life of buildings and equipment exceed the repayment period, some additional returns would presumably accrue to the contract producer's investment. However, total returns to management, labor, and capital for contract operations in Table 13.2 reflect only direct employee compensation estimates.

Returns to capital, management, and operator labor are fundamentally inseparable in owner-operated farming enterprises although separate returns for different production factors are often "estimated." At 1992 hog prices, returns to management on MIR hog farms were estimated at a negative $0.43 per cwt. although the twenty-four-year average shows a positive $3.58 (Plain). The difference is approximately equal to the $4 difference between 1992 hog prices and the $46 long-term average assumed for total returns. The returns to management and capital for the MIR hog farms in Table 13.2 reflect 1992 returns adjusted to reflect the long-run average returns to management. Returns to labor for MIR hog farms reflect reported compensation for hired labor.

Estimated returns to management, capital, and labor per person employed are more than 25 percent higher for MIR hog farms in Table 13.2 than the direct employee compensation per person in the contract operations. Some of this difference is quite likely due to the fact that returns to management and equity capital accrue to the farmers in independent hog operations but accrue to corporate managers and investors in the contract operations. However, even the most ardent advocates of contract production freely admit that well-managed, independent hog operations can compete with large, specialized hog operations.

Glenn Grimes of the University of Missouri, who has studied the economics of large-scale hog production over several decades, concludes: "The lowest-cost one-third of producers are competitive with the best large producers" (Grimes 1994a). The comparisons of economic returns per person for MIR and contract units in Table 13.2 do nothing more than confirm this conventional wisdom. Well-managed, independent hog farms can employ more people at compensation levels comparable to those offered by contract hog production.

Comparing MIR hog farms to contract hog production units is like comparing apples to oranges. One represents whole-farm operations, the other represents specialized hog enterprises. In one, the equity capital and management is on-farm; in the other, most of the capital and management comes from the outside. One set of assets represents an investment in a specific set of buildings and equipment; the other represents a wide variety of capital assets at various stages of depreciation. So how can such comparisons have any real meaning? The comparisons have meaning precisely because the two systems represent two very different, but very realistic, futures for hog production in Missouri.

One alternative is to promote large-scale, contract production as a means of increasing hog production in the hope of retaining or regaining employment in hog production. The other is to promote more intensive management as a means of improving the competitiveness of smaller, independently owned hog operations. Still another strategy for the future is to develop a "new paradigm" for pork production. These strategies require very different kinds of natural, financial, and human resources and may result in very different kinds of hog production systems.

Economic returns to management reflect returns associated with decision making. Mechanized, specialized, and tightly controlled production systems allow room for very little individual management input and thus provide very little opportunity to earn a true return to management. Operations with greater potential returns to management tend to be diverse, complex, dynamic systems with a great deal of flexibility for managers to make decisions that impact performance. The realistic choices for the future are not between apples and apples, but rather between apples and oranges. It is more important that comparisons reflect realistic alternatives than that they be clear and easy to make.

Hog producers have a variety of potential paradigms for hog production in the twenty-first century. To support one model of twenty-first century hog production and not support others implies the only choice is between apples and nothing. Hog farmers and others who live and work in rural communities should be allowed to choose their own future. If they choose apples over oranges, it will have been their choice. However, given a choice between apples, oranges, and bananas, they just might choose some of all three.

Implications for the Future

Corporate-owned, contract hog production is a reality of the current agricultural economy. It seems quite likely that corporate, contract hog production will become more common over time in spite of anything that its opponents may do to slow its spread into new areas of the country. The emergence of large-scale, specialized hog operations simply continues a long-term trend toward industrialization of the agricultural economy. Industrialization at first appears to increase productivity of human resources through mechanization and mass production technologies. However, over time, industrial technologies replace more and more labor with mechanization. Over time, the management function also becomes more concentrated among fewer and fewer people.

The traditional economic assumption has been that more efficient production, in general, will increase total economic output by enough to provide new jobs for displaced workers in newly emerging sectors of the economy. However, the growing number of displaced workers in the American economy, who now range from underemployed to permanently unemployable, has begun to raise serious questions about the traditional economic assumptions with respect to gains from further industrialization. The productive employment of people may be the most fundamental economic and social problem that the industrial development model is inherently incapable of solving.

Rural America cannot retreat to an earlier time when cost competition was less keen, full-time family farms were the norm, and agricultural communities were strong and growing. However, there is clear evidence that independently-owned, modest-size, family-operated hog farms can be commercially competitive with current contract production units, at least in the short run. The new paradigm for farming arising from the issue of sustainable agriculture supports the goal of economically viable, ecologically sound, socially responsible systems of farming. Social responsibility includes a commitment to providing quality employment opportunities on independently owned, small- to moderate-size family farms. There is clear evidence that successful, modest-size, family-operated hog farms contribute more to the economic and social well-being of rural communities than do their corporate counterparts.

As a rural economic development strategy, it would seem that a goal of improving independent hog farmers' management capabilities should receive at least as high a priority in the short run as would contract hog production. The goal of developing a new sustainable paradigm for agriculture, including hog production, may be even more important over the longer run. Greater reliance on intensive management creates more quality employment opportunities in rural areas by enhancing the productivity of people rather than replacing people with capital investments and large-scale, mass-production technologies. Empowerment of people to be productive is the foundation upon which the new paradigm of sustainable agriculture must be built.

Some will demand concrete evidence of the success of this new paradigm before they will act. According to Barker, some typical responses to those who propose new paradigms include: "That's impossible." "It's too radical." "We tried something like it before and it didn't work." "I wish it were that easy." "Let's get real, okay?" "How dare you suggest that what we are doing is wrong!" One may look to the decentralizing, demassifying, and otherwise deindustrializing of the rest of the U.S. economy for evidence that the industrial era is coming to an end. However, those "who choose to change to a new paradigm early, must do so as an act of faith rather than the result of factual proof, because there will never be enough proof too convincing in the early stages" (Barker, p.199).

Those who wait until the value of a new paradigm can be proven will lose any advantage to those with the courage to change in the face of uncertainty. Independent hog producers do not have the luxury of time to wait and see if something else will work. They must find a new paradigm for farming soon or they will be doing something other than farming for a living. The fundamental question is whether they can expect real help from the academic and scientific community in meeting this challenge or whether they will be advised to accept the "inevitability" of industrialization just as the industrial era is drawing to a close.

Note

Portions of this chapter also appear in *Pigs, Profits and Rural Communities* by Kendall Thu and E. Paul Durrenberger. State University of New York Press, © 1998.

References

Barker, J. 1993. *Paradigms: The Business of Discovering the Future.* New York, N.Y.: Harper Collins.

DiPietre, D. D. 1992. "The Economic Impact of Increased Contract Swine Production in Missouri." *Missouri Farm Financial Outlook 1993*, pp. 71–78. Department of Agricultural Economics, University of Missouri–Columbia, November-December.

Drucker, P. 1989. *The New Realities.* New York, N.Y.: Harper and Row.

Dunham, D. 1994. *Food Cost Review, 1993.* Washington, D.C.: U.S. Department of Agriculture, Economic Research Service, Agricultural Economic Report 696.

Ehlmann, G. M., and N. A. Hein. 1993. *Missouri Farm Business Summary, 1992.* FM 939, Extension Division, University of Missouri–Columbia.

Glover, R. S. 1988. "Farmers Pay the 'Price' for Advances in Biotech." *Atlanta Constitution,* December 17, section A, p. 21..

Grimes, G. 1994a. "Smaller Pork Producers Can Still Compete." Park Ridge, Ill.: American Farm Bureau, March 17.

———. 1994b. "Hog Outlook." *Missouri Farm Financial Outlook 1995*, pp. 24–34. Department of Agricultural Economics, University of Missouri–Columbia, November-December.

Ikerd, J. E. 1989. "Sustainable Agriculture." *Proceedings of the Annual Outlook Conference,* pp. 679–90. Washington, D.C.: U.S. Department of Agriculture.

Plain, R. 1993. "1992 Missouri Hog Returns." *Farm Management Newsletter,* p. 8. Department of Agricultural Economics, University of Missouri–Columbia, December.

Reich, R. B. 1991. "The Real Economy." *The Atlantic Monthly,* February, pp. 35–52.

Senge, P. M. 1990. *The Fifth Discipline.* New York, N.Y.: Doubleday Publishing Co.

Stein, C. 1991. "Corporate Giants Try to Cut Themselves Down to Size." *Raleigh News and Observer,* December 14, p. 12.

Toffler, A. 1990. *Power Shift.* New York, N.Y.: Bantam Books.

U.S. Department of Agriculture. 1895. *Yearbook of the United States Department of Agriculture, 1895*. Washington, D.C.: U.S. Government Printing Office.

————. 1990. *Agricultural Chart Book*. Washington, D.C.: Agricultural Handbook 689.

————. 1993. *Hogs and Pigs*. Washington, D.C.: U.S. Department of Agriculture, National Agricultural Statistics Service, December.

U.S. Department of Commerce. *1992 Census of Agriculture—Missouri State and County Data*. Washington, D.C.: Bureau of the Census.

PART IV
FOREIGN INVESTMENT, CONSUMER IMPACTS, AND AGRICULTURAL COOPERATIVES

14 Vertical Integration in Agribusiness Foreign Investment

KINGSLEY BASH and STEPHEN P. DAVIES

Three conditions often cited to explain foreign investment—location, ownership, and internalization advantages—combine elements of classical trade, industrial organization, and transaction cost theory (Dunning). According to neoclassical trade theory, benefits of foreign investment depend on the terms of trade, being based on input costs, and technology differences. However, trade theory fails to explain why multinational firms flourish when technological advantages are fleeting, transport costs are low, and inputs and products are mobile.

In contrast, industrial organization theory suggests that direct investment in foreign affiliates arises because it is more profitable than domestic production for export. Foreign investment allows multinational firms to exercise competitive advantages, extend collusive networks, erect competitive barriers, and earn monopoly profits. An important source of competitive advantage is the ability to coordinate functions vertically, capture scale economies, erect barriers to entry, and operate at lower cost than local competitors. However, industrial organization models fail to explain how vertical coordination influences organizational structures and incentives or why direct foreign investment involves intermediate contractual arrangements between the extremes of spot-market contracts and fully internalized ownership.

Organizational form and contract choice in foreign investment are informed by insights from transaction cost economics. Williamson (1991) argues that organizational form varies systematically with the attributes of transactions. We argue that transaction costs influence contract choice. Frank and Henderson discuss several types of vertical coordination contracts—spot market, market-specific, production management, resource-providing, and financial integration—with increasing levels of coordination between vertically interdependent enterprises. The purpose of this study is to examine factors influencing contract choice in agribusiness direct foreign investment. The objective is to determine whether transaction cost conditions significantly influence multinationals' equity ownership of foreign affiliates.

In the first section below, we examine the determinants of ownership level (or contract choice) as seen through the transaction cost paradigm. In the second section, a theoretical model is developed that combines elements of industrial organization and transaction cost theory to explain the level of ownership in foreign investment. The model is tested in the third section using industry-level financial information on U.S.-based multinationals and their foreign agribusiness affiliates, provided by the Department of Commerce, and World Bank estimates of national economic conditions. The final section provides a summary and some implications and avenues for further research.

Transaction Costs and Contract Choice

To explain the choice between intermediate contracts such as licensing, franchise, and joint-venture agreements, we draw on institutional economics. Market power consideration of industrial organization was extended by Williamson's analysis of transaction costs and hierarchical efficiencies. Buckley; Casson; Graham; and others further developed the "new institutional economics" approach to foreign investment, using transaction cost and contract choice analysis. While its foundations are based in neoclassical microeconomics, the transaction cost approach is also based on the theory of the firm (Coase) and the assumption that vertical coordination is critical to the organization of firms. Transaction cost theory emphasizes the fixed costs of risk and management, and shows how vertical coordination can increase profits by reducing transaction costs. Transaction cost theory, in effect, gives a contractual representation of vertical coordination (Sauvée).

Three conditions are needed for transaction costs to become important to contract choice. Two are behavioral conditions—limited cognitive competencies (bounded rationality) and self-interested, guileful propensities (opportunism). When bounded rationality gives one market participant an exploitable advantage over another and market participants are opportunistic, self-interested, and guileful with a tendency to cheat each other given opportunity and incentive, contracts are an important means of aligning incentives (Williamson 1985). Contract choice also depends on the existence of sunk costs in investment-specific assets (asset specificity). Asset specificity pertains to physical assets such as capital equipment,[1] but also to intangible assets such as management skills, market information, advertising, and research capabilities. Despite opportunism and bounded rationality, contracting conditions may nevertheless remain competitive as long as asset specificity is low, due to the existence of alternative users and the threat of switching. However, once a contract is established and investment-specific assets become sunk costs, incentives for opportunism increase. Contracting conditions change. The relationship between buyer and seller undergoes a "fundamental transformation" to small-numbers bargaining (Williamson 1985).

Attempts to analyze multinational foreign investment contract choice should thus reflect the combined effects of asset specificity, bounded rationality, and opportunism. Williamson calls this the "world of contract," in which information is costly and imperfect, transactions are rife with potential opportunism, and sunk costs lose value. When all three conditions exist, planning is necessarily incomplete because of bounded rationality, promises break down because of opportunism, and assets become sunk costs because of asset specificity. Harmonizing contractual relationships to promote continuity and adaptability becomes an important source of economic value.[2]

Transaction Cost Model

We used a regression model incorporating transaction cost and industrial organization effects on multinational firms' ownership of foreign affiliates. The model tests a proposition arising from the transaction cost approach: that transaction costs influence vertical coordination. A critical assumption is that vertical coordination is reflected in vertical financial ownership and that ownership can be measured by multinational firms' equity in foreign affiliates, as estimated by the U.S. Department of Commerce. This suggests a model (Jones and Hill) in which the costs and benefits of vertical financial ownership are supply and demand curves for assets in foreign affiliates (Figure 14.1). Marginal ownership costs, represented in the first equation, include intercept-shift variables to capture the effects of changes in investment size and proxies for transaction cost variables—sunk costs to indicate asset specificity, labor intensity for opportunism, and investment experience to measure bounded rationality. The second equation, representing marginal ownership benefits,

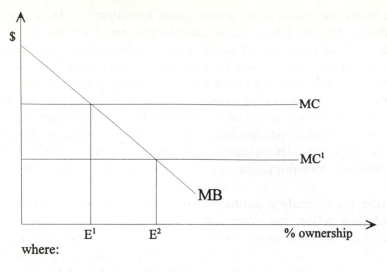

where:

marginal ownership costs = f(sunk costs, investment experience, labor-intensity, size of affiliate assets);

marginal ownership benefits = f(affiliate profits, investment experience); and

the equilibrium condition is: marginal costs = marginal benefits.

Figure 14.1 Foreign investment contract choice model

includes a proxy variable for ownership benefits (affiliate profits) and a shift variable for investment experience.

The industrial organization and transaction cost approaches are essentially complementary, but they emphasize different aspects of the multinational's profit-maximizing objective. While the industrial organization paradigm involves market power considerations, transaction cost theory holds that firm organization is designed to reduce the combined costs of market transactions and that internal sunk costs, bounded rationality, and opportunism influence multinationals' strategies regarding ownership of foreign affiliates. Under certain conditions, they predict different outcomes. The resulting sign of the coefficient associated with each variable sometimes indicates whether the ownership effect is more consistent with industrial organization or transaction cost theory. Market power considerations suggest that investment size and profitability also increase ownership while transaction cost considerations suggest they reduce it.

In the long run, marginal ownership benefits are expected to decline as multinationals exhaust the hierarchical efficiencies of ownership. In the long run, marginal ownership costs may either increase because of multinationals bidding up equity prices or decline because of ownership cost economies. In the short run, however, marginal ownership costs are likely to remain constant. In any case, the endogenous cost variable is missing from the marginal cost curve, so it is convenient to assume a zero slope. Given constant marginal ownership costs, we can identify the equilibrium point (E^1) at the intersection of the marginal cost and market power ownership influences, as illustrated in Figure 14.1. At some optimal level, the constant costs of ownership equal its declining benefits.

Data Sources

The model was tested using information from benchmark surveys conducted by the U.S. Department of Commerce[3] on large nonbank U.S. multinationals and their nonbank foreign affiliates. The sample includes foreign agribusiness affiliates that are at least 10 percent owned by U.S.-based multinationals. The sample includes farms, farm input suppliers, and food and beverage processors and distributors, but excludes the tobacco, alcohol,[4] grocery, and restaurant industries. To overcome data suppression problems,[5] thirty-one countries were aggregated into five regions; sixteen agribusiness industries were aggregated into six industry subsectors[6] (Table 14.1). The 1982 and 1989 surveys provide a unique opportunity to pool cross-sectional data, isolate structural effects, and measure investment behavior in the 1980s.

Frank and Henderson discuss ways to measure vertical coordination—value added to sales, industry linkages through production functions, and input-output models. We used another measure of vertical coordination—equity ownership. While coordination need not be accompanied by increased equity ownership, the reverse is generally true: equity ownership usually increases administrative coordination. The dependent variable chosen to represent vertical financial coordination in our model is the percentage of affiliate assets owned by U.S. multinationals.

To the extent that transaction costs can be measured, their effect on ownership can be quantified. Despite their size[7] and apparent importance to contract choice, transaction costs are difficult to measure. Transaction costs

Table 14.1 Industry and country categories

Subsectors	Industries
Farm inputs and farm production	Agri-chemicals
	Farm and garden machinery manufacturing
	Wholesale farm and garden equipment
	Farm, forestry, and fishing
Milling and baking	Grain and flour mills
	Bakeries
Textiles, paper, and lumber	Textile mills
	Pulp and paper mills
	Timber mills
Food and beverages	Meat and dairy products
	Preserved fruits and vegetables
	Leather products
	Beverages
Food processing	Other food and kindred products
Food distribution	Farm raw materials
	Wholesale grocery distribution

Regions	Countries
Europe	France, Italy, Germany, Switzerland, Denmark, Finland, Belgium, Norway and Sweden, Netherlands, Spain and Portugal, Other Europe
English-speaking	United Kingdom, Australia and New Zealand
Bordering United States	Canada, Mexico
Latin America	Argentina, Brazil, Central America, Colombia and Venezuela, Other Western Hemisphere
Asia	Japan, Indonesia, Malaysia, Philippines, Thailand, and Taiwan, Other Asia

resulting from risk and sunk costs are largely invisible. It is not clear how asset specificity can be measured systematically (Schmallensee). Transaction costs depend on highly specific industry, country, and period conditions. Product characteristics; host country technical capabilities; market infrastructure and support services; firm, industry, and macroeconomic conditions; sociocultural characteristics; business institutions; politics; and the behavior of individual decision makers may also influence transaction costs.

Direct measurements of transaction costs are scarce. Financial data rarely break out the transaction costs of negotiating and managing contracts. Instead of directly measuring transaction costs, researchers devise ways to assess their effects in a comparative institutional framework in which alternative contracts are compared to determine whether organizational and institutional relationships appear to be organized in ways that reduce transaction costs. For example, we used a variety of dummy variables to determine industry, country, and period effects on ownership.

Our initial hypothesis was that the level of ownership in foreign affiliates depends on industry, firm, and national economic conditions. Proxy variables were selected to reflect industry and national economic conditions, such as differences in industry structure, product maturity, information and technology, foreign investment policies, and other country conditions affecting market power and transaction costs. Firm-level differences in investment management were relegated to the error term. Proxy variables are discussed below and defined in Table 14.2.

1. Asset specificity is measured by sunk costs[8] in both fixed physical assets and proprietary intangible assets. Sunk costs in foreign agribusiness affiliates, measured by affiliate assets as a percentage of sales, range from 9 to 109 percent, with a mean of 64 percent.

2. Foreign investment experience is measured by an industry's assets in a particular country as a percentage of the industry's global foreign investment. For example, one country had only 2 percent of an industry's global foreign assets while another country had 43 percent.

3. To measure the effect of opportunism on contract choice, we assume that opportunism increases with the number of people involved in a transaction, i.e., that opportunism increases with labor intensity. The labor intensity of foreign agribusiness affiliates, measured by the affiliate's labor costs as a percentage of operating costs, ranges from 0.3 to 33 percent, with a mean of 13 percent.

Table 14.2 Transaction costs and proxy variables

Contracting condition	Proxy variable	Description
Asset specificity	Sunk costs	Asset specificity is indicated by sunk costs, measured by assets as a proportion of sales. Sunk costs include both physical assets such as plant, property, and equipment, and intangible assets such as R&D, brand names, goodwill, and management skills.
Inverse of bounded rationality	dfi experience	The inverse of bounded rationality is indicated by the industry's direct foreign investment experience.
Opportunism	Labor intensity	Opportunism is indicated by labor intensity, measured by the ratio of labor costs to total costs of goods sold, and selling, general, and administrative expenses.
Investment size	Average size of affiliate assets	Investment size is indicated by affiliate assets, measured by the average size of affiliate assets.
Profitability	Return on sales	The profitability of foreign investment is indicated by affiliate profits, measured by return on sales (ROS) in foreign affiliates.

4. Investment size is measured by the average value of assets in foreign affiliates, ranging from $3 million to $366 million, with a mean of $42 million.

5. Affiliate profits (net income as a percentage of sales) indicate investment profitability. In 1982 and 1989 the profitability of foreign agribusiness affiliates ranged from 109 percent to minus 93 percent of sales, with a mean of 23 percent.

Overall Econometric Performance

The sample used in this study includes 189 observations from two cross-sectional surveys, conducted in 1982 and 1989, of foreign agribusiness affiliates in six industries and twenty-two countries. LIMDEP™ statistical analysis software was used to investigate factors influencing the level of multinational ownership of foreign affiliates. Three models were tested: classical pooling, fixed-effects, and random-effects models. The classical pooling model combined observations into a single group, implicitly assuming that transaction cost effects on ownership did not differ among countries, industries, or periods. This is a highly restrictive assumption; as such, the results of the classical pooling model often gave incorrect signs and generally were not significant.

A fixed-effects model was used to relax the classical pooling assumption of a common intercept for all countries, industries, and periods while maintaining common slope coefficients. The fixed-effects model had a higher adjusted R^2 than either the classical pooling or random-effects models. White's test[9] and the Breusch-Pagan test indicated that heteroskedasticity was not significant at the 5 percent level. The Ramsey reset test provided weak evidence of specification error at the 5 percent level.[10] The random-effects model increased adjusted R^2, but was rejected because it made opportunism effects insignificant.[11]

The results of the marginal cost equation are presented in Table 14.3. Four proxy variables for marginal cost effects and four dummy variables for outlier observations[12] explained 34 percent (adjusted R^2) of the variation in ownership. All coefficients are significantly different from zero at the 5 percent confidence level. The results of the marginal benefits equation are presented in Table 14.4. One proxy variable for marginal ownership benefits (affiliate profits), a transaction cost variable for bounded rationality (investment experience), and four dummy variables explained 37 percent (adjusted

R^2) of the variation in ownership. The elasticity of ownership with respect to investment experience is 0.1. Affiliate profit effects are significant at the 5 percent confidence level but are relatively inelastic. Consistent with both transaction cost and market power considerations, high profits are associated with low levels of ownership. At average profits, the elasticity of ownership with respect to changes in affiliate profits is -0.08. The next section reviews the directions and magnitudes of these coefficients in detail.

Market Power and Transaction Cost Influences in DFI Contract Choice

In the following paragraphs, the coefficients are reported for each variable in the marginal cost equation along with predicted effects based on market power and transaction cost considerations. A summary of the main results is contained in Table 14.5, in which the expected directions from each theory are compared with actual results. The signs of coefficients for three proxy variables—experience, labor intensity, and affiliate size—are consistent with transaction cost theory. The signs on two variables—experience and labor-intensity—are consistent with market power theory. Both transaction cost and market power theories fail to predict sunk cost (asset specificity) effects on internalization.

Asset Specificity

Both transaction cost and industrial organization approaches predict that increasing asset specificity leads to increased ownership. The market power approach maintains that asset specificity can provide multinationals proprietary advantages to appropriate rents in foreign markets. The transaction cost approach assumes that multinational contract choice depends, at least in part, on the level and type of sunk costs. Multinationals own foreign affiliates to protect their investments in market information, brand awareness, and goodwill from degradation by free riders (Davidson) and dilution of international brand position (Anderson and Gatignon). The higher the sunk costs, the higher the expected level of multinational ownership of affiliates. Asset specificity, indicated by sunk costs and measured by the book value of affiliate assets as a percent of sales, has significant ownership effects. Sunk cost effects have a quadratic functional form. Evaluated at its mean, the elasticity of ownership with respect to sunk costs is -0.06, similar to that of affiliate size. As sunk costs increase, ownership declines at a decreasing rate.

Table 14.3 Marginal ownership costs, foreign agribusiness affiliates (1982 and 1989)

Dependent variable		U.S. ownership (MNE-owned assets/total affiliate assets)	
Number of observations	189	Mean of LHS	79%
R-squared	39%	Standard deviation of LHS	0.182
Adjusted R-squared	34%	Standard deviation of residuals	0.147

Variable	Coefficient	Standard error	Elasticity of ownership
Constant	0.875	0.048	
Sunk costs	-0.447	0.146	-0.06
Sunk costs squared	0.184	0.084	
dfi experience	1.933	0.436	+0.11
dfi experience squared	-3.373	1.259	
Labor intensity	0.519	0.239	+0.09
Affiliate size	-0.0011	0.0003	-0.06

Dummy variable	Coefficient	Standard error
Asia	-0.117	0.032
1989	0.070	0.023
Farm inputs and production in the Netherlands, 1982	-0.519	0.154
Milling and baking in Central America, 1989	-0.325	0.149
Textiles in the United Kingdom, 1989	-0.308	0.148
Food and beverage processing in Australia and New Zealand, 1989	-0.345	0.149

Table 14.4 Marginal benefits of ownership, foreign agribusiness affiliates (1982 and 1989)

Dependent variable		U.S. ownership (MNE-owned assets/total affiliate assets)		
Number of observations	189	Mean of LHS		79%
R-squared	37%	Standard deviation of LHS		0.182
Adjusted R-squared	34%	Standard deviation of residuals		0.148

Variable	Coefficient	Standard error	Elasticity of ownership
Constant	0.809	0.025	
dfi experience	1.146	0.399	0.02
dfi experience squared	-2.493	1.227	
Affiliate profits	-0.269	0.057	

Dummy variable	Coefficient	Standard error
Asia	-0.120	0.031
1989	0.053	0.022
Farm inputs and production in the Netherlands, 1982	-0.363	0.149
Milling and baking in Central America, 1989	-0.305	0.150
Textiles in the United Kingdom, 1989	-0.337	0.149
Food and beverage processing in Australia and New Zealand, 1989	-0.361	0.149

Table 14.5 Transaction cost and market power effects on U.S. multinational firms' ownership of foreign agribusiness affiliates

Contracting condition	Proxy variable	Market power	Expected effects		Actual effects
			Transaction costs		
Asset specificity	Sunk costs	+	+		−
Inverse of bounded rationality	Investment experience	+	+		+
Opportunism	Labor intensity	+	+		+
Investment size	Average affiliate assets	+	−		−
Investment profitability	Affiliate ROS	+	−		−

The unexpected effect of sunk costs in reducing ownership may be due either to an inefficient proxy variable or to differences in the asset specificities of tangible and intangible assets (Casson). Previous empirical tests of asset specificity used intangible assets. For example, Contractor (1984) and Gomes-Casseres used advertising expenditures and sunk research costs to measure asset specificity. Conventional measures of intangible asset specificity emphasizing assets committed before the investment occurs ignore the sunk cost effects of physical assets invested after the contract is established. The proxy variable used in this study to measure sunk costs—affiliate assets/affiliate sales—combines physical assets such as plant, property, and equipment with intangible assets such as advertising, research, and goodwill.

Bounded Rationality

A multinational firm entering a new market has high information costs. Its bounded rationality increases management costs and the risk of opportunism in foreign affiliates. The potential benefits of direct ownership increase.[13] As it gains experience, the multinational may not be content to let its foreign affiliates run the international side of the business. The multinational becomes more confident, assertive, desirous of control, and willing to take risks. It may increase ownership to leverage the overhead costs of headquarters staff, technology transfer, and management training required for international operations by increasing ownership (Davidson). Both the transaction cost and market power approaches correctly predict that ownership increases with experience. Measured at its mean, the elasticity of ownership with respect to experience is 0.11 and has a quadratic functional form. Ownership increases with experience, but at a declining rate. Based on ownership elasticities, experience effects are greater than those of sunk costs, labor intensity, and investment size.

Opportunism

The transaction cost approach assumes that people are opportunistic, pursuing self-interest with guileful intent and tactics. As opportunism increases, contracting costs of open-market transactions increase the potential gains from direct ownership. Multinationals increase ownership to reduce opportunistic behavior and align incentives. The potential for opportunism is indicated by the degree of labor intensity, measured by the ratio of labor costs to total operating costs. Both the transaction cost and industrial organization approaches correctly predict that labor intensity increases ownership. The elasticity of ownership with respect to labor intensity is 0.09.

Investment Size

Market power and transaction cost theories predict contradictory investment-size effect on ownership. Market power theory maintains that multinationals use proprietary advantages to appropriate rents in imperfect foreign markets. Large investments, exploiting economies of size and creating barriers to competition, are an important source of proprietary advantages and barriers to entry. Transaction cost theory, on the other hand, suggests that risk increases with investment size.[14]

Multinational firms can reduce risk by reducing their ownership share in large foreign affiliates. As marginal ownership costs fall, the marginal cost curve shifts back and ownership declines. The transaction cost approach correctly predicts that investment size reduces ownership. The elasticity of ownership with respect to size is -0.06.

Country, Industry, and Period Effects

Country, industry, and period effects were tested by stratifying observations by one group and taking appropriate deviations from means while testing the significance of dummy variables representing other groups. Two country and period effects were significant: (1) ownership in foreign affiliates was 7 percent higher in 1989 than in 1982, on average, and (2) ownership in Asian agribusiness affiliates was 12 percent lower than in other countries. Aside from Asia, however, country differences had little influence on ownership. Certain industry effects in selected countries were also found, but these did not add up to systematic industry difference. Therefore, we concluded to our surprise that transaction cost and market power effects on ownership are consistent across countries and industries, suggesting that multinational ownership of foreign affiliates depends more on transaction cost and industrial organization influences than on location advantages or industry characteristics.

The Marginal Benefits Curve

Both market power and transaction cost theories suggest that multinationals use hierarchical efficiencies to maximize profits. Based on market power theory, the very existence of multinationals depends on their ability to exercise proprietary advantages in foreign markets; foreign affiliate ownership allows multinationals to appropriate a larger portion of profits. The market power approach predicts a positive correlation of profits with ownership while transaction cost theory predicts a negative relationship. Transaction cost theory suggests that joint ventures provide hierarchical control at relatively low governance costs. The negative coefficient on profits suggests that as multinationals increase ownership, the governance costs increase faster than control benefits, thereby reducing affiliate profits. The elasticity of ownership with respect to profits was -0.08. The negative sign on profits in our marginal benefits results is consistent with transaction cost theory. The one shift variable included, aside from industry and location effects, was for experience, which was significant and had an elasticity of 0.1.

Conclusions

Transaction costs are a useful guide to choosing the level of equity ownership of foreign affiliates. Labor intensity and investment experience increase ownership of foreign agribusiness affiliates; affiliate size and sunk costs reduce it. Experience reduces the costs of both open-market transactions and internal governance. The model indicates that the costs of governing internal transactions decline faster than open-market transaction costs. Ownership increases with labor intensity, indicating that multinationals increase ownership to better align incentives in labor-intensive affiliates. Over their full range, sunk cost effects on ownership can be represented by a ∪-shaped curve. Ownership declines as affiliate size increases, casting doubt on the argument that multinationals seek market power through ownership of large affiliates. High ownership levels are associated with low affiliate profits, indicating that multinationals do not internalize foreign affiliates to gain a greater proportion of economic rents. Joint ventures may provide adequate control at lower governance costs than internalized subsidiaries, making joint ventures more profitable than subsidiaries.

Perhaps more important than the significance of transaction cost and market power effects on ownership are the effects the model failed to indicate. While transaction costs and multinational ownership levels vary between countries and industries, the elasticities of ownership with respect to transaction costs are not significantly different. The consistency of market power and transaction cost effects on ownership across industries and most foreign countries either indicates that the industry categories used in this model do not capture industry differences or that the determinants of contract choice and ownership levels are similar in a wide range of agribusiness industries. Aside from Asia, U.S. multinationals tend to react the same way to changes in transaction cost conditions, regardless of the country in which they are operating. (Low ownership levels in Asia indicate ownership benefits decline in cases in which sociocultural differences between multinationals and foreign affiliates are large). Multinationals reduce ownership in large affiliates where sunk costs are high. They increase ownership as they gain foreign investment experience, and they increase ownership in labor-intensive affiliates to align incentives. This is not to say that country-specific factors such as foreign investment policies are unimportant to contract choice—foreign investment policies may explain the very presence of a multinational in a foreign market as well as its level of ownership in foreign affiliates. However, the way firms react to changes in transaction cost conditions does not depend on differences in investment policies.

Regardless of industry, multinationals' investment in foreign affiliates tends to react the same way to changes in transaction cost conditions. This has important implications for public direct foreign investment policy and private investment strategy. Industry norms exist to guide investors in choosing the proper level of ownership in foreign affiliates although these norms vary from one industry to another and from one country to another. Governments attempting to promote direct foreign investment should acknowledge the existence of industry norms in foreign affiliate ownership. If imposed indiscriminately on all industries, a policy designed to promote foreign investment in a single target industry will tend to have similar effects in nontarget industries. If the policy involves changing transaction costs, it will tend to affect all agribusiness industries in the same way. Thus a reduction in transaction costs in the grain distribution industry will tend to have similar effects throughout the grain-marketing channel on grain mills, bakeries, input suppliers, and farmers.

While this investment model is useful for predicting transaction cost and market power effects on ownership, it has several weaknesses. The variables shifting the marginal cost curve are well-represented, but the actual marginal cost curve is invisible. Future transaction cost models should include a proxy for marginal ownership costs. One potential candidate is the price of foreign affiliate assets. Stock prices of foreign affiliates may be unavailable, but the prices of similar firms could serve as proxies. A second weakness of the model is that variables shifting the marginal benefits curve and changing the optimal level of ownership are not fully specified. For the model to become a useful tool for investment analysis, factors such as industry-specific cost and output price information should be included. Future models should also test whether traditional proxies for asset specificity, emphasizing intangible assets such as sunk advertising and research costs, perform better than the proxy used in this study (sunk costs), which combines intangible and physical assets.

Notes

1. Joskow found that asset specificity pertains to investments in physical assets, evidenced in the ownership of coal mines by utility companies.
2. The message to multinationals that emerges under these conditions is to organize transactions to economize on bounded rationality while simultaneously safeguarding them against the hazards of opportunism and asset specificity, suggesting a different economic problem than the microeconomic imperative to maximize profits (Williamson 1985).
3. Contractor (1990) used 1982 U.S. Department of Commerce benchmark survey data to analyze the effects of investment policy liberalization on direct foreign investment.
4. Tobacco and alcohol firms operate under regulations and restrictions more similar to those of pharmaceutical markets than to food and fiber markets in the agribusiness sector.
5. The U.S. Department of Commerce is required to suppress any information that would otherwise reveal the activities of individual firms or their foreign affiliates. For example, a large increase in foreign investment in Columbian milling and baking affiliates might reveal the terms of a private transaction that would otherwise remain confidential.
6. The concept of agribusiness as a distinct economic sector of related industries is relatively new, so generally accepted classifications of agribusiness subsectors do not exist. Agribusiness firms are sometimes grouped into three convenient categories based on their relative positions in the marketing channels in the food and fiber sector—farm inputs, farm production, and processing and distribution. The procedure used in this study to aggregate industries into subsectors is based on comparisons of affiliate size, capital intensity, and functional proximity in the value-adding chain of agribusiness firms. (For example, farm inputs and farming operations are grouped together as are farm raw materials and wholesale grocery distributors). The procedure used to aggregate countries was based on geographic proximity, resulting in regions such as Scandinavia, Latin America, and Asia.
7. North and Wallace estimate that transaction costs represent more than 30 percent of U.S. gross national product.
8. Sunk costs refer to investments that would be of substantially less value if redeployed should the original transaction be prematurely terminated.
9. White's heteroskedasticity test statistic (2.5) was less than the critical value (6.0), indicating that heteroskedasticity was not significant at the 5 percent level.
10. The test statistic (4.69) of the Ramsey reset test was less than the critical value at the 5 percent level (4.73) but greater than the critical value at the 1 percent level (3.05).
11. The random-effects model requires that the variance of the error term is not correlated with the variance of the independent variables (reference). This turns out to be another highly restrictive assumption. For example, the variation in affiliate size is greater in large countries than in small countries. The variance of the error term should reflect this size difference. The results from a Hausman test also suggested at the 5 percent level that the

fixed-effects model was a better specification than the random-effects model. The random-effects model was therefore rejected. (See Greene, pp. 307–12, for a discussion of the Hausman test).

12 Four dummy variables were farm inputs and agricultural production in the Netherlands in 1982, textiles in Columbia and Venezuela in 1982, textiles in the United Kingdom in 1982, and food and beverage processing in Australia and New Zealand in 1989.

13 Experience effects on ownership are not without controversy in multinational literature. Like the transaction cost approach, market power theory suggests that experience increases ownership. The multinational increases ownership of foreign affiliates to protect its competitive advantages and appropriate a larger share of economic rents. The counter argument—that experience reduces ownership—is based on the assumption that inexperienced multinationals have an ethnocentric bias causing them to install their own nationals in key positions in foreign affiliates, a goal that may be easier to achieve by ownership than by negotiation. With experience, the multinational firm grows accustomed to sociocultural conditions in foreign affiliates and gains confidence in local managers. Transaction costs in open-market contracts decrease. The need for control declines. The multinational is increasingly willing to delegate control to foreign agents and partners, reflected in low levels of multinational ownership of foreign affiliates.

14 The effect of investment size on ownership may also be due to portfolio considerations: to reduce investment risk, multinational firms may reduce ownership in a few large affiliates and diversity into several small affiliates.

References

Anderson, E., and H. Gatignon. 1986. "Modes of Foreign Entry: A Transaction Cost Analysis and Propositions." *Journal of International Business Studies* 17(3):1–26.

Buckley, P. J. 1992. *New Directions in International Business: Research Priorities for the 1990s.* Aldershot, England: Edward Elgar.

Casson, M. 1992. "Internalization Theory and Beyond." *New Directions in International Business: Research Priorities for the 1990s,* ed. P. J. Buckley, pp. 1–27. Aldershot, England: Edward Elgar.

Coase, R. H. 1952. "The Nature of the Firm." *Readings in Price Theory,* ed. K. E. Boulding and G. J. Stigler, pp. 331–51. Chicago, Ill.: Richard D. Irwin.

Contractor, F. J. 1984. "Choosing between Direct Investment and Licensing: Theoretical Considerations and Empirical Tests." *Journal of International Business Studies* 15(3):167–88.

———. 1990. "Ownership Patterns of U.S. Joint Ventures Abroad and the Liberalization of Foreign Government Regulations in the 1980s: Evidence from the Benchmark Surveys." *Journal of International Business Studies* 21:55–73.

Davidson, W. H. 1980. "The Location of Foreign Direct Investment Activity: Country Characteristics and Experience Effects." *Journal of International Business Studies* 11(2):9–22.

Dunning, J. H. 1988. *Explaining International Production.* London, England: Unwin Hyman.

Frank, S. D., and D. R. Henderson. 1992. "Transaction Costs and Determinants of Vertical Coordination in the U.S. Food Industries." *American Journal of Agricultural Economics* 74:941–50.

Gomes-Casseres, B. 1989. "Ownership Structures of Foreign Subsidiaries: Theory and Evidence." *Journal of Economic Behavior and Organization* 11:1–25.

Graham, E. M. 1992. "Theory of the Firm." *New Directions in International Business: Research Priorities for the 1990s*, ed. P. J. Buckley, pp. 72–80. Aldershot, England: Edward Elgar.

Greene, W. H. 1993. *LIMDEP Reference Guide*. Castle Hill, New South Wales, Australia: Econometric Software.

Harrigan, K. R. 1985. "Vertical Integration and Corporate Strategy." *Academy of Management Journal* 28:397–425.

Jones, G. R., and C. W. L. Hill. 1988. "Transaction Cost Analysis of Strategy-Structure Choice." *Strategic Management Journal* 9:159–72

Joskow, P. L. 1985. "Vertical Integration and Long-Term Contracts: The Case of Coal Burning Electric Generator Plants." *Journal of Law, Economics and Organization* 1:33–80.

North, D. C., and J. J. Wallace. 1986. "Measuring the Transaction Sector in the American Economy, 1870–1970." *Long-Term Factors in American Economic Growth*, ed. S. L. Engleman and R. E. Gallman, pp. 95–148. Chicago, Ill.: University of Chicago Press.

Sauvée, L. 1994. *Vertical Coordination in Agribusiness: Concepts, Theories, and Applications*. Bulletin 694, Office of Agricultural Research Programs, Purdue University, September.

Schmallensee, R. 1988. "Industrial Economics: An Overview." *Economics Journal* 98:643–81.

U.S. Department of Commerce. 1987. *U.S. Direct Investment Abroad: 1982 Benchmark Survey*. Washington, D.C.: Bureau of Economic Analysis.

———. 1992. *U.S. Direct Investment Abroad: 1989 Benchmark Survey*. Washington, D.C.: Bureau of Economic Analysis.

Williamson, O. E. 1985. *The Economic Institutions of Capitalism: Firms, Markets, Relational Contracting*. New York, N.Y.: Free Press.

———. 1991. "Comparative Economic Organization: The Analysis of Discrete Structural Alternatives." *Administrative Science Quarterly* 36:269–96.

World Bank. 1986. *World Development Report*. New York, N.Y.: Oxford University Press.

———. 1991. *World Development Report*. New York, N.Y.: Oxford University Press.

15 The Peanut Program and Pass-through of Prices, Conjectural Variations, and Consumers' Welfare Gain

SATISH Y. DEODHAR and STANLEY M. FLETCHER

Rising government costs and concerns by consumer groups are causing major reforms in agricultural commodity programs in the United States. Certainly, the U.S. peanut program is no exception. As reported by the U.S. Department of Agriculture (1995), the administration, in its efforts to curtail costs, would like to convert the peanut program to a no-net-cost program. Some other supporters of the reforms have claimed, based on a U.S. General Accounting Office report, that the high support price of farmers' stock peanuts is costing U.S. consumers up to $500 million a year. On the other hand, those who oppose the reforms point out that by "consumer," their opponents mean the first buyer, i.e., manufacturers, and there is no assurance that any reduction in the support price would be passed on to the final consumers (Nelin).

Clearly, there is a need to evaluate the impact of a reduction in the support price of farmers' stock peanuts on final consumers. Zhang, Fletcher, and Carley studied transmission of peanut prices in 1995. Studies have also been conducted on other commodity markets by Gardner; Kinnucan and Forker; Holloway; and Palaskas that aimed at explaining the mechanism of farm-retail price spread. However, except for Holloway's study, none of them takes into account the imperfectly competitive market structure, and Holloway's work does not capture the vertical relations that characterize the imperfectly competitive processed food markets. In a 1996 paper, McCorriston and Sheldon tied together the relation between vertically related, imperfectly competitive market structures, product differentiation, the degree of price pass-through, and consumers' welfare variation. Their study shows that in an imperfectly competitive industry, only a fraction of a price change is transmitted to successive stages of production and, therefore, the increase in consumers' welfare turns out to be lower than it would be under perfectly competitive conditions. In applying the model to the banana import market for

319

the United Kingdom, they estimated price pass-through, conjectural variations, and welfare gain; however, they considered only a single stage in the production process.

In following McCorriston and Sheldon, two stages of production are considered for the peanut industry, albeit without any product differentiation. It is shown that the degree of price pass-through, and the resultant change in consumers' welfare, will be lower, the higher the degree of market imperfection in the peanut industry. Using a conjectural variations approach, various degrees of market imperfection (collusion, Cournot-Nash, and competitive) are incorporated into the price transmission process. Various degrees of market imperfection are considered because there is evidence that the peanut industry is imperfectly competitive. In a vertically related, two-stage structure of the peanut industry, the top six manufacturers control more than 75 percent of the U.S. market for peanut butter, and the top three shelling firms account for more than 80 percent of peanut shelling (Fletcher, Zhang, and Carley). Our study focuses on the peanut butter industry, for more than 50 percent of the total quota peanut production in the United States is used in manufacturing peanut butter (Carley and Fletcher). Furthermore, data for the other peanut sectors are not available.

This paper is organized as follows: The first section describes the methodology for the price transmission process. The second section presents the variation in consumers' surplus that will result under various market structures because of changes in the peanut price policy. The third section summarizes and draws conclusions.

The Degree of Price Transmission

As modeled by McCorriston and Sheldon, and originally by others (Singh and Vives; Dixit 1988, 1987), a partial equilibrium analysis is considered where the economy is divided into the peanut sector and a competitive numeraire sector. Further, there is a continuum of consumers of the same type with a utility function separable and linear in the numeraire good, and income effects are ignored. The subutility function for peanut butter is described by a quadratic and concave functional form:

$$U(Q_2) = aQ_2 - \frac{b}{2}Q_2^2 \qquad (1)$$

where Q_2 is the quantity of peanut butter and a and b are positive parameters of the utility function. The subscript 2 refers to the second stage in the vertically related peanut industry. The utility-maximizing behavior on the part of consumers provides the condition that the price of peanut butter (P_2) must equal marginal utility $U'(Q_2)$. Therefore

$$P_2 = a - bQ_2. \tag{2}$$

Equation (2) is nothing but the inverse demand function for peanut butter. Similarly, profit of a representative firm i in stage 2 is given by

$$\pi_{2i} = (P_2 - \alpha P_1 - C_{2i})q_{2i} \tag{3}$$

where P_1 is the price of shelled peanuts, C_{2i} is the other constant marginal cost of production,[1] q_{2i} is the quantity of peanut butter produced by the representative firm i, and α is a ratio that represents the amount of shelled peanuts used to produce one unit of peanut butter. Suppressing the subscript i, the profit-maximizing condition for the representative firm is given by

$$(P_2 - \alpha P_1 - C_2) + q_2 \frac{dP_2}{dq_2} = 0. \tag{4}$$

Assuming n_2 symmetric firms[2] at stage 2 and aggregating the above condition over n_2 firms, we get

$$(P_2 - \alpha P_1 - C_2) - Q_2 D_2 = 0 \tag{5}$$

where the term D_2 incorporates the slope of the demand function and the strategic interaction among firms, i.e., the conjectural variations term for a representative firm. D_2 has the form:

$$D_2 = \frac{b}{n_2}(1 + (n_2 - 1)V_2). \tag{6}$$

The conjectural variations term V_2 represents the conjectures of the representative firm about how its rival firms will react to the change in its own output. As the Folk Theorem asserts (Friedman), in a repeated game played by firms, any outcome, ranging from competitive through Cournot-Nash to collusive, is a possibility, depending on the nature of strategic interaction among firms. If firms collude, their behavior resembles that of a monopolist and the value of V_2 will be 1. On the other hand, if they demonstrate perfectly competitive behavior (Bertrand behavior), the value of V_2 will be $-1/(n_2-1)$, implying that firms are price takers, having no effect on the market price. Similarly, if firms show Cournot-Nash behavior, i.e., they assume other firms will not react to any change in their own output, the corresponding value of V_2 will be 0.[3]

Substituting the value of Q_2 from the inverse demand function (2) into (5), we get

$$P_2 = (\frac{b}{b + D_2})(\alpha P_1 + C_2 + \frac{a}{b} D_2). \tag{7}$$

Further, by substituting the value of P_2 from equation (2) into equation (5) and expressing the value of Q_2 in terms of Q_1, we get the derived inverse demand function for shelled peanuts:

$$P_1 = \frac{a - C_2}{\alpha} - \frac{b + D_2}{\alpha^2} Q_1. \tag{8}$$

The profit for a representative firm (sheller) at stage 1 is given by

$$\pi_1 = (P_1 - \delta P_0 - C_1)q_1 \tag{9}$$

where P_0 is the price of the farmers' stock peanuts used by shellers, C_1 is the other marginal cost of production, and δ is a ratio that represents the amount of farmers' stock peanuts used to produce one unit of shelled peanuts. Once again, the profit-maximizing condition for the representative sheller is given by

$$(P_1 - \delta P_0 - C_1) + q_1\frac{dp_1}{dq_1} = 0. \tag{10}$$

Aggregating the above condition over n_1 symmetric firms gives

$$(P_1 - \delta P_0 - C_1) - Q_1 D_1 = 0 \tag{11}$$

where the term D_1 incorporates the slope of the derived demand function for peanuts and the strategic interaction among firms at stage 1, i.e., the conjectural variations parameter V_1. D_1 is given by

$$D_1 = \frac{b + D_2}{n_1 \alpha^2} (1 + (N_1 - 1) V_1). \tag{12}$$

The interpretation of the term V_1 is similar to V_2. By substituting the value of Q_1 from equation (11) into the derived inverse demand equation (8), we get the following relation:

$$P_1 = \frac{[(a - C_2)\alpha D_1] + [(b + D_2)(\delta P_0 + C_1)]}{\alpha^2 D_1 + b + D_2}. \tag{13}$$

From equations (7) and (13), we get the price transmission equation as

$$\frac{dP_2}{dP_0} = \frac{dP_2}{dP_1} \frac{dP_1}{dP_0} = \frac{b \alpha \delta}{\alpha^2 D_1 + b + D_2}. \tag{14}$$

Further substituting for D_1 and D_2, we get the final form of the price transmission formula:

$$\frac{dP_2}{dP_0} = \frac{\alpha \delta n_1 n_2}{[(n_2 + 1) + (n_2 - 1) V_2] [(n_1 + 1) + (n_1 - 1) V_1]}. \tag{15}$$

The above equation shows that the degree of price transmission from the farmers' stock peanut price to the peanut butter price is a function of the number of firms at the two stages of the production process; the degree of market imperfection or the strategic interaction between firms at the two stages of peanut processing; the quantity of peanuts used per unit of peanut butter; and the quantity of farmers' stock peanuts used per unit of shelled peanuts. As the proportion of peanuts used in peanut butter decreases, so does the degree of price transmission. In the limit, as α (or δ) approaches 0, there will be no price transmission. Clearly, if no peanuts are used in producing peanut butter, the question of price transmission does not arise in the first place.

Assuming for the moment that the values of α and δ are equal to 1, it can be shown that the degree of price transmission varies from 0.25 to 1 as the nature of competition among firms varies from collusive to perfectly competitive. If the firms were to act in a collusive manner, the V_is would be 1, and the degree of price transmission would collapse to 0.25. If firms were behaving in a perfectly competitive manner, the value of transmission would be 1, and, if the firms were behaving in a Cournot-Nash manner, the value would be between the two extremes, depending on the number of firms. It can also be deduced that as the number of firms increase, the degree of price transmission approaches 1. For the peanut industry, given the overwhelming concentration of six firms in peanut butter manufacturing and three firms in the shelling process, the degree of price transmission will be 0.25 for collusive behavior, 0.63 for Cournot-Nash behavior, and 1 for competitive behavior.

In terms of elasticity, the price transmission elasticity will be equal to the share of the value of peanuts in the value of peanut butter if firms demonstrate perfectly competitive behavior, i.e., $(dP_2/dP)(P_0/P_2) = P_0/P_2$. For any behavior that is less than perfectly competitive, this elasticity is bound to be lower than this number. With a vertically related, and apparently imperfect, market structure in the peanut industry, the pass-through of prices is likely to be incomplete. Consequently, the welfare gains to consumers, due to lowering the support price of farmers' stock peanuts, will be lower than in the perfectly competitive case. Therefore, it becomes imperative to measure the extent of the welfare gain to consumers under different degrees of market imperfections and different degrees of price pass-through.

The Extent of Welfare Variation

Given the linear demand function in equation (2), the change in consumers' surplus is measured by calculating the area of the trapezoid under the peanut butter demand function attributable to a change in the peanut butter price. The change in consumers' surplus is given by

$$\Delta CS = \Delta P_2 (Q_2 + \frac{\Delta Q_2}{2}).$$ (16)

Substituting for ΔP_2 in terms of ΔP_0 from equation (15) and for ΔQ_2 in terms of the elasticity of demand for peanut butter (η_d), we get the following form:

$$\Delta CS = Q_2 (1 + \frac{\eta_d}{2P_2} \Omega) \, \Omega$$ (17)

where the term Ω represents

$$\Omega = \frac{\alpha \delta n_1 n_2}{[(n_2 + 1) + (n_2 - 1)V_2] \, [(n_1 + 1) + (n_1 - 1)V_1]} \Delta P_0.$$ (18)

Therefore, the change in consumers' surplus due to a change in the farmers' stock peanut price is a function of the elasticity of demand for peanut butter; the number of firms in the two stages of production; the conjectural variations at the two stages of production; the price and quantity of the peanut butter; the quantity of peanuts used per unit of peanut butter; the quantity of farmers' stock peanuts used per unit of shelled peanuts; and the absolute change in the support price for farmers' stock peanuts.

To perform simulations of the changes in consumer welfare, values of parameters were selected from various sources. One unit of shelled peanuts produces 0.95 units of peanut butter; therefore, the value of α is equal to 1/0.95 or 1.05. Similarly, one unit of farmers' stock peanuts produces 0.75 units of shelled peanuts; therefore, the value of δ is equal to 1/0.75 or 1.33 (National Peanut Council). Since the peanut processing industry is overwhelmingly dominated by six firms producing peanut butter and three firms performing the shelling operation, values of n_2 and n_1 are taken to be 6 and 3, respectively. The price of peanut butter, $1.93 per pound, the average price between 1989 and 1993, was obtained from the U.S. Department of Labor. Similarly, the quantity of peanut butter was obtained from the U.S. Department of Agriculture. The elasticity of U.S. demand for peanut butter is estimated to be about unitary elastic (Fletcher, Zhang, and Carley). To check the sensitivity of our estimates with respect to this parameter, we have used a range of values for the elasticity of demand. Given these initial values, the extent of consumers' welfare change was simulated for different levels of reduction in the support price of farmers' stock peanuts and different degrees of market imperfection. In this study, changes in consumers' welfare due to reductions in the farmers' stock peanut price from the current level of $678 per short ton to $610, $550, and $450 are reported. There is a purpose in choosing these prices. It is likely, in the immediate future, that the support price will be lowered to $610 (Johnson). It is also argued that the support price will be further reduced, but farmers do not have to accept a price lower than $450, which is the Mexican grower price (Gamble). An intermediate price of $550 is also utilized because this price was supported by the peanut shelling organization in the farm bill debate.

Tables 15.1 to 15.3 consistently show that as the degree of market imperfection increases, the increase in consumers' surplus gets smaller and smaller for a given level of price reduction. For instance, with perfectly competitive firm behavior and unitary elastic demand, consumers' surplus increases by $37.00, $70.38, and $127.59 million when prices are reduced to $610, $550, and $450, respectively. For the intermediate case of Cournot-Nash firm behavior, the corresponding increase in consumers' welfare is $23.68, $44.88, and $80.86 million, and, for the collusive firm behavior, there are modest increases by the amounts of $9.16, $17.30, and $30.95. The tables also show that the changes in consumers' welfare are not significantly different in magnitude when the value of the elasticity of demand is varied around unity.

At present, it is mandatory for peanut butter manufacturers to have 90 percent peanut content in the peanut butter. However, increasingly, peanut butter manufacturers are adapting to consumer tastes and concerns. Major brands have started producing reduced-fat peanut spread that contains significantly lower peanut content (Tufts University). This reduction in peanut content will reduce the value of α to about 0.7. Therefore, we also generated estimates of the consumers' welfare change under the assumption that peanut manufacturers produce only the low-fat peanut spread. The increase in consumer welfare is correspondingly smaller, compared to regular peanut butter. Obviously, as the peanut content goes down, so does the degree of price pass-through, reaching 0 in the limiting case where no peanuts are used. The variations in consumers' surplus are reported in Tables 15.4 to 15.6.

Table 15.1 Change in consumers' surplus under perfectly competitive firm behavior

Change in price[a]	$\eta_d = -0.5$	$\eta_d = -1$	$\eta_d = -1.5$
From $678 to $610	36.77[b]	37.00	37.22
From $678 to $550	69.59	70.38	71.18
From $678 to $450	125.06	127.59	130.12

[a] Farmers' stock peanut price, dollars per short ton.
[b] All values expressed in million dollars.

Table 15.2 Change in consumers' surplus under Cournot-Nash firm behavior

Change in price[a]	$\eta_d = -0.5$	$\eta_d = -1$	$\eta_d = -1.5$
From $678 to $610	23.59[b]	23.68	23.77
From $678 to $550	44.55	44.88	45.21
From $678 to $450	79.82	80.86	81.91

[a] Farmers' stock peanut price, dollars per short ton.
[b] All values expressed in million dollars.

Table 15.3 Change in consumers' surplus under collusive firm behavior

Change in price[a]	$\eta_d = -0.5$	$\eta_d = -1$	$\eta_d = -1.5$
From $678 to $610	9.15[b]	9.16	9.18
From $678 to $550	17.25	17.30	17.35
From $678 to $450	30.79	30.95	31.11

[a] Farmers' stock peanut price, dollars per short ton.
[b] All values expressed in million dollars.

Table 15.4 Change in consumers' surplus under perfectly competitive firm behavior, reduced fat peanut butter, i.e., α = 0.7

Change in price[a]	$\eta_d = -0.5$	$\eta_d = -1$	$\eta_d = -1.5$
From $678 to $610	24.46[b]	24.56	24.66
From $678 to $550	46.22	46.57	46.92
From $678 to $450	82.81	83.94	85.06

[a] Farmers' stock peanut price, dollars per short ton.
[b] All values expressed in million dollars.

Table 15.5 Change in consumers' surplus under Cournot-Nash firm behavior, reduced fat peanut butter, i.e., α = 0.7

Change in price[a]	$\eta_d = -0.5$	$\eta_d = -1$	$\eta_d = -1.5$
From $678 to $610	15.70[b]	15.75	15.79
From $678 to $550	29.63	29.78	29.92
From $678 to $450	52.98	53.44	53.91

[a] Farmers' stock peanut price, dollars per short ton.
[b] All values expressed in million dollars.

Table 15.6 Change in consumers' surplus under collusive firm behavior, reduced fat peanut butter, i.e., α = 0.7

Change in Price[a]	$\eta_d = -0.5$	$\eta_d = -1$	$\eta_d = -1.5$
From $678 to $610	6.09[b]	6.10	6.11
From $678 to $550	11.49	11.51	11.53
From $678 to $450	20.49	20.56	20.63

[a] Farmers' stock peanut price, dollars per short ton.
[b] All values expressed in million dollars.

Summary and Conclusion

The degree of price pass-through from the farm gate to the retail store is very important from the consumers' point of view. Gardner; and Zhang, Fletcher, and Carley have studied the pass-through under the assumption that markets are perfectly competitive. Though Holloway used a conjectural variations approach to incorporate market imperfections, he did not take into account the vertical linkages in the food industry. In this study, a modified version of the simulation model by McCorriston and Sheldon was developed. Assuming a homogeneous product, peanut butter, and the degree of price pass-through, the resultant changes in consumers' welfare were estimated in view of the likely changes in the farmers' stock peanut support prices. The results show that the degree of price pass-through and gain in consumers' welfare, due to lowering the peanut support price, will be lower the higher the degree of market imperfection in the peanut industry. Further, the lower the peanut content in peanut butter, the lower will be the gain in consumer surplus.

As noted earlier, peanut butter accounts for more than 50 percent of peanut products. Allowing for the additional consumers' gain in peanut candy and snack peanuts, the total consumers' gain is not likely to be anywhere near $500 million. Moreover, to the extent that national brands differentiate themselves and create brand loyalty, the degree of price transmission will be lower, and, therefore, our results can be taken as the upper bound on the changes in consumers' welfare.

Notes

1 With a few firms controlling the total production, it is assumed that individual output levels are large enough and, in the relevant output range, constant marginal cost and average costs are identical. A similar assumption is made for the shelling operation.
2 That is, firms have identical costs and, therefore, have the same output levels. The justification for this assumption is that an uneven distribution of firm sizes can be translated into a distribution of symmetric-size firms by using the numbers-equivalent of the Herfindahl index.
3 Conjectural variations are not completely satisfactory from a game-theoretic point of view since they describe dynamics based on a static model. However, Schmalensee describes it as a reduced-form parameter that summarizes the intensity of rivalry that emerges from complex patterns of behavior. Perloff opined that it is designed to describe rather than explain a market outcome.

References

Carley, D., and S. Fletcher. 1991. *Factors Affecting Consumption of Edible Peanuts and Impact on Farmers in the United States.* Research Bulletin 405, College of Agriculture and Environmental Science, University of Georgia.

Dixit, A. 1987. "Optimal Trade and Industrial Policy for the U.S. Automobile Industry." *Empirical Methods in International Trade*, ed. R. C. Feenstra, pp. 141–165. Cambridge, Mass.: MIT Press.

———. 1988. "Anti-Dumping and Countervailing Duties Under Oligopoly." *European Economic Review* 32:55–68.

Fletcher, S. M., P. Zhang, and D. H. Carley. 1994. *Potential Impact on Peanut Farmers and Food Manufacturers from Changes in Peanut Prices.* Faculty Series FS–94–09, Department of Agriculture and Applied Economics, University of Georgia, August.

Friedman, J. W. 1971. "A Noncooperative Equilibrium for Supergames." *Review of Economic Studies* 38:1–12.

Gamble, W. 1995. "Should the U.S. Peanut Quota Support Price Be Lowered?: No." *The Peanut Grower*, February, p. 8.

Gardner, B. L. 1975. "The Farm-Retail Price Spread in a Competitive Food Industry." *American Journal of Agricultural Economics* 57:399–409.

Holloway, G. J. 1991. "The Farm-Retail Price Spread in an Imperfectly Competitive Industry." *American Journal of Agricultural Economics* 73: 979–89.

Johnson, B. 1995. "Tough Battle in Progress to Save Peanut Program." *The Peanut Grower*, November, p. 25.

Kinnucan, H. W., and O. D. Forker. 1987. "Asymmetry in Farm-Retail Price Transmission for Major Dairy Products." *American Journal of Agricultural Economics* 69:285–92.

McCorriston, S., and I. M. Sheldon. 1996. "The Effect of Vertical Markets on Trade Policy Reform." *Oxford Economic Papers* 48:664–72.

National Peanut Council. 1994. *Peanut Industry Guide*, vol. 30. Raleigh, N.C.: SpecAg Publications.

Nelin, M. 1994. "Protecting the Peanut Program." *The Peanut Grower*, July, p. 18.

Palaskas, T. B. 1995. "Statistical Analysis of Price Transmission in the European Union." *Journal of Agricultural Economics* 46:61–9.

Perloff, J. M. 1992. "Econometric Analysis of Imperfect Competition and Implications for Trade Research." *Industrial Organization and International Trade: Methodological Foundations for International Food and Agricultural Market Research*, ed. I. M. Sheldon and D. R. Henderson, pp. 59–105. North Central Regional Research Project NC-194 Publication 334, Ohio State University, July.

Schmalensee, R. 1989. "Inter-Industry Studies of Structure and Performance." *Handbook of Industrial Organization*, ed. R. Schmalensee and R. Willig, vol. 2, pp. 951–1009. Amsterdam, The Netherlands: North-Holland.

Singh, N., and X. Vives. 1984. "Price and Quantity Competition in a Differentiated Duopoly." *Rand Journal of Economics* 15:546–51.

Tufts University. 1994. "From the Peanut (Butter) Gallery." *Diet and Nutrition Letter*, April.

U.S. Department of Agriculture. 1995. "Commodity Marketing and Programs." *1995 Farm Bill: Guidance of the Administration*. Washington, D.C., May 10.

———. Various, 1989–1994. *Peanut Stock and Processing*. Washington, D.C.: National Agricultural Statistics Service.

U.S. Department of Labor. Various. *CPI Detailed Report*. Washington, D.C.: Bureau of Labor Statistics.

U.S. General Accounting Office. 1993. *Peanut Program: Changes Are Needed to Make the Program Responsive to Market Forces*. Washington, D.C., February 8.

Zhang, P., S. M. Fletcher, and H. C. Carley. 1995. "Peanut Price Transmission Asymmetry in Peanut Butter." *Agribusiness* 11:13–20.

16 Dairy Cooperatives' Role in Vertical Coordination

K. CHARLES LING and CAROLYN BETTS LIEBRAND

In animal agriculture, such as the poultry and egg industries, investor-owned firms have been the primary force behind vertical integration. The dairy sector has been the major exception. Long ago, dairy farmers integrated forward into marketing channels in a major way. Dairy producers have achieved this through farmer-owned, farmer-controlled, and farmer-used dairy cooperatives. Their experience can be a useful model for other agricultural industries facing the pressure of vertical integration.

Results of a 1993 U.S. Department of Agriculture survey indicate that dairy cooperatives handled 82 percent of the nation's milk at the first-handler level in fiscal 1992 (Ling and Liebrand). In 1993, dairy cooperatives' milk payments to farmers constituted 85 percent of the nation's cash receipts from milk production (Kraenzle).

Dairy farmers' integration at the first-handler level usually entails a tacit or explicit marketing agreement with a cooperative that designates it as the exclusive marketing agent for the farmer's milk production. The majority of dairy cooperatives perform only bargaining functions, but they represent only 25 percent of cooperative milk volume (Table 16.1). Prices members receive for their milk usually include minimal deductions because bargaining cooperatives incur minimal marketing expenses.

The remaining dairy cooperatives operate one or more plants and, to varying degrees, are further integrated down the market channel. Transmission of milk prices to farmers is somewhat more indirect because most of these cooperatives "reblend" their earnings before paying members for milk. The blend price is calculated and paid to farmers after adding premiums and/or marketing earnings to, and subtracting expenses and/or marketing losses from, the total value of the milk pool.

333

Table 16.1 Dairy cooperatives by type of operation, 1992

Type of operation	Number	Proportion of total dairy cooperatives	Proportion of total cooperative milk volume
		--------------- Percent ---------------	
Bargaining only	135	51	21
Bargaining with receiving facility only	44	17	4
Operating at least one processing/manufac- turing plant	86	32	75
Total	265	100	100

In 1992, dairy cooperatives with processing/manufacturing operations handled 75 percent of the total volume of milk marketed by cooperatives (Table 16.1). These cooperatives manufactured major shares of the nation's "hard" dairy products: 65 percent of the butter, 81 percent of the dry milk products, and 43 percent of the cheese (Table 16.2). However, their presence in the fluid and "soft" product categories was rather limited: 16 percent of packaged fluid milk, 13 percent of cottage cheese, 10 percent of ice cream and ice milk, and only 3 percent of yogurt.

How Dairy Cooperatives Integrate

Based on the functions dairy cooperatives perform in the market channel, vertical integration by dairy cooperatives can be classified into six categories. Each category shows a different level of vertical integration and involves different market opportunities and risks. (The categories are for the purpose of this paper only, which may differ from conventional categorization.)

Table 16.2   Cooperative shares of national production of milk and milk products, 1992

Product	Cooperative share (percent)
Member milk	80
Milk delivered to plants and dealers	82
Butter	65
Dry milk products	81
Cheese	43
Dry whey products	48
Packaged fluid milk	16
Cottage cheese	13
Ice cream mix and ice milk mix	13
Ice cream and ice milk	10
Yogurt	3

Bargaining Cooperatives

These cooperatives operate as bargaining associations and refrain from product processing/manufacturing. Bargaining cooperatives operate under the philosophy that dairy producers' place in the market is producing milk and that the role of dairy cooperatives is to secure the most profitable outlets for the milk and in jointly preparing milk for market at the first-handler level. Further processing and sales of dairy products are left to other handlers. Business risk for bargaining cooperatives is low as long as there are buyers for milk. At the same time, the cooperatives only have a limited opportunity to capture more of the consumer dollar. Members make minimal financial commitment in their cooperatives because little capital is needed for bargaining operations. They are takers of the milk price determined when the economic law of supply and demand for milk is played out in the marketplace. Their strength is in numbers; in this case, the volume of milk cooperative members collectively control. Government administered milk prices serve as a floor and the starting price in the bargaining process. Milk payment is usually pooled.

In 1992, this category included 135 pure bargaining cooperatives and 44 bargaining cooperatives that operated receiving stations without other plant operations (Tables 16.1 and 16.3). Together, the 179 cooperatives represented 68 percent of dairy cooperatives but only 25 percent of milk marketed by all cooperatives. Most were small cooperatives in terms of milk volume. The majority were in the Northeast and the Upper Midwest.

Bargaining-Balancing Cooperatives

These cooperatives bargain for milk prices and manufacture the surplus into commodity dairy products for supply balancing. The main function of these cooperatives is selling milk and performing related services to other handlers. A bargaining-balancing cooperative operates much like a bargaining cooperative except that it has plant facilities to service handlers' needs and/or to balance milk supply. Having the capability to dispose of surplus milk substantially strengthens these cooperatives' bargaining position. Surplus milk is usually made into storable "hard" products—butter, powder, and cheese—that are supported by the federal government's price-support program.

In recent years, continuing declines in the government support prices for dairy products have had the effect of making supply balancing operations unprofitable or, more commonly, a losing proposition. Furthermore, a balancing plant is usually a high-cost operation because the facility is used only part of the year and usually at low capacity. The impact of these factors on cooperatives depends on what proportion of a cooperative's total milk volume goes into supply balancing operations. A large cooperative with a modern, efficient manufacturing plant(s) that services fluid milk and soft product customer-handlers and balances only a small proportion of its milk may be able to absorb the cost of supply balancing. However, many balancing plants are old and inefficient.

A smaller cooperative with an outmoded plant(s) may be able to live off the depreciated assets and "milk the old plant" for a while. Eventually, the plant has to be replaced. The cooperative then finds it does not have the financial ability or enough milk volume to sustain a modern plant. As a result, some bargaining-balancing cooperatives have merged with a larger cooperative or

Table 16.3 Share of cooperative milk by operating category of dairy cooperatives

Category	Number	Proportion of total dairy cooperatives	Proportion of total cooperative milk volume	Proportion of total milk processed/manufactured by cooperatives
		------	Percent	------
Bargaining	179	68	25	0
Bargaining-balancing	24	9	17	11
Undifferentiated hard-product manufacturing	5	2	4	8
Niche marketing	29	11	2	4
Fluid processing	7	3	4	8
Diversified	21	8	49	70
Total*	265	100	100	100

* Totals do not add to 100 percent due to rounding.

have abandoned their balancing operations and become bargaining cooperatives. Others have divested their own plants but have invested in, or have joint ventures in, milk processing facilities, thus maintaining an outlet for milk in excess of what they can sell.

Some other bargaining-balancing cooperatives have attempted to cover their high cost of operations by going into the consumer market, thinking that the solution was in capturing a higher share of the marketing margin. In many cases, they have underestimated the fierce competitive nature of the consumer market and the financial resources needed to break into that market and have ended up in further demise.

In 1992, there were twenty-four bargaining-balancing dairy cooperatives (Table 16.3). They accounted for 9 percent of dairy cooperatives and 17 percent of all milk marketed cooperatively. Their share of the milk processed or manufactured by cooperatives was 11 percent. Seventy-five percent of their milk was sold to other handlers, and the remaining 25 percent manufactured in their own plants (Table 16.4). They operated seven plants for American cheese, seventeen for butter, and eleven for powder (Table 16.5).

Table 16.4 Proportions of milk sold raw and processed/manufactured by operating category of cooperatives

Category	Milk sold raw	Milk processed/ manufactured
	Percent	
Bargaining	100	0
Bargaining-balancing	75	25
Undifferentiated hard-product manufacturing	19	81
Niche marketing	13	87
Fluid processing	10	90
Diversified	43	57

Table 16.5 Number of plants owned and operated by groups of dairy cooperatives that perform processing/manufacturing functions, 1992

Function	Category					
	Bargaining-balancing	Undifferentiated hard-product manufacturing	Niche marketing	Fluid processing	Diversified	Total
			Number			
Make American cheese	7	2	14	0	57	80
Make Italian cheese	0	0	3	0	43	46
Make process cheese	1	1	0	0	8	10
Churn butter	17	4	5	2	20	48
Package fluid milk	0	0	4	27	44	75
Make dry products	11	4	1	2	34	52
Make dry whey products	3	2	2	0	33	40
Make cottage cheese	0	0	1	8	16	25
Make ice cream	0	0	3	18	16	37

Undifferentiated Hard-Product Manufacturing Cooperatives

These cooperatives capture processor margins by manufacturing undifferentiated, commodity dairy products in their well-run, large-scale modern plants. They sell little milk to other handlers. Most of the milk supply is used in their own plants.

Margins are slim to nonexistent in making commodity products. So three things are required to operate a successful manufacturing cooperative:

1. A very efficient large-scale plant(s) that takes advantage of modern technology and economies of scale.
2. A very large volume of milk that allows the cooperative to operate its plant(s) at or close to maximum capacity.
3. A ready market for manufactured products, including the Commodity Credit Corporation.

Undifferentiated hard-product manufacturing cooperatives have very large-scale, state-of-the-art, efficient plants. They are usually operated at or near capacity and at very low cost. However, because these plants are usually used for high-volume manufacturing of butter, powder, and cheese, the operations are not flexible enough to take advantage of changes in market opportunities. The continuing declines in the government support prices for dairy products affect market product prices and have made manufacturing operations less profitable. However, recent relaxation of trade barriers may help cooperatives manufacturing butter and powder find new and promising markets in the international arena.

There were five dairy cooperatives in this category in 1992 (Table 16.3). They represented less than 2 percent of dairy cooperatives but handled 4 percent of cooperatively marketed milk. Their manufacturing volume accounted for 8 percent of milk processed or manufactured by all cooperatives. These cooperatives sold only 19 percent of their milk to other handlers and manufactured the other 81 percent (Table 16.4). Table 16.5 shows the plants mainly manufactured American cheese (2), butter (4), and powder (4).

Niche Marketing Cooperatives

These cooperatives capture processor margins and at least some marketing margins. They manufacture and market differentiated products as their main line of business. They typically process all of their members' milk in their own plants. These cooperatives are mostly located in the traditional dairying areas of the country. They manufacture and market specialty or branded cheese and other dairy products for particular market niches. They are usually long-established cooperatives with small-scale plants; many need to be modernized.

Niche marketing cooperatives face both domestic and foreign market pressures. Domestically, as milk production shifts to lower-cost regions and milk supply tightens in the traditional milksheds, competition for the available supply can be financially stressful for these cooperatives. On the international front, the relaxation of Section 22 import quotas may bring more for-eign-produced specialty cheese into the United States to compete with the products of these cooperatives.

Regardless of these pressures, the few cooperatives with well-established brands and high-quality premium cheese no doubt will continue to flourish. Other, less entrenched cooperatives will be under mounting pressure to improve their operating and marketing efficiency. Many of them are likely to merge with cooperatives that have more financial resources and marketing expertise.

Twenty-nine cooperatives, or 11 percent of all dairy cooperatives, were in this category in 1992 (Table 16.3). Their share of cooperatively marketed milk was 2 percent. Their processing volume was 4 percent of the milk put through plants owned and operated by cooperatives. On average, they processed 81 percent of their members' milk and sold the remaining 19 percent to other handlers (Table 16.4). The majority of their plants made cheese (Table 16.5).

Fluid Processing Cooperatives

These cooperatives also capture processor margins and at least some marketing margins. Processing fluid milk products is the main business of these cooperatives. As with niche marketing cooperatives, fluid processing cooperatives typically process all of their members' milk in their own plants.

The continuous state of structural adjustment in the fluid milk processing industry is caused by several factors. Per capita fluid consumption has been in long-term decline. Aggregate demand has been growing since it hit bottom in 1982, but at a slow pace. Excess plant capacity in the industry makes it a very competitive business. Above all, dominance of retail outlets by supermarket chains and by dairy/convenience store chains tends to depress processor margins.

To survive in this environment, a firm must be a low-cost, high-volume, and very efficient operator. It must continually upgrade its plant(s) to take advantage of new technology and economies of scale. This requires ample financial resources and a management team that is on constant alert regarding the market pulse and operating efficiency. Few cooperatives are expected to remain in the business of processing fluid products as their main line of operation.

Some fluid processing cooperatives deliberately keep membership below a certain level and purchase milk from outside sources when necessary to avoid the cost of supply balancing or disposing of surplus milk. Together, they processed 90 percent of their members' milk and sold the remaining 10 percent to other handlers in 1992 (Table 16.4). Fluid processing cooperatives are usually long-established firms. Most are small-scale businesses—only two are relatively large-scale, modern operations.

In 1992, seven cooperatives, or 3 percent of all dairy cooperatives, specialized in processing fluid products (Table 16.3). Their share of cooperative milk was 4 percent. Their processing volume was 8 percent of the milk that was processed or manufactured by cooperatives. They operated twenty-seven fluid processing plants and eighteen ice cream plants (Table 16.5).

Diversified Dairy Cooperatives

These cooperatives are the most vertically integrated. They bargain for milk prices, process and market both differentiated and commodity products, and balance the residual—a combination of bargaining-balancing, undifferentiated hard-product manufacturing, niche marketing, and/or fluid processing cooperatives.

Most of the diversified dairy cooperatives did not start out as such. They grew into this category gradually through the years. Originally, many were bargaining-balancing or undifferentiated hard-product manufacturing cooperatives. Many diversified into related dairy enterprises as a defense mechanism for adapting to market evolution and changes in government policies. The pace of growing into diversified dairy cooperatives quickened in the mid-1980s as the government promulgated market-oriented dairy policies and as the cooperatives reacted to fast-changing consumer tastes and preferences.

Most of the diversified cooperatives are dominant in terms of member milk volume. Each cooperative operates a system of plants that process or manufacture a variety of dairy products. They typically sell a substantial amount of milk to other handlers while maintaining a steady volume for their own processing or manufacturing plants to fully use available capacity. The residual surplus milk is usually used in their balancing plant(s) to manufacture butter and nonfat dry milk. Some cooperatives are sophisticated marketers of consumer products.

Diversified dairy cooperatives have an advantage in being able to shift milk to the most profitable enterprises. A diversified dairy cooperative must have a multiplant processing complex and a sufficient supply of milk to use the plants. The business requires ample financial resources and an able management team.

In 1992, there were twenty-one dairy cooperatives in this category. While that number represented only 8 percent of dairy cooperatives, their milk accounted for 49 percent of total cooperatively marketed volume (Table 16.3). Their share of milk processed or manufactured by cooperatives was 70 percent. Collectively, they sold 43 percent of their members' milk to other handlers and processed the other 57 percent in their own plants (Table 16.4). Most cooperatively owned milk processing and manufacturing plants were operated by diversified dairy cooperatives (Table 16.5).

Prospects for Vertical Integration

Dairy cooperatives market more than 80 percent of the nation's milk supply. With the energy unleashed by a more market-oriented dairy economy, they are going to do more with their milk and add value to it. Their presence in the market channel will be more prominent. In the future, most dairy cooperatives will move in one of two divergent directions—to more or less vertical integration. Many will merge with, or evolve into, diversified dairy coopera- tives while others, usually small cooperatives, will divest and become bargaining cooperatives. Some large cooperatives will remain in the bargaining-balancing mode as long as their balancing operations are a relatively minor part of their operations.

Some farmers are striving to form organic or other niche marketing cooperatives. While these cooperatives may provide limited benefits to their select group of members, they are not likely to be a major factor in the foreseeable future.

Diversified dairy cooperatives will handle the major share of the nation's milk volume. The market will be more vertically integrated by these cooperatives. In the process, they will confront a fast-changing business environment and many unprecedented challenges, including:

1. *Less or No Government Support.* When the government support price for milk was high, it essentially set market prices for milk and milk products. The market was very stable. Since the early 1980s, government policy has been to reduce surplus production by reducing production capacity and support prices. Price fluctuations have become more common and sometimes volatile. Inventory management has been a challenging task, especially for cooperatives that age cheese. The 1996 farm bill further reduced the government's role in the dairy market, thus challenging farmers to manage their own industry.

2. *Globalization of Market.* Greater market access under the Uruguay Round of the General Agreement on Tariffs and Trade and the North American Free Trade Agreement thrusts the dairy industry into international competition. The world dairy market will be an increasingly important factor in making business decisions.

3. *Rule Changes.* Rules and regulations concerning labeling, food safety, environmental protection, etc., have been undergoing major overhauls in response to advancements in biological and food sciences and increased public concerns. Complying with new and changing regulations raises the cost of doing business. In addition, federal market orders have changed frequently in recent years. The order system will continue to undergo some major overhauls in the near future.

4. *Consumer Relations.* Discerning and adapting to consumers' shifting tastes, preferences, and perceptions of food nutrition will challenge the dairy industry. Consumers' demand for better quality and more services also must be satisfied.

5. *Employee Relations.* Employees are increasingly demanding that work should also fulfill their personal needs, such as family, flexible work schedule, alternative workplace, etc. To attract and retain quality employees, businesses have to satisfy these needs while maintaining smooth and efficient operations.

6. *Organizational Strategies.* The traditional cooperative that is both a producer political organization and a business entity may not be conducive to the decision making demanded by a dynamic marketplace. This is especially true for the diversified dairy cooperatives.

The challenge is to devise a structure that allows for maximum management flexibility while maintaining producer control over the business and the organization. Darigold Farms/Darigold, Inc., Land O'Lakes/Country Lake, and Agri-Mark/Cabot represent three different models.

7. *Joint Ventures and Business Alliances.* There has been a renewed awareness of the advantages of operating as a cooperative under the Capper-Volstead Act. Recently, several marketing-agencies-in-common have been forged for sharing market information (Dairy Marketing Cooperative Federation, Dairy Marketing Information Association, and Western Cooperative Marketing Association) or jointly marketing products (DairyAmerica). Also, many joint ventures and business alliances have been formed between cooperatives and, in some cases, between cooperatives and investor-owned firms to serve some common needs (most notably, several cooperatives' joint ventures with Leprino Cheese). Some other cooperatives, such as Mid-America Dairymen and Dairylea, invest in investor-owned firms to gain market access and improve earning potential.

8. *Capital Requirements.* Acquiring and maintaining modern, efficient plants and marketing consumer dairy products require substantial capital. Currently, member equity in the manufacturing and processing cooperatives (undifferentiated hard-product manufacturing, niche marketing, fluid processing, and diversified cooperatives) averages about $3 per cwt. As dairy cooperatives further integrate down the market channel, capital requirements will be much, much higher. As a general rule, capital in a dairy cooperative is mainly supplied by members, mostly through retained earnings or capital retains. The need for capital in the cooperative often conflicts with the need on the farm. The pressure to revolve equity to members may not allow the cooperative to be adequately capitalized. To get ahead of the game, dairy cooperatives must generate more earnings.

9. *Diversity in Milk Production Units.* Dairy farms have grown more divergent in size and production practices. Arguments among members for equitable versus equal treatment tend to create tension within a cooperative. It is difficult to satisfy every member's needs when the characteristics of dairy farms are diverging.

Conclusions

Economic reality is forcing dairy farmers to manage their industry and earn more dollars from the marketplace. Dairy cooperatives have been effective vehicles for farmers integrating down the market channel. In the future, dairy cooperatives will control an even larger share of the nation's milk supply. They will continue to grow and diversify and reach closer to consumers to capture a greater share of the consumer dollar.

The next several years will be very challenging. However, cooperatives that have ample capital, astute management, and a forward-looking board of directors will find the challenge both exciting and rewarding.

For other agricultural industries that are facing vertical integration by investor-owned firms, dairy cooperatives are examples of how farmers can legally take matters into their own hands. Vertical integration through cooperatives has enabled dairy farmers to capture margins from the marketplace that otherwise would go to middlemen. By working together in cooperatives, dairy farmer members can better control their own economic destiny.

References

Kraenzle, C. A. 1995. "Cooperatives' Share of Farm Marketings Hits 10-Year High." *Farmer Cooperatives*, February, pp. 4–5.

Ling, K. C., and C. B. Liebrand. 1994. *Marketing Operations of Dairy Cooperatives*. Washington, D. C.: U.S. Department of Agriculture, Agricultural Cooperative Service, Research Report 133, April.